DEGLOVED

Life is just a big journey. I'm glad we got to do some adventuring with you! ← Adelaide

To the first responders, the hospital staff, and my family

DEGLOVED

Cherish
EDITIONS

First published in Great Britain 2020 by Cherish Editions

Cherish Editions is a trading style of Shaw Callaghan Ltd & Shaw Callaghan 23 USA, INC.

The Foundation Centre

Navigation House, 48 Millgate, Newark

Nottinghamshire NG24 4TS UK

www.triggerpublishing.com

Text Copyright © 2020 Adelaide Perr

British Library Cataloguing in Publication Data

A CIP catalogue record for this book is available upon request from the British Library

ISBN: 9781913615055

This book is also available in e-Book format:

ePUB: 9781913615062

Cover design by Bookollective

Typeset by Lapiz Digital Services

AUTHOR'S NOTE

Prior to 2014, the only broken bones I had were a few fingers. My pinkie finger was in third grade while playing dodge ball and my index finger was off the coast of Africa during my time in the Coast Guard. Seeing your finger go in a different direction is no joke, but I will fully admit that I had no experience with trauma prior to the crash that you will read about. After the crash, I realized that what I experienced behind closed doors was vastly different than what most people saw. Most people focused on my physical injuries, which healed quickly. Meanwhile, the real struggle was the emotional toll the crash took on me. I felt the need to share my story because I think it will help others who have gone through trauma and those who are there for support. Maybe, *just maybe*, it will make those who share the road more compassionate toward each other.

This is a book from my memory. If I recall correctly, I began writing *Degloved* around January 2015, several months after my time in the hospital. I have done my best to interview others, many are mentioned in the book. Some interviews were done early on; others happened years later. Additionally, I have returned to documents such as the police reports, newspaper articles, the two inches worth of paper I wrote to my family when I couldn't talk in the hospital, the medical reports, emails, and more. That being said, I may have messed up details in a few places (let's all just blame it on the heavy dose of pain drugs I was on for those first five weeks).

To protect their privacy, I have changed the last names of the medical staff and police officers, although I speak very highly of these people. I have also changed the full name of the driver and the passenger in his car. While this information is public knowledge, I did not want to cause them harm.

ABOUT CHERISH EDITIONS

Cherish Editions is a bespoke self-publishing service for authors of mental health, wellbeing and inspirational books. As a division of Trigger Publishing, the UK's leading independent mental health and wellbeing publisher, we are experienced in creating and selling positive, responsible, important and inspirational books, which work to de-stigmatise the issues around mental health and improve the mental health and wellbeing of those who read our titles.

Cherish Editions is unique in that a percentage of the profits from the sale of our books goes directly to mental health charity Shaw Mind, to deliver its vision to provide support for those experiencing mental ill health. Find out more about Cherish Editions by visiting cherisheditions.com or by joining us on:
Twitter @cherisheditions
Facebook @cherisheditions
Instagram @cherisheditions

You can also find out more about the work Shaw Mind do by visiting their website: shawmind.org or joining them on:
Twitter @Shaw_Mind
Facebook @shawmindUK

Your Local Mental Health & Wellbeing Charity

CONTENTS

CONTENTS

CHAPTER 1
UPON IMPACT

*'I was following Adelaide Perr and witnessed the accident,
the severity of her injuries ... I will simply say it really was
the worst single thing I have ever witnessed and left an
indelible memory of absolute horror.'*
Scott, cyclist, 13th March 2015

There was no sign when I woke up on 18th October 2014 that the
day's events would forever change my relationships and alter how
I interact in the world. It was my favorite kind of day: a brisk but
sunny Saturday with invigorating cool air and a slight scent of dead
leaves. I left my boyfriend, Kennett, behind in bed while I walked
our seven-month-old puppy, Maybellene, along a bike path and
up a tiny dirt hill that led to the dog park. When I returned to the
two-bedroom apartment forty-five minutes later, Kennett was in
the kitchen flipping plate-sized pancakes. Decked out with peanut
butter, banana, and a heavy drizzle of honey, this was our standard
Saturday breakfast. We ate on the couch, at times resting our plates
on the coffee table while we perused the internet.

Kennett and I had met three years earlier, and I was quick to fall
in love with how dedicated he was to cycling. I was a trail runner,
but Kennett had already been an elite cyclist and bike commuter for
seven years. Within a few months of our relationship, Kennett bought
me my first road bike. He was the one who taught me how to ride in
a pack and how to draft off him on the way to the grocery store so I
could keep up. When I began training for bike racing during our first

year together, Kennett became my coach. Saturday rides were dates for Kennett and me, even if we didn't ride together the entire time.

By this particular Saturday, we had lived together for two years. We shared our current apartment with Kennett's brother Galen, and his girlfriend Joslynn. All three of them worked for a coffee shop in our neighborhood, while I worked in the bike industry writing content for websites. What little time we had outside of training was spent with family or playing with Maybellene, a new addition to the house as of July. As athletes, Kennett and I kept our lives simple and full of routines, such as the Saturday pancakes. Nights were spent eating salad and dessert in front of a Netflix show so that we could get to bed early; eating on the couch was a necessity – our dining room was filled with bikes rather than a proper table. Long rides over the weekend were just another piece of the weekly ritual we had created for ourselves.

As the final bites of pancake were devoured, Kennett and I discussed our separate rides for the day. He was going to enjoy an off-season ride with friends who planned to climb Lefthand Canyon, a narrow two-lane mountain road that gains over 3,000 feet in elevation over 16 miles. In my off-season from cycling, I was training for the HITS Lake Havasu Triathlon. The 2.4-mile swim, 112-mile bike ride, and 26.2-mile run were only three weeks away. One last long, flat ride was meant to boost my confidence. I liked tagging along with Kennett and his fast friends, so I decided to ride the first few miles in their pack before separating.

We went upstairs to change into our bike kits. I was testing out my old blue triathlon shorts to see if they'd be at least marginally comfortable over a long ride. I put on Kennett's old King of the Mountain Jersey that he had won while racing at the Sea Otter Cycling Classic the previous year and gifted to me. Even though the short sleeves were a little too snug against my triceps, I loved the red polka dots on this jersey and felt spunky wearing it. Because it was fall, I'm sure we debated what other articles of clothing were necessary. I opted for a pair of black arm warmers and a vest that was given to me by Kennett's team the previous season. The form-fitting vest, brightly colored with the Swedish and United States flags, looked better than my other cycling apparel and made me feel lean and confident. Both the jersey and the vest would later be cut off my body, not salvageable enough to put in the plastic bag with my blood-soaked shoes and other items.

Grabbing the bikes, we headed out of our apartment via the inside stairwell and out to the street. We coasted a block down our residential neighborhood to the coffee shop where Kennett worked on the corner – a hotspot for cyclists leaving town on group rides. Like so many others, this is where we would meet up with our friends. I pulled up next to the brick-walled corner and sat on my bike waiting for the full group of guys to form. Our friend Matt stood in front of me, and because I had my triathlon bike, a conversation about racing came up. He had at one point been a triathlete, but he'd since become a pro cyclist and occasionally trained with Kennett. I'll never forget Matt encouraging me to get a coach that morning. After watching my cycling progress over the winter and spring, he believed I could go places as an athlete, and that meant the world to me. It was the last time I was told I was a powerful cyclist before the crash. In the months that followed, I often returned to that conversation in my mind and used it as motivation to regain my strength.

Word spread between our small group of eight that we were headed out. We navigated through the black wrought-iron patio furniture outside of the coffee shop. With a chorus of clicks and beeps, we all clipped into our bikes and hit the start button on our GPS units. My Garmin screen showed speed, average speed, distance, time, and power output. I would use all of these data points to stay on track for a steady-effort ride.

The group organized into a pack that rode two people side-by-side. I stayed out of my aero bars, which allow a triathlete to lean on their elbows and extend into a lower, more aero position, and kept my hands closer to the brakes, allowing me to react quickly to the movements within the pack. The upright position also ensured I could see around the riders directly in front of me. We got through the last two stoplights in town, turned left onto the shoulder of US Highway

36, and headed north. While designated as a highway, US 36 is only a two-lane road. Each side has a paved shoulder that varies between 5 and 10 feet wide, making room for cyclists, even though the speed limit for cars is 65 mph.

I rode at the back of the pack next to Matt so I wouldn't push too hard for the first fifteen minutes of my planned five-plus-hour ride. At the turn for Lefthand Canyon, the guys looked over their shoulders to check for traffic behind and then slid over a lane while waving a quick goodbye to me as I continued along US 36.

Once I was alone, I glanced down at my Garmin and refocused on executing my ride. I wanted to see if I could hold an average pace above 20 mph for just over 100 miles. My plan was to complete four loops on rolling-to-flat roads. I wanted to feel comfortable with the distance; doing the ride as a series of 25-mile loops gave me the option to cut it short if my energy was dragging. When I parted from the boys, I was only 2 miles in to my first lap, so I settled into a steady effort. Every twenty minutes or so I'd eat a gel or part of a Clif Bar and wash it down with water. I spent most of my time hunched over my aero bars.

My ride got progressively quieter as I turned off US 36 east to US 66, which was equally busy but had a consistent 10-foot shoulder that provided a greater buffer from the cars. When I turned south onto 75th Street, a quieter, two-lane road, I passed the Purple Door Market. I made a mental note to stop at the small store on my second lap and refill on water. Turning onto Neva Road I had to push a little harder to hold my average speed on the false flat that took me by a field of horses to the north and a trailhead to the south.

I finished the first lap at the intersection of Neva Road and US 36 in an hour and ten minutes, which was right on schedule. Cresting the hill, I looked behind me for other cyclists before making a right turn to start my second lap. I began calculating where Kennett might be on the road. For motivation and a mental reprieve, he had agreed to meet me after riding with his friends by doing my loop in the opposite direction until he saw me. I estimated that I'd see him on this lap. The key would be to make sure he didn't pass me when I stopped at the Purple Door Market.

As is probably the case for almost every local rider, I'm normally happy to leave the noise and car exhaust of US 36 behind me. The road serves merely as a means to another destination. Given the bright blue sky and warming rays of sunshine, I was just another one of the thousand or more cyclists taking advantage of perfect riding weather on October 18th, 2014. That day I thought it was odd that, despite being on the busiest road I'd travel as part of my ride, it was my favorite section. Maybe the rolling terrain was simply more engaging than the straight roads ahead, or maybe it was the patches of sun that warmed me through my vest. Whatever it was, I specifically remember being calm, content, and proud of my willpower to push through what would be a hard ride.

Still gauging my speed, I naturally slowed on the climbs, picked up my pace during the flat sections, and relaxed when I had the momentum of going downhill. Trying to keep my effort consistent, I ended up playing an irritating game of leapfrog with another cyclist. I passed him on a downhill only to have him come around me shortly after. Within a few minutes I was in front again. I later learned that the guy who I had been trading spots with was Scott, an important witness ... and nearly a second crash victim.

After passing Scott the second time, I tucked into my aero bars and took a deep breath. The upcoming section of road, which heads north into the town of Lyons, was my last downhill to rest until the next lap around. As I approached the junction of US 36 and Hygiene Road, a two-lane country road off to the right, I moved left from the shoulder of US 36 into the right-hand turn lane that existed for those traveling east onto Hygiene Road.

Moving into the turn lane would deter cars from cutting me off with a right hook, while also providing a straight, safe trajectory through the intersection and back to the highway's shoulder again. Since US 36 is the larger road, there is no stop sign for north or southbound traffic; only cars approaching from Hygiene have to stop in order to get onto US 36. Those defensive riding tactics had become second nature to me. I knew the rules of the road and that my movement into the center of the turn lane clearly told drivers my intentions.

When I was 50 feet out from the intersection, a large red obstacle appeared in my vision. I knew it was a car, but it drove several feet past the stop sign so abruptly that when it stopped directly in my lane of traffic, my situation was momentarily surreal. Given that I was on a 6% downhill, my speed was around 35 mph. My hands jumped up from the aero bars to my bullhorns, the standard place for a person's hands to rest on a bicycle, where I grasped the brakes so tightly that they locked against the rims of my wheels. Slowing wasn't a good enough option; I needed to stop. The feeling of my rear tire skidding out from underneath me sent an electrifying sense of panic throughout my body. I knew my control was gone, that I could no longer correct the situation, and that I was going down. My mind went blank. When my body slammed into the red Fiat, Scott was behind me by mere seconds. With those extra moments, he was able to swerve to the left and into the other lane, narrowly avoiding the red car and oncoming traffic. Behind him, tires screeched as another car swerved to miss the Fiat.

While I don't recall the impact, I know I went straight through the driver's-side window. My face shattered the glass into thousands of shards. Those pieces sliced my face open before they settled onto the vehicle's seats, between the folds of the stick shift, and across the soon-to-be-bloody blacktop. In addition to the driver, there were two passengers in the Fiat, drivers from other cars, and nearby cyclists who watched the scene unravel. One passenger of the Fiat, Brian Clifford, jumped out of the car and ran to my side. He pressed a blue-and-white plaid shirt against what was left of my cheekbone. The driver, Larry Rush, was shaken and stood back.

Away from the chaos, my clear water bottle with a yellow cap came to a stop down the hill. Kennett had filled the water bottle for me earlier that morning; seeing it would be his first sign that something was amiss.

Among the people who assisted me and directed traffic, there was someone who dialed 911. At 11:48 am Sergeant Bill Fisher from the Boulder County Sheriff's office received the radio call. In five-to-ten-second-long updates from the dispatcher he learned it was a head and facial trauma case. Much later, this call would stick with him, because his own girlfriend had previously sustained similar trauma while in a car crash. However, he didn't have time to process any of this as he flipped on his lights and sirens. As he sped north along US 36, a helicopter was called to transport me to Craig Hospital in Denver.

By 11:50 am, just two minutes after receiving the call, Fisher was on the scene with a first-aid kit. He found me propped up against the driver's side wheel. As the only police officer on the scene, he focused his attention on providing medical care, relying on bystanders to deal with diverting traffic. As I went in and out of consciousness, he assured me I was doing a good job staying calm. 'Stay with me. What is your name? Take a few breaths for me.' My grip on his hand was strong.

I tried to say Adelaide multiple times, but he couldn't make out the garbles. I finally gave up on my middle name, which I go by, and spouted out my first name, which is Sara. According to Scott, I also asked, 'Why is there so much blood?' My unanswered question has since been: how was I able to speak at all?

In the end, an ambulance was able to reach me faster than the helicopter. When the paramedics arrived, one of them rushed over with a bandage. 'I want to get this on her face,' he insisted. Officer Fisher tried to convey that doing so probably wasn't going to be feasible. As the paramedic began removing the flannel shirt, my face came off with it. With a greater understanding, the paramedic agreed. 'Okay, we'll leave the shirt there for now.'

All official documents described the bleeding from the left side of my face as significant, extensive, brisk, and severe. Another term used for such injuries is 'degloved'. Picture peeling off a glove, except replace the image of a glove with the image of skin and soft tissue. Officer Fisher wrote in his after-action report that it was a level-one trauma incident. As such, I had to be transported to a designated level-one trauma center. These hospitals are required to have a helipad along with twenty-four-hour emergency care, including trauma surgeons, oral surgeons, plastic surgeons, and, most important to me at the time, maxillofacial and anesthesiology care.

It took just four minutes from the time of impact until I was loaded into the ambulance. Only another seven minutes passed until I was wheeled through the emergency room doors of Longmont United Hospital, 7 miles due east of the crash. The EMTs weren't sure I'd stay alive for those crucial minutes. My only post-crash memory of that day is being slid into the ambulance on the stretcher. Through my blurry vision I could see the sky outlined by open ambulance doors. I heard the voice of an EMT and will never forget his harrowing words: 'Her face is peeled off.'

What haunts me more than those final words from the EMT is what I can't recall. The details I've written about what happened after I hit the window – those aren't my memories, because I don't have any. I learned the full picture of the scene only through reading police reports and having conversations with Scott and Officer Fisher in the years since. What was I thinking during those moments of consciousness? What did I want to ask but couldn't due to my injuries? Did they tell me where I was headed? Did I realize there was so much blood because I was bleeding to death?

CHAPTER 2
FAMILY

*'Patient appears in severe pain, distress ... Patient alert
and oriented to person, place, and time ... Mental state is
sluggish ... She denies pain other than to her face.'*
Emergency Room records

The type of violent trauma that I went through is something I've
only consciously experienced while watching movies. I haven't
even been near someone close to death before. Thus, the most
emotionally charged details are not from my memory, not from
what I was told about the crash scene, but from hearing how my
family learned I was in a critical condition. It has been through
their painful, heart-wrenching stories that I have been able to
comprehend how dire my situation was.

Kennett was the first person to learn of my crash. While riding to
meet me, he had been daydreaming about racing and lunch. He was
getting increasingly tired and eager to spot me so he could head home.
The longer he went without seeing me, the more concerned he grew
that I wasn't merely riding slowly, but that I'd turned around early and
called it a day. However, in the back of his mind was laid a third, more
disturbing possibility.

He recalled riding past an intersection earlier in the week that was
busy with emergency vehicles. A cyclist had been hit and sustained
minor injuries. Kennett tried to ignore such similar possibilities,
but as he approached the intersection of US 36 and Hygiene,
he saw flashing lights at the top of the hill. Hyper-aware of his

surroundings, he spotted an abandoned water bottle with a yellow lid on the pavement in front of him. His stomach dropped. *I drink a lot of water while riding and he knew I wouldn't leave a bottle behind.* Up ahead, the sight of two police cars at the intersection made his heart start pounding.

I had been rushed away by the ambulance around noon and Kennett had arrived at the scene at just past 1:30 pm. The police were there, getting witness statements and investigating the evidence, including my 50-foot skid marks left on the road. Kennett rode up to the intersection and pulled off to talk with one of the officers.

'What happened here? Was a cyclist hit?' Kennett asked.

'Yes, a car pulled out abruptly and the cyclist T-boned it,' the officer said, gesturing to the red Fiat moved off the road into the grass.

'Was it a man or a woman?' There was a sense of urgency to confirm it had not been me.

'The victim was a female. She went through the driver's side window. Her injuries were … ah, substantial.'

'What was her name?' Kennett practically shouted.

'From what I was told, she wasn't in a condition to give her name.'

'What color hair did she have? How old was she? What did she look like?' Kennett's heart was beating even faster now, with hot and cold flashes flushing up and down his body. His vision seemed to narrow and the pit of his stomach was approaching the ground.

'Sorry, I don't know. I wasn't here when she was. She was taken to the hospital an hour and a half ago. To Longmont United.'

'Do you know what color her bike was?' Kennett asked.

'Blue.'

Kennett did some quick bike math. *She was taken to the hospital at 12:00. It's 1:34 right now. If it's Adelaide, she would have just started her second lap by then, so the timing matches.*

The color of the bike, the timing, the water bottle – it all should have been enough for Kennett to realize I was likely the victim. Yet he stayed in denial. Irrationally, he decided if he went out of his way to the hospital, the victim would not be me. Sort of like bringing an umbrella to ensure it doesn't rain. Kennett asked for a ride from the officer and was told he'd have to wait another fifteen minutes or so for the investigation to wrap up before anyone could drive him. The officer also noted that his bike wouldn't fit in the squad car.

'That's fine,' Kennett replied. 'I'll dump it in the bushes over there,' and he began walking into the grass to leave his bike behind.

She hadn't been able to give her name, and the impact to her face was 'substantial'.

These last two details made Kennett's stomach churn, his heart race, and his legs weaken as he walked into the bushes. Just about to lay his bike on the ground, Kennett asked three bystanders if they knew what had happened and who the driver was. One guy said yes. Kennett asked for a description of what the victim looked like. There was a brief pause before one guy spoke up.

'I think her name was Adelaide.'

The shock hit Kennett, and he didn't say or do anything for several seconds. *Serious facial trauma and she hadn't given her name, meaning that she's either unconscious or dead.* Kennett's thoughts immediately turned to the worst, and he assumed someone else riding nearby had ID'd me. Turning to the driver, he screamed, 'What the fuck!' Rush stumbled backward to avoid an attack.

Kennett stopped himself from doing anything further and the police officer rushed to step in front of Kennett to make sure. Kennett's worry outweighed his rage, however, and his immediate need was to be at the hospital.

Frantically grabbing his bike, Kennett rode through the grass to get back on the pavement. The police officer, who needed to stay at the scene with the driver for further questioning, yelled out some directions for Kennett as he left. Kennett sped downhill toward Longmont, sobbing uncontrollably in between screams. The screams, which lasted for almost the entire 7-mile ride to Longmont, were without expletives, or words at all. He figured I'd be dead or paralyzed when he got there.

On his ride, Kennett blew through the same red lights as the ambulance had. He tried to recall the last time he had given me a hug. He felt guilty for getting me into cycling, as if he could have predicted what had just happened. His mind questioned what life would be like without me. The screaming and crying interfered with his breathing, but there was nothing he could do to calm himself. It no longer mattered that he was tired from riding for too long without food; he just kept pedaling as hard as he could.

At Longmont United Hospital he ran his bike through the double doors and asked where the emergency room was. A chaperone guided him through the corridors to the ER with her arm around his shoulder. He was cold from sweat and he no doubt struggled to walk on the tiled floors in his cleated bike shoes. Rubbing his back, she asked him what had happened. He couldn't tell her because he was too upset and didn't know many facts himself. Kennett was told to leave his bike at the front desk before being guided into a private room where a doctor briefed him on my condition.

The emergency room doctor calmed Kennett with the good news first: I was alive and, to their knowledge, I had not sustained damage to my brain, spine, or limbs. When first wheeled through the doors I had been conscious. Then he described the brunt of my injuries.

My face had been shattered in numerous areas – cheekbone, nose, eye socket, septum, and jaw. Glass had ripped my upper lip back all the way to my left shoulder. The doctor's eyes teared up as Kennett cried, and after describing all of the injuries, he gave Kennett a long hug.

Kennett was then walked into the room where I laid sedated, waiting for my first surgery. Nurses were using a hand-held pump to fill my lungs with air. Doctors were still assessing me. Kennett couldn't see my injuries because they were covered with bandages. He took my hand, which was cold and white, apart from a few splotches of dried blood. Dr. Walker, a white-haired older trauma surgeon, introduced himself.

Kennett was asked to sign an approval for surgery. Then he was guided to the center desks of the ER, where for the next hour various insurance documents and contact information sheets were placed in front of him to fill out. Even the answers to questions he should know seemed particularly difficult to recall. A short, motherly woman with chin-length brown hair came by with pretzels and ice water for Kennett. She introduced herself as Laura, the hospital chaplain. She also handed over a pair of hospital socks with the grippers on the bottom so that he could remove his cycling shoes.

Officer Henderson, the investigating officer from the crash scene, arrived in the emergency room to speak with Kennett. He explained what he believed had occurred in the crash. He and others from Colorado State Patrol had been concerned about Kennett. They may have been worried Kennett would get hit running red lights to get to the hospital or harm himself if he found out I had died. Whatever the reasoning, they expressed that they were glad to have found him.

Attempting to get a few calories into his mouth but lacking dexterity, Kennett accidentally dropped the cup of pretzels. Having so many people nearby was overwhelming. Since Kennett does not carry his phone with him while riding, someone let him use a nurse's desktop computer to access contact information on Facebook. He became frustrated by how long it took to reach someone. He tried my parents, my sister, his brother Galen, and his parents.

Finally, Kennett was able to get ahold of Galen, who gave him the phone numbers for my sister Lydia, and her fiancé Jeff, who both lived locally, and my parents, who were in Pittsburgh. Kennett had to make the first phone calls to my family. Meanwhile, back at the apartment, Galen and Joslynn packed up items at home to bring to the hospital for Kennett.

Kennett left voicemails on my parents' home phone before calling my mom's cell. Her pre-paid phone is used for outbound calls and travel. Even when she's on a trip, chances are she doesn't have reception. Luckily, she happened to be near her purse in the kitchen when the call from Kennett came in. My parents were getting ready to go out for dinner with their friends.

My parents, Raymond and Kathleen, still live in the house I grew up in. It's a red-brick house with white siding along the front second level. The side porch that extends out on the left is an open-air room in the summer. By October, the forest green awnings had probably already been taken down for the season. While it's a suburban house, it has an older east-coast style with windows that get stuck when the humidity is high; floorboards that creak when you are trying to sneak into the kitchen for a snack; and only one-and-a-half bathrooms.

My dad was out walking our family dog, Chloe, a fourteen-year-old, sable-colored sheltie. He strolled up the 50-yard hill to get back home, stopping briefly to talk to a neighbor. When opening the door to go inside, he saw my mom in the kitchen on the phone. She wasn't in tears, but my dad saw her intent focus on what was being said on the other line. My dad stayed quiet and let her finish the conversation.

When my mom hung up from the phone call with Kennett, she relayed the news to my dad and crumpled to the ground. More than once she told my dad she wanted to get in the car immediately and drive to Colorado. It didn't make sense because the trip takes at least two days, but she wanted to take action, any action, to help her daughter. My dad booked a flight for my mom to leave the next morning. He would make arrangements for Chloe and fly out Monday; he could linger in denial for an extra day.

Within an hour of learning the news of the crash, my parents received a call from the emergency room doctor, Dr. Monroe. My dad handed the phone to my mom because she is adept at speaking about medical issues. My mom's understanding of human anatomy stems, in part, from her undergraduate degree in biology and her time as a volunteer EMT. Dr. Monroe told her there was damage at my spinal accessory nerve and a severed sternocleidomastoid. The spinal accessory nerve activates the sternocleidomastoid, which allows the head to turn from side to side. He also told my mom there was a risk I had sustained a spinal injury. He continued with an explanation of the extensive damage to my jaw and soft tissue. From their conversation, my mom had a clear understanding of my condition.

'When are you coming into town and where are you planning on staying?' Dr. Monroe asked.

'I have another daughter who lives in South Boulder. I'll be staying with her.'

'That's twenty minutes from Longmont United. You should consider staying closer to the hospital. There are several hotels within five minutes.' Although he didn't directly say it, he was implying that it was important my mom be able to get to the hospital quickly should my condition worsen. At the time, I was already part way through my first surgery.

Another phone call came in from Dr. Walker. In a calm tone, he also described my injuries. My mom just sat on the carpeted stairs, looking blankly into the living room and listening. Dr. Walker offered her a bit of relief. His own daughter had been in a similar accident and he spoke not only through the lens of a trauma surgeon, but also with the compassion of a fellow parent who understood the shock my parents were experiencing.

At some point that afternoon my mom left a voicemail trying to reach Lydia, my sister, who lives 7 miles south of me. After that there was nothing they could do for me until my mom arrived Sunday morning and my dad on Monday.

At this point, both Kennett and my mom had left voicemails for Lydia, who is five years older than me. Despite our age difference, Lydia and I are occasionally confused for being twins, and I like to think we have a similarly tight bond. I'm cognizant of when my movements mirror hers – I stop mid-sentence to tell Kennett, 'I'm talking like Lydia.'

She was in college by the time I entered high school, but I'd occasionally visit her for a sushi dinner at the University of Pittsburgh or for a weekend in New York City once she took a finance job. Our relationship reached a new level when she emailed me on a summer night in 2009: 'Want to go on an expedition?'

I was twenty-two and in the process of honorably separating from the Coast Guard in Charleston, South Carolina. Lydia was still living in New York City but was looking to make a change. Through several more emails we decided to do a bike tour together and bought two Surly touring bikes with panniers to carry our gear. By October she had moved in with me. Our goal was to ride to Alaska, and while that didn't pan out, Lydia and I still ended up spending the entire month of January 2010 on the road together, traveling from Charleston, South Carolina to Baton Rouge, Louisiana. The farthest apart we got from each other during the trip was within yelling distance across the grocery store aisles. We both moved to Boulder after our bike tour. Initially, it was an adjustment to not know Lydia's whereabouts on a minute-to-minute basis. To this day we still rely on each other being nearby.

Before she even knew about my crash, Lydia had been having a bad day. She and Jeff had run the Dirty Bismarck, a 14-mile dirt trail on the south end of town, and she had rolled her ankle. During their run across the mesa they had both noticed a Flight for Life emergency medical helicopter fly over. They didn't know it at the time, but the helicopter had likely been the one called to save me. Later, she found herself busy doing housework.

My sister and Jeff have a friend in law enforcement who heard my name over his radio. He sent them a text message explaining that my name had been mentioned with regards to a bike, but didn't know any details. Since my sister knows me so well, her first thought was that my bike must have been stolen because I had left it carelessly unlocked – again. She told Jeff she would deal with me later. They found out I was in the hospital when their friend was able to update Jeff with a phone call.

Once Lydia learned that I was seriously injured, she went to rinse off the sweat and dirt from her run. Standing under the warm water, she slumped down and cried. She didn't know how badly I was hurt, but her body was also in pain and she later wondered if perhaps at that moment she was hurting more than me. She was accurately describing the secondary trauma that she, and others, experienced. When I was in the crash, my body went into shock, releasing cortisol and norepinephrine to help me manage the acute pain. After I was admitted to the hospital I was also sedated. My body went so far as to wipe my memories of that afternoon. Those who experience secondary trauma do not benefit from the body's protective measures. They don't produce the same critical hormones needed to manage pain and they are never injected with medication. My sister was not the only one experiencing secondary trauma; Kennett was still managing the shock on his own at the hospital.

With my parents and Lydia notified, Kennett was done making phone calls. Galen and Jos were on their way to the hospital. Lydia and Jeff were shortly behind. Laura, the chaplain, had remained with Kennett the entire time. Now she took him to the O.R. waiting room and provided him with some blankets. When Galen and Jos arrived, they gave Kennett huge hugs and handed over some clothes and snacks they had brought. Laura guided Kennett to a bathroom with a bathtub so he could warm up before getting dressed in his street clothes. In the quiet room he cried some more. When he could catch his breath for long enough, he would take a sip of San Pellegrino lemonade or some of the protein mix that Galen had brought along. Once dressed and snug in his blue puffy jacket, Kennett emerged to see my sister and Jeff in the waiting room. A sense of relief hit him. The past several hours had been the most alone he had ever felt. Finally, he was warm, had some food, and was in the company of loved ones.

When Lydia got to the hospital, Kennett gave her details of what had happened. After learning the extent of my injuries, she stepped into the hallway to call my parents. My dad told her she needed to stay strong so that she could make decisions that would help me. Given that I was in surgery and would be for a while, Lydia reasoned with my dad that she still had time to indulge in feeling sad.

Lydia is an organizer. She is the person in our family who can book plane tickets and come up with an itinerary that is perfect – a trip without any hiccups. In the hospital she fell back to doing what she does best – researching to make sure I was with the most skilled plastic surgeon. She looked at the website of Dr. Carter, who was in the operating room with me, and was pleased to learn he was not only an accomplished facial surgeon but that his passion was in figurative and portrait sculpting. This impressed Lydia so much that once I was awake in the hospital, she shared the results of her investigative work with me. In surgery, Dr. Carter and the medical team picked glass from my face as they stitched up my soft tissue with around 700 stitches. Contrary to what I had initially assumed, they never went in to fix my bones during the first surgery. That would happen another day.

Midway through the eight hours, Dr. Carter came into the waiting room to give Kennett, Lydia, Jeff, Galen, and Joslynn an update. Other assistant surgeons and nurses provided more frequent updates. At 9 pm the family split up to go for a quick bite to eat at the nearby Wahoo's Fish Tacos and Noodles and Co. before returning to wait some more.

After surgery, Dr. Carter debriefed them, showing them before-and-after photos on his digital SLR camera. My spinal accessory nerve, the one for moving the neck from side to side, had been dangling in the open air against my neck muscle, and was millimeters away from being severed. But I was in the clear; it had not been damaged. While my left eye socket had been shattered, my eye itself was going to be okay. My tongue had been bitten in half down the center lengthwise and was missing a chunk.

The largest concern was my lip. When it ripped down my face, it was torn away from blood vessels supplying oxygen to keep the tissue alive. Dr. Carter ordered leeches be sent to the hospital's pharmacy to help save my lip. Leeches, which are closely related to earthworms, draw blood. They release proteins and peptides that thin the blood and bring it to the surface. Post-surgery, they kept blood clots from forming, which in my case was crucial to keep the left side of my lip from necrotizing – turning a black/purple color and dying. Lydia was fascinated that leeches would be the best solution possible given all of the medical technology available.

At the end of a long night, they were all allowed into the intensive care room to see me. The nurses said even though I was sedated and wouldn't remember anything later, there was a slight chance I would be responsive. While I was patched up and more alive-looking than before surgery, I was still in a sedated coma with my arms in restraints in case I became agitated. Kennett cried at the contrast of how cheerful I'd been that morning compared to my current monster-like state.

There were no nurses standing by to use a hand pump, but I had a ventilator to make me breathe. My tongue stuck out past my broken front teeth and my lips curled upwards around the ventilator tubes, giving me an odd grinning expression that eventually made Kennett smile. My bruised and swollen eyes were taped shut. Glossy Frankenstein stitches, shimmering from a thick slathering of antibacterial ointment, covered the entirety of the left side of my face. While that area had taken the brunt of the impact, my entire body was swollen from surgery. I resembled the Michelin Man. My hands were bruised all the way through to the palm from applying so much pressure to the bike's brake levers. My hair had been chopped off so they could have clear access to my neck, yet dried blood remained on the strands that hadn't been touched.

As a polite gesture to make one-sided conversation, someone thought to ask me, 'Do you want a Vitamix?' I squeezed their hand. It later became a joke that I seemed thrilled at the thought of getting such an expensive gift. I would be getting a Vitamix regardless, because it would be a while before I could chew solid food again. I wasn't awake, but it was apparent in my hand squeezing and my small body movements that I knew they were beside me. After about five minutes, the others left Kennett alone with me. Kennett took my hand and asked, 'Will you marry me?'

A few tears rolled down my face. I gently squeezed his hand and nodded my head. I have no memory of this first proposal, but I cherish it nonetheless. When I was physically at the worst point in my life and I had an enormous emotional recovery yet to come, Kennett told me he would stay by my side. As Kennett tried to leave, I became increasingly more agitated. Lydia and Jeff, who were waiting outside the room, kept telling Kennett he needed to go home for some sleep. When he said goodbye, my weak limbs hit the restraints. To calm me back down he told me he would be waiting just outside my room. Everyone left the hospital for the night. Kennett made it to bed around 1:00 am. Lying next to Maybellene, he cried himself to sleep.

CHAPTER 3
THE PROPOSAL

'KP came over last night. I asked if he considered me his girlfriend. He said this weekend he was calling me his lady friend with his teammates but when asked if he was getting dropped off at his girlfriend's house he said yes. So I guess I have a boyfriend.'
Journal entry, February 4th, 2013

In October 2012, my best friend Kim had a roommate move into her apartment in Boulder, Colorado. His name was Kennett. I'd see him when I went over to Kim's for dinner or to hang out, but it's easiest to track the progression of our relationship by holidays. For Halloween, Kim invited me to a house party she and Kennett were going to in Denver. It was the first time I did more than acknowledge him in the living room of their apartment, but nothing happened over Halloween. It merely opened the door for the three of us to spend time together again, playing Egyptian Rat Screw or watching a movie.

On his birthday, November 16th, our trio was supposed to go out for Mexican. Kim purposefully backed out, so instead Kennett and I went to The Kitchen Next Door, a casual farm-to-table restaurant on downtown's Pearl Street. Neither of us had asked the other one out. Neither of us knew how interested the other person was. After dinner we braved the chilly air and strolled east along the pedestrian-only road, past the restaurants and window shops. Our hands bumped against each other, the energy between us building ever so slightly.

Our first kiss came later in the night while watching *Catch Me If You Can* on the couch at his house. A week later we shared Thanksgiving together with friends, though it took until New Year's for us to agree that we were going to be a couple.

We were lying in bed late one evening about a month into dating when I decided to share one of my more challenging qualities with him. The room was dark, so he couldn't see me. My mom uses a similar tactic of initiating uncomfortable conversations – she does it in the car because she can't make eye contact while driving. My head was spinning.

'Hey, Kennett, just so you know, I have bipolar II. I switch between being hypomanic and depressed.'

His response was minimal. 'Oh, okay.'

'I've experienced symptoms since high school, but I just got diagnozed this past August. Just in case you want to back out before I grow too attached to you.'

He hadn't seen me in a depressed, irrational state yet and he didn't know much about bipolar II, so this information meant little to him. He remembered his friend growing up had bipolar, but all that he'd learned from that experience was that sometimes his friend bailed on plans last minute. The conversation went better than I had thought it would – simply because Kennett didn't have any real idea what bipolar is, or the drastic emotional distress and self-doubt that its victims suffer from. While I was on medication and understood the disorder better than I had in previous years, I knew that Kennett would start noticing my mood swings as we spent more time together. I didn't want to scare him off like I had with other boyfriends in the past.

One time when I was in college, I had set off for an afternoon run with my boyfriend at the time, which should have been a great way to unwind from a day's worth of classes. Instead, as the sidewalk started to follow a long uphill, my heart rate increased and I found myself hyperventilating. We weren't going fast, but I still couldn't keep up. I was getting teary-eyed and overwhelmed. He didn't understand what was causing me to break down sobbing. To be fair, I didn't understand my behaviors either. My emotions were running haywire without explanation – I didn't fail a test, learn that a family member was hurt, or experience any hardship. I simply lost control of my brain for an afternoon. All I could recognize was that I needed someone close by because it was scary to lose control of my emotions. We headed onto a wooded cross-country trail and I could barely pick up my feet. Annoyed because these occurrences were becoming almost normal, he took off running and left me behind. I stumbled to the nearest boulder off the trail and cried so hard I was convulsing.

When I was diagnozed, I learned these experiences were part of atypical depression. I wouldn't necessarily *feel* depressed, but I'd have symptoms such as sleeping too much, overeating, paranoia, mood reactivity, and lethargy. Over time, I chose to explain the disorder to Kennett and how it manifested so that he could identify it. I could explain it rationally ahead of time, but it was difficult for me to share what went on in the midst of a bipolar episode. 'I can be like Cameron in *Ferris Bueller's Day Off* when he's sitting in the chair on the diving board just staring into space. Even though I might be struggling to talk or even move, I'll have thoughts racing through my head.'

Adapting to my relationship with Kennett was exciting, and for the first several months together I lived mostly on the optimistic side of the bipolar spectrum – a state of hypomania. In February, Kennett invited me to join him for Bike to Work Day, which consisted of riding between food stations with the rest of his co-workers throughout downtown Boulder. The food stations weren't far apart, and I was able to keep up as we skirted down side streets among other bike commuters.

This was my introduction into his lifestyle, which included being a car-free bike commuter. I was enamored with Kennett for this alone. Ever since my sister and I had done our month-long bike tour in 2010, I had wanted to give up my car. Life slowed down when I was riding. After our bike tour I realized that biking opened up doors for exploring. Within my bike tour with Lydia there were smaller adventures, such as when we passed near St. Marks National Wildlife

Refuges along Florida's Gulf Coast and learned that the whooping cranes would be migrating through. We ended up staying with locals and joined them to see the endangered cranes being led to their winter migration spot by ultralights, just like in the movie *Fly Away Home*. Rarely when I commuted in Boulder were days on the bike that exciting, but I still often saw wildlife on the road, which made the journey just as enthralling as the destination.

I also realized that going places locally didn't necessarily take longer than driving. Despite knowing the positives of bike commuting, it required a change in habits, and up until meeting Kennett, I never followed through with it for more than a few days. Inevitably I'd hit a bad spell of bipolar and be left with barely enough energy to walk around the house.

Now that I was taking medication to help with my bipolar, I was better able to adopt some of Kennett's good habits. This included bike commuting and consistently training. After Bike to Work Day, Kennett invited me for more commuting rides. Those times, I wasn't always fast enough to keep up, so in late spring Kennett bought me a beautiful matte black-and-red Ridley road bike. Commuting together, I'd joke the only reason he was ahead was because he had more expensive wheels.

When the spring came, Kennett would leave for a long Sunday ride and I would set out on a run. I'd been running since I was deemed old enough to join my dad for his regular 4-mile loop through town. Now I was following in Lydia's footsteps by ultra-running, and she suggested I join her for a race in June. It would be my first 50-mile ultra-marathon, so I had a reason to stay on top of training. After this last planned trail race, I transitioned into biking with the hopes of racing the next season. It was exciting because, with the use a power meter, I could track my improvements in a way I couldn't on running trails. Kennett would pace me on climbs like Flagstaff, a series of switchbacks up a local mountain, or Sunshine, a canyon road with an average grade of 6% and ramps significantly steeper than that. With Kennett's help, I was regularly setting new personal bests. Between commuting and training, the bike was how we spent time together, what we joked about, and was a way we showed support for each other.

While riding connected us, Kennett's national racing schedule did not. I struggled being left behind when he traveled. During our first April-through-September together, he would leave for a four-day stage race and come home only to leave the following week – a schedule he had grown accustomed to during the past seven years.

I missed him when he left. I saw other couples who went on weekend adventures to the mountains, but Kennett would be off in Arkansas, Minnesota, Oregon, or some other random state. There would be a movie in the park, but I'd go as the third wheel with friends because Kennett would be in the team van driving to his next race. During his trips I often fell into a depression. Even when he wasn't missing a social event, the abrupt change when Kennett left threw me off my routine and triggered my bipolar disorder.

Being disappointed about a boyfriend leaving for trips isn't unusual; I know several friends who have struggled with this. However, my emotions tend to be more intense than average due to bipolar disorder. The first time Kennett witnessed this was when he traveled to Philadelphia for a one-day race in June. When Kennett called from a parking lot outside the hotel, he wanted to tell me how exhilarating it was getting into the lead break-away with a lap to go. Meanwhile I was irrationally crying about how he was gone – to the point where Kennett thought our relationship was over. If I couldn't handle him going away, how were we going to make it as a couple?

Now, after years of spending time with me, Kennett will say his trip to Philadelphia was the first time he comprehended the severity of my bipolar. He'd seen my moods shift a few times in the spring. Once, I grew angry because he wanted to bail on a restaurant dinner we had planned with my sister and Jeff, because he was sick. I had rationalized my behavior to him by explaining, 'I don't do well with last-minute changes to dinner plans.' This seemed like a minor frustration in comparison to my call after his Philadelphia race, but it was yet more evidence. As Kennett started to understand these incidents together, he realized what he was up against with my mood swings.

Despite the rough phone conversation and a few minor disputes like the one we had over dinner plans, we did stay together, and when Kennett's lease was up in July, he moved in with me. I did my best to support him even when I struggled, writing him good-luck notes and giving him small gifts to open each time he traveled. At the end of his racing season, my mind eased. I told myself, *That wasn't as bad as it seemed. He only travels for a few days at a time. I managed to create my own routines when he was gone, and I can do it again. I won't be so upset next year. I'll get my act together and support him better.*

It was a year since I had met Kennett; we were living together, and we had lasted through a full season of his bike racing and almost weekly travel schedule. He sent out his race resume to find another team in 2014 and heard back from a new professional team that was starting out of Uppsala, Sweden. He was ecstatic about getting a spot on the team; his dream of racing professionally, which he had been working toward for six years, was finally coming true. But what stability we had as a couple went out the door once he signed that contract.

Earlier that fall when I had made up my mind about being more supportive of his racing, I hadn't considered that he might be gone for months on end, let alone the entire year. Moreover, it became clear that winter that the team's administration was massively disorganized, and we had no idea when he would leave for Sweden, what races he would do, if he'd return mid-season to the States, and whether he'd be home for good by the following autumn. Because of these new stresses, I became inconsolable. October through January, I frequently broke down. The worst was when he would go for a five- or six-hour weekend ride. Even if I left the house and did my own ride, I would be back two or three hours before him. In December, the sun would go behind the mountains just before five. I'd look out our window as the sky darkened and wait for him to return. Each time, I'd try to pull myself together enough to ask how his ride went and to not bring up how this was another day we didn't spend together.

By the time his cleats clicked up the stairs and into the apartment, I would have already lost my resolve. Even if I made it through dinner and a movie, I'd be crying before bed. Kennett was having an increasingly difficult time managing the stress that my bipolar was causing. He began worrying about what state of mind I'd be in when he came home from his rides, and even began cutting them short on occasion because the anxiety would essentially ruin his workout. In his mind, I was dragging him down into my own depression and ruining his ability to train, relax, and enjoy his life. He began resenting me when I was doing poorly day after day, which only made it harder on me when I would catch a stony look on his face through my own tear-blurred eyes. *Did he want to live with this stress, this depression, this anxiety about my moods until the day he died?* With each passing week, he felt more trapped as our relationship solidified, time-wise, and increasingly guilty for having thoughts of leaving me. Would I completely go to pieces if he left me? Would I kill myself? He was damned if he stayed with me, damned if he left.

Midnight trips for a half-gallon of ice cream soothed the emotions until next time, but both of us worried how many next times there would be. Kennett was finally reaching his dream of being paid to be on a team that was invited to prestigious races in Europe. That he had to spend stressful nights while I cried about it detracted from his achievement and made him feel guilty for accepting the contract offer. Sugar from the ice cream magnified my mood swings, but at least on those nights we'd go to bed as best friends.

In the midst of the turmoil around Sweden, I occasionally worked for the owner of a local race timing company who got it into my head that I could plan a race. He mentioned that, if I ever did, he would partner with me. I came home on October 14th, 2013 in a hypomanic state and told Kennett that, despite never having competed in a bike race before, I wanted to promote one. After emailing the director of Bicycle Racing Association of Colorado, I learned there was a meeting for all race directors on 15th October – the very next day. We decided to hold the race in late February, even though it was a crapshoot with weather. It would allow us to kick-start the season and hopefully get a big turnout. Throughout the winter I searched for sponsors, got permits, and advertised what would become the Gebhardt Automotive Cycling Classic.

Looking back on that winter, I recall more time training with Kennett and planning the race than moments spent crying. Every Saturday, we would leave our apartment fully bundled for riding in the cold weather, our pockets filled with fuel and a second pair of gloves. Together we'd roll into the parking lot of Gateway Fun Park, where twenty to a hundred of the fastest cyclists in town would meet for a 65-mile loop on rural roads to Carter Lake.

Right off the bat I'd be pushing my threshold to keep up with the peloton until I got dropped. I'd talk with Kennett's friends as the pack shifted, and over several rides they became my friends too. Kennett told me this was the first time he'd ever worried about the safety of anyone else in the peloton. We didn't spend much time together on the Gateway ride, but I got to briefly be a part of his cycling world, I got my butt kicked by fast cyclists, and I got out in the sunshine. It calmed my brain, and I became addicted to the sport and all that went along with it. Kennett once again saw the adventurous side of me he had fallen in love with, and cycling became an activity we could bond over again, instead of being a contentious subject.

In January of 2014, my Honda broke down, and rather than repair it, I became a car-free bike commuter. I also got a job in the bicycle industry as a copywriter. In February, and again in March, we traveled to Tucson to train and race. We biked to meet friends and run errands regardless of inclement weather or dark nights. Our daily lives were bike-centric and our vacations, which helped keep us from focusing on Kennett's leave date, became chances to train in warm locations. My bipolar hadn't disappeared; however, it seemed like bike racing and my new bike lifestyle were having a tremendous impact on my brain chemistry.

I finally understood Kennett's love for the sport. Through racing, I learned the intoxicating feeling of attacking a field full of other adrenalized cyclists, and the fear of getting caught before the finish line. I met his cycling friends and found that, even when Kennett left town, I'd still have other people to ride with. Maybe if we were both racing, albeit on different continents and at different levels, we'd still have a strong bond when the season ended. All of these minor points of connection mattered because neither one of us was confident about what would happen once Kennett actually left.

The date Kennett was supposed to leave for Europe ended up becoming a moving target – the first sign of many that team management was drastically unprepared. Kennett arrived in Sweden sick with bronchitis and found the team in total disarray, lacking any sponsors, equipment, or a race schedule. Something either shady or downright illegal was going on with funding for the riders' meager salaries, which were paid late, as well. He and two of his American teammates were set up in a run-down college dorm. It was far from ideal, and something that added to the stress was Kennett's knowledge that I was quickly deteriorating back home in Boulder.

We kept to our plan of talking on Skype daily, but the distance between us wore on me from week one. Like in Philadelphia, there were calls when Kennett assumed our relationship was irreparable. Most of the time he just assumed we would mutually end the relationship because I couldn't handle him being away and he couldn't change the fact that he was going to be gone. However, during one video chat, I was crying and told him that I couldn't do it anymore. I slammed my laptop shut, ending the conversation just minutes into its start. After I regained composure, I became fearful that I'd lose Kennett if I didn't get back to him soon. Since he was either no longer online or simply didn't want to talk to me again, I reached out to his teammate on Facebook. Meanwhile, Kennett had contemplated what had happened and decided that we were officially broken up. He'd had breakfast and got ready to ride, when, about an hour after I had ended the call, his teammate told him that I needed him to contact me. We got back on Skype and I apologized for my irrational behavior. I have always managed to gather myself quickly enough to apologize when one of these arguments occurs, whether now in Boulder or years ago when Kennett was in Sweden.

After three weeks away, Kennett was still sick and unable to race or train, the team was making no progress getting equipment or sponsors, and the management's bold lies became easier to see through. With no reason to stay in Sweden, and our relationship on the brink, he decided to come home. I bought his plane ticket.

I wasn't entirely to blame for the bad experience Kennett had in Sweden and I didn't wreck his chances of bike racing in Europe by having him return to Colorado. The team quickly unraveled further over the next month, and by June it was completely dissolved. He rode for other teams in the United States for the rest of the year, his dream of racing professionally in Europe cut short.

At the end of the season in September I told myself, *I've had enough practice. I've been through two years of Kennett traveling nationally to race. He isn't going to Europe next year, so I'll cope much better through race season. Maybe next year I'll even sign up to compete in the women's category three field for some of the same races as him.* That is what I thought when I was being positive. Other days, I'd think more along the lines of telling myself that it might be too late. *Even if I cope better next year, who's to say Kennett wants to continue putting up with me? He was fine when I first told him about my bipolar, but he didn't understand it. Now he's seen all my crazy sides and I may be too much for him.*

On several different fall nights before my crash, I asked Kennett if he was going to leave me because of a bad mood swing. He assured me that he would stay by my side during a bipolar episode, no matter what. Mostly, I was thinking ahead to next year's race schedule and what would happen if I lashed out at him for leaving town. I even had the nerve to bring up marriage. I knew getting engaged was a big step for Kennett to consider, but I wanted reassurance that I wouldn't lose him.

Kennett had considered asking me to marry him, mostly because I kept bringing it up. Yet, he wasn't sure he was ready. He was still settling in from having been a nomadic bike racer for seven years and had never been in a relationship before. His focus that fall turned to submitting a race resume to team directors so that he could have a spot racing nationally in 2015. Even in the off-season he was continuing to train. Given where he was putting his attention, I assumed marriage was still far from his thoughts.

Disaster has a way of forcing a hand – making a decision that has been turned over in the mind for months on end without resolution. As Kennett raged toward Longmont United on October 18th, gut-wrenching images popped into his head – an empty bed, my bikes collecting dust in the living room, a sad hound dog waiting by the door for me to come home. He suddenly wished that he had already asked me and made up his mind. 'If she's alive,' he told himself, 'I'll marry her.'

CHAPTER 4
LOVED ONE DOWN

'Early on, one of the social workers told me that in her
judgment, probably the best case would be you would
spend several weeks in the hospital and then she would make
arrangements for you to go to a special facility in Denver for
brain injuries. She thought you would be there for at least
several months. We did not talk about the worst case.'

Dad

From Saturday through Wednesday I remained in a dark hospital room. Under the control of a respirator, my chest rose and fell. My eyes were taped shut and my face was covered with ointments and gauze. A halo of matted hair surrounded my swollen face on the pillow. IVs extended from my left bicep and the cocktail of drugs running through my veins made sure I wouldn't wake up, wouldn't dream, and wouldn't have any memories as a coma patient.

Those awake, both family members and people who had heard about my story from afar, were the ones plagued with the uncomfortably intense emotions. The type of sick-to-your-stomach feelings that demand priority over all other thoughts and coexist only with a sense of dread about what the future holds.

My mom flew into the Denver airport on Sunday morning while I was recovering from a successful first surgery. Lydia picked her up from the airport and, at my mom's request, they drove straight to the hospital. Though the 50 miles were mostly highway, it seemed to drive like city-traffic gridlock.

Lydia and my mom entered through the hospital's main sliding doors, past a grand piano, and across a large atrium, which housed a Panera-like cafeteria to the left. A narrow hallway, with cream-colored walls and cheerful artwork, led to the ICU. Another door took them to the waiting area where they checked in at the visitor's desk, washed their hands in the stainless-steel sink, and got buzzed in through the heavy wooden door to intensive care.

ICU was set up in a square, with rooms on the outside walls and a nurses' station in the center. My sister led my mom to the room; a left, then a right, and then there I was, several doors down on the left-hand side. Each room had a sliding glass door separating the patient from the hallway, which allowed massive medical devices to be moved in and out. As my mom looked through the glass, she could see equipment and monitors crowding my bed.

My mom paused at the door for a split second. Her eyes focused on all the IVs in my arm. Lydia stepped aside to let her go first. The nurse, Jodi, had her attention focused on me and didn't initially notice I had visitors. My mom asked Jodi, 'Can I walk around and see her face and hold her hand?'

'Sure, that's alright. I'm monitoring her medication right now because we're having a difficult time keeping her sedated.'

As my mom came around the bed, she gently touched my fingers, the only part of my hand not taped over to hold the IV lines in place. 'It's okay. It's okay. I couldn't get here any faster. We're here …'

In response to my mom's arrival, I grew agitated and a small tear rolled down from my one open eye. My mom wasn't sure if the tear signified that I was in pain, relieved to see her, or terrified that her presence meant my injuries were severe. I imagine it must have been all three combined. I wish I could have told my mom, 'Don't worry, I've had enough pain medication. If I could, I would give you a hug.'

Monitors were beeping to notify Jodi that my heart rate was dropping below 50 bpm. My mom noticed and wanted to make life easier on the medical staff – to keep the family's nuisance levels to a minimum so the doctors and nurses could do their job efficiently.

'Jodi, would it be best if we left for now? We can go to the waiting room and give you time to get her settled.'

'Thanks, that would be great. We've been struggling to keep her sedated all day. I know she's an athlete, but her heart rate is actually so low that the medication levels needed to sedate her could cause her heart to stop.'

On the way out of the door, another nurse asked my mom, 'We realize your daughter is a healthy athlete, but are you sure she doesn't take drugs? It shouldn't be this difficult to keep her asleep.'

'No, she really doesn't. She's reluctant to even take bipolar medication.'

In the room, Jodi turned her attention back to my care. She was relieved my mom knew that controlling sedation medications and fluid levels is a fine balancing act. Given the shock I'd experienced in the past twenty-four hours, my body wasn't capable of regulating itself. My mom's willingness to leave and her compassion toward the nurses throughout the afternoon kept Jodi calm on what proved to be a stressful day at work.

In the waiting room my mom spent her time thinking through the possible outcomes. Would her daughter be paralyzed when she woke up? What would the extent of her daughter's brain damage be? How would she react when she learned of her own injuries?

By Sunday afternoon other visitors were beginning to come, including my friend Kim. On Saturday, Kim spent the night in Estes Park, an hour drive into the mountains. Before bed she opened Facebook and saw a *Daily Camera* article, 'Boulder cyclist severely injured after crash with car on US 36.' Reading further into the body of the newspaper article she learned that the cyclist was me. She sat upright in bed and started screaming. After calling Kennett for an update she decided her family would return early from Estes Park so that she could stop by the hospital during Sunday's visiting hours.

While my mom instructed all visitors to keep the conversation away from the crash, knowing that in some extremely rare cases coma patients remember parts of their time sedated, Kim actually wanted me to remember something from my days sedated – something funny. In the ICU room she tried to inject humor into her stilted one-way conversation with me. She was probably the only person to attempt that.

For Kim, seeing me in the hospital bed helped her believe that I would eventually recover. Having a visual, despite that disfigured visual being difficult to look at, seemed to solidify the fact that I was alive. For some people, ignorance is bliss, and hiding from a problem is their way of coping. For Kim, seeing what my injuries looked like prevented even worse thoughts from creeping into her mind.

After leaving me, she continued to experience my crash in ways not easily seen. Besides coming to visit me in the hospital twice and hanging out with me in the months that followed, Kim's schedule was not *changed* as a result of my crash. Everything and everyone around her remained normal, while her emotions went haywire. And, unlike my immediate family, she didn't know who to talk with about her thoughts.

She was far enough removed from the crash that she didn't feel comfortable sharing with others why she was so bothered and distracted over the next several weeks. Not only did she feel for me, but she kept replaying what it must have been like for Kennett, who was her old roommate, to have ridden up on the scene. Kim had a hard time stifling her nerves.

In Kim, the crash brought out a, 'Holy shit – I'm not invincible' mentality. This was a shared sentiment that many people had, although there were different variations depending on who it was that was processing my crash. Some friends had a loop playing in their head that sounded like, 'Is it selfish of me to still ride now that I have a family? What if I get hit and my kids grow up without a parent?' Another was, 'Holy shit – I can't always protect my child.'

For instance, the same Sunday my mom was cursing every delay in reaching the hospital and Kim was returning early from Estes Park, my co-worker Tim was spending time with his daughter. Months later, in a letter to the judge, he wrote:

'My daughter and I were gearing up for a bike ride when my phone started buzzing. Through several texts and phone calls, I learned that my friend and co-worker, Adelaide Perr, had been seriously injured while riding. At the time, I didn't know many details or much about her injuries. What I did know is that I was heading out the door for a ride with my 12-year-old daughter ... We went for the ride. I tried to enjoy it, but I spent most of my time and energy watching out for her and teaching her what I could about cycling safety on the roads. Other than riding around our neighborhood, she hasn't been on her bike since. It's easy to be overprotective as a parent. I hope I'll feel more comfortable about her on the bike. But since Adelaide was hurt, I struggle with introducing my daughter to a healthy recreational activity that could get her killed.'

Both my dad and Kennett's dad Curt, were facing Tim's fear in real time. On Monday, they each flew into Denver. Up until arriving at the hospital my dad had kept a very upbeat outlook that, while my injuries were serious, I'd recover just fine. Then he actually saw me lying unconscious in the hospital bed. He learned from doctors that I might not have full mobility in my legs, and this couldn't be ruled out until they performed a neurological test when I was awake.

Furthermore, my dad was astonished at how long my treatment was estimated to be. The social worker told my dad they could expect me to stay several weeks in an outpatient treatment facility on top of multiple weeks in the ICU. My dad began to worry – would his daughter ever make a full recovery?

While I wasn't Curt's daughter, I'd spent plenty of time with him over holidays and summer visits to Oregon. Curt knew from talking on the phone with his younger son Galen, that this was a 'loved-one-down' scenario and that Kennett would need support. He simply needed to get to Boulder to assess the situation and figure out how he could help.

In the past, Curt had been on rescue missions and had lost friends in mountaineering and kayaking incidents. Out of all the family members, he had the most experience with these types of situations.

Curt intended to keep Kennett calm and help him maintain realistic expectations. Even though I was missing, our home was just as full because Curt was sleeping on the futon. Conversation nearly ceased in the apartment because most topics felt extraneous and frivolous.

Since Lydia, Jeff, Jos, and Galen all lived in Boulder, they had to balance being present in the hospital for family with their daily responsibilities. Jos and Galen thought long-term and planned for when I'd return home. They covered Kennett's coffee shop shifts and kept the house clean – everything they could do to prevent Kennett from becoming overwhelmed. Taking care of Maybellene, who knew something was wrong herself, became a joint effort.

My parents stayed in the guest bedroom at Jeff and Lydia's house, although Lydia has almost no recollection of them being there. On Monday, she went to work. Months later, lacking all memory of the day, she tried to find notes from an important client meeting she had attended. Not only had her memory failed her about what had occurred during the meeting, she realized she hadn't even taken notes to fall back on.

Instead, Lydia's attention was on keeping a positive energy in the hospital room and processing the crash herself. She brought in a small set of speakers so she could play music while I was in the coma. She collected a variety of family photos, which she printed and posted on the wall across from my hospital bed. Her iPad was ready to go for when I woke up and was able to read a book.

Within the first day or two, Lydia rode her bike up to the site of the crash and walked around the intersection for about half an hour. There was still a big red stain on the asphalt from my blood. It made her sick to see, but she won't tell me many details because she isn't keen to delve into the painful memories she does have.

My sister's choice was to get back on the bike as soon as possible after my crash. For others, including strangers, my crash was the final straw that made them give up riding altogether. My story spread to cyclists worldwide when Kennett's blog was shared on Facebook and then made it onto a website called Drunk Cyclist. In fact, several of my parents' neighbors in Pittsburgh learned of my crash through this site. Reading his first-hand account made people's stomachs tighten and tears roll silently down their faces. It also brought the crash a little too close to home for many.

Kelly was one person who had stumbled upon Kennett's blog. I met her months later through a friend. She told me she had ridden the same route as I had that morning. As Kelly wrote in her letter to the judge,

'I left on my ride that day without saying bye to my husband, or telling him I loved him because I was slightly annoyed he wouldn't get out of bed. It could have been me that left with words unspoken ... Since that day, I ride a little slower, a little more cautious, but mostly I ride a little more in fear. I now primarily stick to roads that have ample bike lanes, good cell phone coverage, and lighter traffic. I make sure to tell my husband I am heading out on the bike and where I am headed. I try to find someone to go with me when I can. Mostly the whole time I ride, I now wonder what did I last say to my husband and family. Was it enough? The answer will always be no because there are no words strong enough for what could happen.'

No one in my family, aside from Kennett, wanted to talk about whether or not I would get back on the bike. Looking down at my potentially paralyzed, unconscious body, it was too difficult to see beyond the hospital. The one person who seemed to be able to avoid tunnel vision was Jeff, who knew I would need a personal injury lawyer. He scheduled appointments with several local attorneys who came to the hospital to meet with my parents and Kennett. Jeff cancelled flights Kennett and I had for an upcoming trip. Essentially, Jeff was the person who took care of all the critical details that would have otherwise been overlooked.

Tuesday afternoon, I went back in for three simultaneous surgeries. The main event was reconstructing all the shattered bones in my face. The other surgeries were to insert the gastronomy tube – a rubber feeding tube that goes through the abdomen to the stomach – along with a tracheostomy tube – a breathing tube in the throat.

The parents, Kennett, Lydia, Jeff, Jos, and Galen all saw me before the surgery and, since surgery was scheduled to be six hours long, they left in search of a meal. My mom was sick with worry after I was wheeled out of the ICU to the surgery room. She thought, *Oh my god, I'd rather sit by myself in the hospital than go out to dinner.* Despite this, my mom joined the whole family as they headed to a coffee shop and, later, for Thai food.

That Tuesday night was the worst night of my dad's life. Once they were all seated at the circular table with their tea and coffee, my dad became overwhelmed. He motioned for the others to join hands while he said a prayer on my behalf. 'Dear God, if you are up there …' While my father doesn't follow any particular faith, it was comforting for him to reach out for a higher power.

Kennett, in contrast, was annoyed that people were so concerned. He had already seen me at my worst when I'd been hit on Saturday, so by comparison Tuesday afternoon was a nice gathering with family. He felt the mood was lighter than it had been and to support this he says they even tried to take a group photo. Now he recognizes that he didn't let his mind wander to the worst-case scenario. The farthest his brain would go down the rabbit-hole was to worry about if I'd ever want to ride my bike again.

After dinner, everyone piled into two cars and drove back to the hospital, where they continued to wait another few hours. When the surgeons finally came out, they said that the operations had been a great success. If only a six-hour surgery could have fixed the psychological damage sustained by me, my family, friends, and other cyclists.

CHAPTER 5
DISORIENTATION

'I was concerned you'd wake up hating the world.'
Dad

Since my Tuesday night surgery had been successful, the nurses gradually brought me out of sedation on Wednesday – day five. As I gained consciousness, my arms flailed and my eyes grew wild like an animal being attacked by a predator. I was too agitated, so they sedated me again and started the whole process over a few hours later.

As a result of the morphine and other drugs I was on, my recollection of waking up is hazy. While gaining consciousness, the image of a red car pulling into traffic replayed over and over in my mind. I remembered seeing the sky as I was rolled through ambulance doors on the stretcher, and I recalled the EMT's words, 'Her face is peeled off.' The sensation of my rear bike wheel slipping out from underneath me was fresh. My vision was blurry for a while, and I couldn't discern what was a dream and what was reality.

While I don't know who was near me when I woke up, I remember having a piece of paper and a black Sharpie in front of me. I couldn't speak because of the tracheostomy. The first few times I was handed paper and pen I drew illegible lines all over, trying to regain my cognition and motor skills enough to construct words. Since I was lying back in bed, I couldn't even see what I was writing. The Sharpie bled through the paper, making what was already almost indecipherable even less possible to read. In and out of consciousness, at one point I thought I had written, 'Osmo', which was the drink mix Kennett and I used. In hindsight, I wasn't sharing any of my nutritional secrets – I was trying to ascertain how I'd ended up in my new surroundings.

Kennett saved almost every sheet of paper I wrote on. The stack, about two inches high, has given me the chance to see what I actually wrote. Across one sheet I scribbled, 'I'm scared', and going in another direction on the page I penned in larger letters, 'BLoooD'. Several times I simply formed a messy set of letters written on top of one another. Looking closely at a piece of paper months later, I saw a distinct 'o' between a mix of other lines. I had been trying to spell out 'Mom'. When Nurse Julie came in to take care of me, I managed to legibly write, 'I trust you.' I understood I was in no position to debate my care. Stranger or not, Julie was going to keep me safe.

After I became more alert, I knew three things: I wasn't dreaming, I was very injured, and my injuries were caused by the car I'd been picturing. Beyond that I had little awareness of the present state of affairs or what the future had in store for me.

When my motor skills improved I wrote to my family about the red car, pulling the brakes, skidding, and hearing the EMT. Those were parts of the story I could discuss in great detail. However, it was news to me that I made impact with the car. I had known almost immediately after the Fiat pulled out that I was going to crash, but when I woke up in the hospital I figured my wheel had skidded out from underneath me and I had subsequently hit the pavement. Not knowing I had shattered a window meant I was also clueless about what injuries I had sustained.

My discovery process took days. I'd write questions or comments, hand my paper over to the other person for them to read, and wait for them to speak back to me. It was through these one-sided conversations that I slowly became oriented with why I was in a hospital bed and what my life had become.

My parents didn't share details with me because they wanted me to focus on recovering. Kennett was more willing to talk, but he couldn't fill me in on every detail in one sitting because I was having trouble staying awake and following along. I came out of sedation thinking I was very much the same person I had always been. Each day it became clearer that my life had taken a drastic change of course that I couldn't back out of.

I made it clear to the nurses and my family that I was only going to look in a mirror when I felt ready to, which didn't help me understand the extent of the damage to my face. Given where the nurses were applying ointment, the stark fact that I couldn't speak, and that leeches were being used to keep my lip alive, I figured looking into a mirror would be equivalent to a child seeing an evil clown. It made sense to wait because the longer I put off looking at my reflection, the more time my face would have to heal itself. I reasoned that I could miss seeing the worst of it if I just kept delaying the inevitable.

This left me guessing: *What exactly does having one's face peeled off mean? How does one fix that? What other injuries are there?* Being in the ICU didn't prevent me from being optimistic. One afternoon, it was just my mom and me. She was standing at the right side of my bed so she'd be close enough to read what I wrote on my pad of paper. I tried to point out the positive, 'Still ... No broken bones.' Pretty much every cyclist I knew who crashed seemed to break their collarbone. I had avoided the collarbone, which in a momentary lapse of situational awareness, led me to think that I had lucked out.

I turned the sheet of paper toward her and her eyes scanned, searching for the spot where I'd last written. The page was already cluttered with previous conversations, so it took her a moment to find my most recent statement. She looked up at me through her reading glasses, 'What are you talking about? You broke all the bones in your face.' She handed me back my paper and slowly listed all the places my face had been shattered.

To which I wrote, 'Really? I forgot about those. Oh yeah ... eye socket ... oh.' I was momentarily disturbed but reality still didn't sink in. With most broken bones, there is a general understanding of the recovery timeline and process. Break an elbow and the rehab includes a sling and learning to be ambidextrous. But for a serious facial injury,

I had no prior experience to help me comprehend what the long-term consequences would be. Furthermore, hydrocodone dulled the pain and kept me on cloud nine. And, by not looking in a mirror, I had essentially put up blinders to prevent getting spooked. So when my mom told me about the broken bones in my face I found it humorous how oblivious I had been, and I found my mom's somber reaction even funnier. I shared the humor with other visitors – how crazy was it that I didn't realize I had any broken bones!

My intent was not to remain in denial of my injuries. I was eager to gather information and slowly process how it would impact me. As long as I didn't have a visual of what I looked like, all the details seemed theoretical. For instance, in another conversation Kennett told me I had bitten off a third of my tongue in the crash. It made sense but I never would have thought to make it part of my inquiries. In the past I'd only noticed my tongue when it got tired from picking out pieces of popcorn or kale lodged between my molars.

When Kennett shared that my tongue had been bitten off, I couldn't open my mouth to check for myself, so I was left with my imagination. I was curious what having only a partial tongue would look like to others and how much it would be noticeable. I spent my alone time considering what taste buds I'd lose. What if I lost the ability to taste sweets? Would that be good or bad? It would be a travesty, but it would be a boost to my health. I'd no longer be tempted by cake. It didn't dawn on me to be worried about how it would affect my speech until the speech therapist walked into my room unannounced, standing at the foot of the bed while I stared back waiting for her to tell me what her job was.

That was the last time I had to see the speech therapist. I wasn't talking in the hospital until Sunday and I left on Tuesday morning, day eleven. My tongue itself wasn't nearly as bad as Kennett was led to believe. It did take a few months for me to distinguish between my 'P's and my 'T's, but it was just as much because I'd broken my jaw as anything else. I didn't have to sacrifice the taste of desserts, and during the months that followed, blended up apple pie and ice cream became a favorite of mine. When my tongue healed, I was left with only an inconspicuous scar.

The only detail I didn't want to hear about was how the surgeons went in above my eye to fix all my bones during Tuesday's surgery. The description Kennett gave me of a medical device going in through my eye socket to access my cheekbone was too vivid, so I cut the conversation short.

All of these graphic details left my mind to wander to unpleasant places, like whether my reconstructed cheek would sit in the same place on my face. Knowing what happened in the crash and during surgeries was one thing; however, seeing the result was a gamble. If I saw my reflection, one of two things would happen. Either I'd learn that my imagination had been running rampant and it wasn't so hideous, or I'd be devastated more than I could possibly handle at the time. Best to remain in steady control of my emotions and avoid the mirror. Instead, I played a guessing game equivalent to the board game Guess Who?, which was popular when I was growing up. *Will I have a scar on my face? Will I have a smoker's hole from the trach? Is my lip coming back to life?* I'd ask these questions to the medical team so that I could get a better approximation of what mystery face I'd be matched with when I finally gained the courage to look at myself.

I managed to make it until Sunday, day nine, before seeing my face. There were so many milestones I had to reach first. Before I could examine the plastic surgery job, I had to come to terms with the idea that the world had continued without me while I was sedated. Learning it was Wednesday and that I had lost five days of my life was shocking. After being told I was fortunate to be alive, my mind frequently slipped into thinking, *What if I hadn't made it? In a way, I ceased to exist for those five days. What if I just had never woken back up?* My mind would spin like this whenever there was a quiet moment.

On the opposite side of the spectrum, I was very much alive in a way I am not sure I've ever experienced outside of sports. The rest of the world seems to fall away when attempting to break through to a new level or set a personal best. In both training and racing, performing at my maximum heightens my sense of presence. In the hospital, day-to-day movements I would have never consciously thought of before became huge accomplishments worthy of writing home about. Worthy enough that I didn't even have to write home about it – everyone would come visit me within a few hours to see my most recent progress.

The first surprise my family got was on Thursday morning, which was day six. Earlier that morning, before the sun had risen and the day shift came to work, Nurse Josh had come into my room asking if I wanted to sit in a chair. I figured the biggest barrier to getting out of bed would be dealing with how many machines I was hooked up to. It was more complicated than that.

First, I had to sit up enough in the bed to slide my legs over the right-hand side. The bed moved underneath me like a waterbed because it was designed to relieve bedsores. Josh walked to one side of me and another nurse went to my other side as I slowly stood, bending forward to protect my stomach from the pain of the gastrostomy tube. They untangled and rearranged the IVs, ventilator, catheter, and blood pressure cord that extended from my body as I used both nurses for support.

Lying in bed for so long had given me foot drop, a condition that caused difficulty lifting the front of my foot to take steps. The drop was one reason the neurologist was concerned I might have nerve damage, but subsequent testing once I became conscious proved that I had full function of all my limbs. On top of that, my calves were completely locked up. Taking the two steps to turn and sit into the chair tested my balance and woke up my weakened legs. Not only had I been confined to a bed for several days, my diet had become liquid and I'd lost twelve pounds.

Because we were undertaking this adventure during the night shift, I felt like we were breaking the rules to have a fun time. I was a rebel simply by hunching over in a chair and wearing a *stunning* hospital gown and pulse oximeter. I couldn't wait to do it again and by mid-morning I had my chance. Much to my parents' surprise, when they arrived around nine, I was able to sit in a wheelchair.

Just the day before, the neurologist had been doing tests to ensure I wasn't paralyzed. Even more unbelievable to them was that I was requesting, or demanding, to see Maybellene. Despite my excitement of getting into a chair, seeing our seven-month-old puppy was the major adventure of that Thursday. Maybellene is a short-haired hound mix, tan with a black saddle and white chest. At the time she was all legs and probably thirty pounds. We adopted her as an emotional support dog for my bipolar, and after my crash I needed her more than ever.

But the intensive care unit didn't even allow flowers in patients' rooms. Maybellene stood no chance of coming in. After some discussion, the nurses decided to let me outside, which was unprecedented. Intensive care patients don't even roam the hallways, so there was an air of enthusiasm among the staff. Who would get to escort me? This was so unheard of that a security guard had to come into the ICU from another area of the hospital to disarm the emergency door.

With help, I got out of my bed and into a wheelchair. I was adorned with a heated, white, woven blanket over my lap; another over my shoulders; and my mom's sunglasses. The lights in my room had been off for days and I had a severe concussion. I put the sunglasses on as soon as I was wheeled into the hallway to protect my sensitive eyes and prevent a headache. On my lap was my trusty blue clipboard with pen and paper.

I was wheeled beyond the glass doors of my room and to the left through the double doors as the security guard stood by. My parents and Kennett walked out first. Nurse Elizabeth, who had been the lucky one chosen to join me outside, rolled my wheelchair around a corner and told me to hold on as we navigated over a crack in the concrete. The uneven sidewalk led us to a small parking lot in the back of the hospital. We joked that the wheelchair needed wider, off-road tires to handle the bumpy terrain. Taking in my surroundings I could see we were near an older neighborhood with residential single-level homes. Elizabeth pointed out her car as we passed by it, parked on the side street. As they turned me again to the left, I saw the mountains. In some spots they were covered yellow by aspen trees while the peaks in the background were already dusted with snow.

Up until then I had been sheltered in the safe cocoon of the intensive care unit with kind, capable nurses. The hospital was like a summer camp. The nurses had become friends and instead of art projects I had relearned simple tasks like writing. Going outside created a crack in my mind where the real world could slowly seep in and remind me that my life was not going to be the same.

My excitement at being outdoors was eclipsed by the thoughts of the world existing without me. I reflected, *I almost never got to see those snow-capped mountains again. The aspens, with their golden leaves flickering in the sun, are still as beautiful as they were two weekends ago when Kennett and I went for our six-hour ride. This is why I love fall. I just missed another one of the best weekends of the year for climbing with him. Now I just need to enjoy that I am able see them at all.*

I appreciated the Front Range in a way only a first-timer to the area could. I know that breathing the fresh, crisp air must have been great that day too, but truly what I remember is the spectacular landscape of blue skies butting up against the white-capped mountains behind the foothills.

A few minutes later, when Maybellene arrived with Jos and Galen, she lightened the mood for everyone. I desperately wanted her on my lap, even though it wasn't possible because of my stomach tube. She, on the other hand, wanted nothing to do with me. I didn't smell like the Adelaide she knew. My hospital odor was more a combination of sour urine and bacitracin. Just like me, Maybellene had no idea where she was. For as much as she missed my presence at home, she ignored me on that visit because she couldn't recognize me. Instead, she devoured miniature dried pears that had dropped from the trees I was parked under. While Maybellene wasn't human, this was the first time I had been looked at strangely. In the ICU, all the nurses and visitors treated me normally, which helped me forget my circumstances.

During my short trip outside, I realized I was lost. I knew I was a patient at Longmont United, but I'd never been near the hospital before. While Longmont gave me enough detail to know I was slightly northeast of Boulder and the mountains told me which direction I was facing, I wasn't sure how I'd get home if left to my own devices. Of all the concerns I could have had while lying in intensive care, this was a silly one. It wasn't as though I would be discharged from the hospital without someone to drive me home. Yet it bothered me that I had no clue what stoplights my family hit on their daily drive to visit me. After my fifteen-minute adventure outside, I got excited for the day when I could finally do the drive home with them.

Hospitals know how disorienting it is to be a patient. They make sure to write the day of the week on the whiteboard in front of you. The clock is also placed in direct view of the hospital bed. With the machines that take blood pressure every two hours of the night, the four-hour pain medication schedule, and the midday naps, it can be impossible to even figure out the time of day. The best way to track time passing was the nurses' shift changes. I didn't want to think much about my life beyond the hospital, but that didn't dissuade me from trying to go outdoors again. Now that I had a taste for it, mountains and natural light seemed irresistible.

Around 5 pm the next day, I calculated the nurses' schedule in my head. They'd start shift change at 6:30 pm so I figured we'd have time for another adventure. I wrote to Kennett, 'Maybe we can get permission to wheelchair outside one more time?' What had begun as Josh getting me out of bed the prior morning ended with me taking every opportunity to explore beyond my ICU room. I was out of bed enough times in the days that followed that Nurse Kris later asked, 'Can you vacuum for us next time you roll around in the wheelchair?'

CHAPTER 6
HALLUCINATIONS

'I think the first week when you're awake will be really bad. Like super terrible, even though I'm really looking forward to it. BUT, I think the second week will be only just a bit terrible. The third week might suck a bit more than the second week though.'

Kennett, journaling to me while I was asleep

Friday night, day seven, was the scariest time I experienced in the hospital. It began with a new set of evening nurses who I didn't trust. Irrationally, I thought they might do something wrong and I wouldn't be able to communicate my schedule or needs with them. My parents had already left earlier in the evening, but Kennett normally stayed with me each night until at least 10 pm. On Friday, I asked him to stay with me longer.

My fear stemmed from the fact that I was on a ventilator to help me breathe. The machine hooked up to a small tube that went into the opening in my windpipe from the tracheostomy. Mucus formed inside the tube over time and had to be suctioned out because it would block my airway, leaving me suffocating in my own phlegm.

That night, mucus built up every twenty minutes, and each time my breathing became labored as my chest filled with fluid. Kennett was in protective mode and hit the nurse's button repeatedly in an effort to speed up the respiratory therapist's response.

She seemed to move at a geriatric patient's pace while pushing her instruments into the room, putting on sterile gloves, and unwrapping the sealed, sanitary tubing. The tedious process seemed to take minutes and, while I fought for enough air, both Kennett and I wanted her to hurry the hell up. Finally she'd connect the pencil-sized tubing to a machine, stick it down the hole in my neck, all the way into my lungs, and clear out the phlegm. Even though the suctioning was performed for less than ten seconds at a time, each procedure was as terrifying as the last. The tubing blocked my airway, so it created the sensation of choking. I also had to be temporarily unhooked from the ventilator, which aided my breathing in the first place.

Throughout Friday night, when I'd close my eyes I'd hallucinate bright, gigantic Mardi Gras characters, who were projected onto the wall and ceiling. Their legs were out of proportion with their upper bodies, as though they were on stilts. The women wore long dresses while the men were in vividly patched clothing. The background was tangerine orange as I watched them dancing to big band music. The dancing was the most grounded element of the hallucination because Kennett and I were listening to my iPod.

My sister had brought me small speakers earlier in the week so we could play music as an activity. I had been a long-time groupie of the singer-songwriter Stephen Kellogg and his band the Sixers, so we played song after song, repeating the same ones over again as the hours went by. I'd been to over ten of his concerts before. I couldn't sing along, but I knew all the lyrics.

In one of the actual concerts I'd attended, Stephen Kellogg and the Sixers played 'Milwaukee' and broke down each element of the music. The pianist did a solo after which Stephen sung. As the piano solo continued he talked about getting scared at life and how friends, family, and the melody help him feel less afraid. When the drums came into the song, he described them as the heartbeat. That is exactly how I listened to each element of the music while in the hospital. Exhausted and anxious from each respiratory episode when I struggled to breathe, Kennett and I broke down crying through lyrics.

And that was how the night continued. We played songs, cried to the lyrics, and I'd describe my imaginary giant people to Kennett with pen and paper. I'd complain that even with my eyes open I kept seeing purple-, red-, and orange-colored fireworks bursting through the darkness. Mucus would fill my lungs, the respiratory therapist would shuffle in, and I'd look for reassurance from Kennett as I endured a few more seconds of choking and violent coughing. The goal throughout it all was simply to make it until the sun rose.

In the morning, Kennett went home to sleep and I took a nap. When my parents came in at nine o'clock, I made my dad play Stephen Kellogg's song 'Father's Day'. I needed the protection of my family, and to listen to the reassuring lyrics of my favorite songwriter to remind me there'd be better days ahead. While that night was the last I struggled to breathe, I had other looming fears that a slow-moving respiratory therapist and pain medication couldn't fix.

It was as though I had been stuck in rough ocean waters and colliding with the Fiat was only the first wave of a set. I managed to come back to the surface without drowning. I was alive and excited to be making almost hourly improvements in the hospital, but I could see another enormous wave approaching. It was only a matter of time before it also crested and came crashing down on me. This second wave was a looming awareness that I was most likely going to suffer from a massive bipolar depressive episode.

By Saturday, my fears were amplified because I had missed a full night of sleep and had hallucinated for the first time in my life when I saw the Mardi Gras characters. *At what point am I going to drop into depression from the stress on my body? Hallucinations are a sign of bipolar I, not II. Is it possible for a person's bipolar to get so severe as to cause the shift from bipolar II to I?* I may not have had all the answers, but my concerns were legitimate. Unlike the crash, where I was in the dark about injuries and recovery, I had past experiences where stress brought on mental instability.

Even before being diagnosed at age twenty-six, I had times where my lifestyle naturally helped keep my brain balanced. Having a regimented schedule, almost no alcohol, and consistent exercise helped my brain immensely during college at the United States Coast Guard Academy. The real trouble came when I graduated in 2008 and was sent to the USCGC *Dallas* in Charleston, South Carolina – my new assignment as an ensign. Upon arrival my biggest goal was to qualify as a deck watch officer, so I could control safe navigation of the cutter. I was also designated as the COMMO, communications officer, and took over planning morale events for the entire crew.

The appeal of the 378-foot Coast Guard cutter was its upcoming patrol to Africa followed by the Mediterranean. It was my chance to travel to places I'd wanted to see since I was a kid, so I'd put the assignment on my wish list despite my hesitation about being underway for extended periods of time. From prior summer assignments as a cadet at the Academy, I knew the confinement and schedule of being underway wasn't conducive to my wellbeing. Sure enough, I became psychologically unstable shortly after we left Charleston. There were plenty of warning signs, but whenever my world went south, I found someone or something to blame for my disposition.

The operations officer, 'Ops', was my immediate superior and as a result he saw my most severe mood shifts. His stateroom was one floor beneath mine. Midway through patrol I made my way down the narrow ladderwell and rapped on his door, which was directly to the right, at the bottom of the stairs. He invited me into his room and shut the door, which wasn't common protocol because it could be interpreted as an inappropriate relationship. However, it was best to hide my tearful outbreaks from the rest of the 130 crew members onboard. His room was the size of a large bathroom. The paint was a light dingy yellow. The bed was directly across the room with a small cubby above it filled with books secured for sea. To the left of the door was his messy desk that was anything but ready for a rogue wave. He always had a mug of coffee either in his hand or on the desk.

I needed someone who could listen to my complaints about the executive officer, XO, who was second-in-command on the cutter. 'Ops, I can't do this anymore. XO yelled at me for my hair being wet. It isn't fair. I'm the only female officer whose hair isn't long enough for a ponytail. When am I supposed to find time to blow-dry my hair when I'm doing doubles trying to qualify as a deck watch officer? I'm not cut out for this! I will never be a good officer.'

'Blow-dry your hair, it's not hard. XO doesn't have it out for you. Once you qualify as a deck watch officer, you'll only have to stand watch once a day and your life will ease up a bit.'

Because I'd only slept for a few hours before my 4 am watch, I'd be garbling my words as I cried. How could I possibly blow-dry my hair when I had to take care of my other responsibilities and pull myself together enough to be around others during my 4 pm watch on the bridge?

The next day, when I found time to stop by Ops' stateroom to check in again, my mood had already shifted drastically. This time, he told me, 'You're right. You might not be great for this job. I talked with Captain and XO and we are thinking it would be good for you to see a psychologist when we pull into port in Rota, Spain.'

'How can you possibly say that?' I responded angrily. 'Aren't you on my side? No, absolutely not! I can't believe you'd ever tell me I'm not cut out to be an officer. I'm completely capable of qualifying for my position.' I stormed out, full of energy and pissed off. Variations of this conversation occurred multiple times. My anger would come and go, but overall I appreciated that Ops continued to talk to me without holding my moods against me and I genuinely thought highly of him.

One time when I stopped by his room, Ops asked me semi-seriously, 'Any chance you are pregnant? My ex-wife acted like this when she was having our kids.'

I laughed at his question and instead attributed my behavior to the stress of being sea-sick, taking malaria meds that intensified dreams, not having much time to exercise, breaking my finger underway, and, of course, my perceived idea that the XO was singling me out. All this added stress to my life, which amplified my bipolar. However, none of these events directly caused my mood swings – those were the result of faulty brain chemicals.

When we returned to homeport in Charleston I decided of my own accord that I needed to either be a highly qualified and respected officer or I needed to find a way out of my five-year commitment to the Coast Guard. At the Academy, a Senior Chief advised us that, as future officers, an enlisted member always needed to be able to walk up to us with either good news or terrible news and expect us to react with the same calm demeanor. His advice stood out to me as a marker to strive for – stable enough to interact with others in a predictable way. As proven by my tearful fits underway, I was failing the enlisted members in my division by not being a steady person they could approach. After we returned that fall, I decided to see a military psychologist on the nearby naval base. It would not go well.

When I walked into the psychiatrist's office, he immediately wanted to check under the sleeves of my blue uniform windbreaker for cut marks, which put me on the defensive. I told him I had a good support network from family and friends but he scoffed at me, telling me I wouldn't be in his office if that were true. After I described my wish to become a better officer or leave the Coast Guard, he said I had options but failed to list them. When I pushed him to learn what he had in mind, he repeatedly told me that we could discuss those mysterious options at another appointment. At the end of the session, after he left the office, I took a moment to wipe tears off my face before walking into the waiting room. His response to my delayed exit was, 'Did you get lost in there?' Not only did I never see the psychologist again, he left a bad enough impression on me that I no longer wanted to seek help. It would take another three years for me to work up the courage to return to a psychiatrist and get properly diagnosed.

In the meantime, I agreed with my command that they could write me a poor Officer Evaluation Report (OER), which would lead to an honorable discharge in August of 2009. I felt like a failure for not completing my time in the Coast Guard but at least there had been a way out. A way that allowed me to keep a more consistent schedule and return to better health. Lying in bed at Longmont United Hospital, I was keenly aware that I didn't have a get-out-early option for my recovery.

My time on the USCGC *Dallas* was significantly different from lying in the hospital bed. For one, with a staff of nurses around the clock, I wasn't even responsible for myself, let alone an entire communications division and the morale on a large cutter.

Yet, there were some common elements between my time underway and my current status in intensive care that scared me. I had spent five days unconscious without medication. I did not know how long I could go unmedicated before I would watch myself unravel. The two years since I had been diagnosed in late summer of 2012 were the most mentally stable I had been. Would I suddenly regress after being off medication?

Standing doubles in the Coast Guard meant I was on the bridge two times a day. (For example, the 8 am to 12 pm watch along with the 8 pm to midnight watch.) The rotation also shifted regularly. I would go from waking up at 2:30 am so I could do my rounds and be on the bridge by 4 am, to suddenly needing to be up for the midnight to 4 am watch. In the hospital, I was up at various hours of the night. The nurses would check my vitals every two hours, which meant I was never able to sleep properly. Taking pain medication and having leech treatment were both on a schedule requiring I be up every four hours. Of course, on Friday I missed sleeping altogether.

When I had horrible nightmares from malaria medicine in the Coast Guard, it reaffirmed my long-standing fears that medication could mess with my sleep and moods. Now, in the hospital bed, I didn't even know what medicine I was taking or the potential side effects.

There was a lot at stake for me. I was already physically in a different condition and I didn't want to lose my sense of self too. I couldn't afford to have a bipolar episode because I didn't want an additional stress on my relationship with Kennett. I wouldn't blame him if the crash and bipolar combined were too much for him. How could I ever be mad at him for wanting to leave me? Even I loathe myself when I'm depressed and I still had no idea what I looked like.

If my mood did plummet, I was worried I wouldn't be able to bring myself back to baseline. A major coping mechanism I have for depression is forcing myself to get some exercise. Getting up and sitting in a wheelchair wasn't going to produce enough endorphins to save me if I became depressed.

In the Coast Guard, I didn't know why I was struggling so much more than my peers. I couldn't identify the triggers, such as lack of sleep or exercise. I wasn't able to tell Ops why I acted like a pregnant woman. At least now I could explain to the medical staff how I was affected by sleep, sudden changes to plans, and more.

At the time I figured if I told enough of the medical staff about my bipolar, we could all work together to create a safe haven and prevent me from having a massive mood swing. Did I make a difference? Probably not. I wrote to nurses that the half-life of my bipolar medicine was eight hours (which I later looked up and found wasn't even correct) to explain why it was important for me not to be missing doses.

The nurses, doctors, and my family were all astonished at how quickly I was out of bed. I was an unusual patient for intensive care because, unlike the many geriatric patients, I was a fit athlete and my health was on the upswing. As a result, everyone who walked into my room seemed to carry a positive vibe with them. Nobody had a crystal ball to determine my future, but spending six weeks in outpatient care wouldn't be part of it.

I was recovering rapidly, however my upbeat attitude waxed and waned on a predictable four-hour opioid schedule. Unlike bipolar, I knew I could control these rapid changes in my outlook with careful monitoring of when I received pain medication. Fifteen minutes after I got a dose, life seemed pretty manageable. Once that wore off four hours later, I was miserable. With the clock sitting high up on the wall in front of my bed I was able to keep close tabs and write 'Meds = 4hrs!' as a shorthand way of communicating to the nurses I was in too much pain.

In conversations with several nurses I redrew a minimalist graph that the psychiatrist who diagnosed me with bipolar had drawn in an appointment. It was a visual of how my blood sugar spikes and crashes more than the average person when they have sugar. When the blood sugar takes a dive, it puts additional stress on the body. I explained to the nurses that the hospital choices of cranberry juice or apple juice were going to spike my blood sugar and make me mentally unstable. The solution was simply to get more chicken broth and less juice.

I was similarly anal about my self-proposed schedule. I took up an entire sheet of computer paper when I told a nurse, 'Not personal BUT FOOD LEECHES MEDS 4 hrs.' Another sheet was filled with an even more direct note, 'MEDS FOOD LEECHES ON TIME.' I figured if I carefully monitored these I could prevent feeling worse later. The leeches were included in my demands because they took about twenty minutes to suck my blood and I appreciated knowing when my next blood-soaked leech encounter for the day would be.

In general I think I was a pleasant, engaging patient, but I had a bossy side. My fears were often about my emotional wellbeing and less about my unseen injuries. However, the medical team's job was to take care of me physically, which occasionally clashed with how I felt my bipolar sensitivities should be approached.

One time I butted heads with Dr. Carter, who visited my room with the intent of taking out some of my stitches. It would have been a noisy disagreement, except I couldn't raise my voice in frustration, so I scribbled my words with extra vigor.

In my mind there were several problems with Dr. Carter showing up in my room. First, I hadn't been notified that work was going to be done on my face. Granted he was the one with an actual schedule to keep. The real problem stemmed from the fact that he wanted to give me fast-acting pain medication before going in to remove stitches. This would be a different pain medication than I was accustomed to and I would be taking it on an empty stomach. I didn't know how this new medication would affect me mentally, which upset me. Plus, I was weak and according to my clock it was time for me to be fed a smoothie through my stomach tube. I asked to eat first and explained that it would only take a few minutes. I wasn't munching on a meal; a nurse was pumping a semi-liquid smoothie into my gastrostomy tube via a 1-inch-wide syringe. Dr. Carter told me he didn't have time. After all, he had other patients to see. So I put up a fight.

I told him I was the patient, it was my body, and I wasn't going to have my stitches taken out until I was fed. The stitches didn't bother me so, as far as I was concerned, it didn't matter when they came out. He told me he probably wouldn't be able to come back until the next day. I let him walk out of the room. Looking back, I'm not even sure if my reasoning made any sense. I do know I picked a fight with the wrong person.

At the time, I didn't realize who Dr. Carter was in the grand scheme of it all. It was the equivalent of a business owner fighting with their only multi-million-dollar client — except maybe worse. It wasn't in my best interest to be stubborn toward the person who had perfectly reconstructed my cheekbone, saved my lip from dying, and carefully placed the stitches in to begin with.

While we didn't get off to the best start when I was conscious, Dr. Carter was positive in all of our interactions. After talking with my parents, he came back in to remove the stitches and never held my silent outburst against me. Crisis averted for the time being.

For all the additional stressors to my body, such as lack of sleep, no exercise, and huge doses of pain medication, I never got depressed in the hospital. Looking back, I think one of the reasons I stayed emotionally stable was because of the caring medical team. For instance, the night nurses I was nervous about on Friday? They ended up spending hours over the weekend reading and talking to me, in addition to taking care of my medical needs. They kept me from feeling alone and sorry for myself in the middle of the night when the hallway lights, beeping machines, and pain kept me from sleeping.

In those early days Kennett and I were surrounded by people who cared, which buoyed us up when it felt like we were drowning. Even in the Coast Guard, when I may have perceived that the XO was out to punish me, my fellow Coasties were looking out for my best interests. I didn't have any prior knowledge to help me prepare for the next set of rough waves on the horizon. It wasn't until later, when I felt a sense of injustice, that my emotions began to tailspin.

CHAPTER 7
GETTING MARRIED

'I feel like I just married you because this is a lot of not fun heavy stuff to deal with. But I am very excited toooooo.'
My note to Kennett in the hospital

Late Thursday morning, the day after I woke up, Kennett made his first appearance of the day. He walked around and stood by the right side of my bed where he could read my writing quickly, which made for an efficient conversation.

I wrote, 'Did you sleep okay?'

'Yeah, each night it's getting a little easier. Maybellene is sleeping in bed with me while you're gone. How are you feeling?'

I gave two thumbs up, which was my quickest shorthand for saying I was doing all right.

'My dad is in the waiting room. He'll come say hi in a little bit. He flew in Monday. He and your dad were on the same bus from the airport and sat next to each other briefly when they were both trying to figure out when to get off the bus. Later that afternoon they met in the waiting room and your dad said, "I know you!"' (Our dads had never met before.)

I smiled, though I wouldn't appreciate the humor of the chance encounter until the following day, when my sister showed me photos of the dads' meeting. They both showed up dressed identically in checkered shirts, jeans, and brown boots. Like two peas in a pod.

'My dad's staying on the futon at the apartment. It's been nice having him here to talk to.'

I scribbled to Kennett, 'I am glad your dad is with you.'

Kennett seemed like he had a secret to tell me and changed the topic quickly, suddenly asking, 'Will you marry me?' I was caught off guard because of the relaxed nature of the question.

Excuse me, did I hear you right? I thought. He hadn't paused the conversation or done anything else to prepare me for it. I responded by writing, 'Are you serious? Or joking?'

'I'm being serious,' Kennett replied.

I wrote in extra-large, one-inch-high letters, 'YES!'

Kennett read over my shoulder and laughed. 'Good, that's the third time I asked you. You don't remember any of the other times?'

'No,' I wrote.

'I proposed the night you were hit. You squeezed my hand and nodded your head. I reminded you multiple times when you were in a coma but you didn't respond. I reminded you we were engaged each night actually. I also asked you yesterday when you were still pretty out of it. You nodded yes again. So now you really can't back out.'

Tears formed in my eyes as the news sunk in.

The fact that Kennett proposed so early on after my crash became extremely reassuring. It's easy to make a relationship work when everything is going fine, but Kennett didn't choose to marry me at my best moment. He decided that, even with my bipolar, injuries, and tears, I was still worth being around. However, I didn't comprehend all of this until left alone for several hours. Initially, as I agreed to get married, all I could think was, *I need to announce I'm engaged!*

If I had been capable of walking and talking, I would have immediately dragged Kennett to the nurses' station so I could re-introduce him as my fiancé, pause briefly for congratulations, and zoom off to find whoever was hanging back in the waiting room.

Instead, I told my parents when they came in and, to my dismay, they didn't seem shocked. That's because Kennett had already asked my dad for my hand in marriage. This story has since become one of my dad's favorites to tell about the crash. On midday Tuesday, prior to my surgery, Kennett asked my dad to walk to the hospital chapel with him. Since they had already taken a few afternoon walks through the neighborhood, the outing was not special in and of itself. However, Kennett chose the spot intentionally. He knew that my dad had, on his own, visited the chapel a few times and felt it was a sanctuary where he could retreat to when emotions ran high.

The chapel was a small, windowless room, warmly lit with elegant light fixtures. There were a few religious pamphlets and statues, but it served as a non-denominational chapel for anyone in the hospital. While in the room, Kennett asked, 'Raymond, I'm going to marry Adelaide, if that's alright with you.'

'Wow, yes. That's excellent! Of course, of course!'

'Well, technically I already asked her, but it was that first night and she was only semi-conscious.'

At that, my dad smiled and gave Kennett a long hug. For several years my dad has told me this story because, when he reflects back on it, he knows how special it was that Kennett had taken the time to ask him. What I didn't realize until more recently was just how unimportant Kennett asking my dad for my hand in marriage was to my dad at that moment. My dad and I had a good laugh when he tried to give me a comparison of how he felt. 'It was like your house is burning down and someone walks up to you and asks, "Can I pick your tomatoes in the backyard?"' My mom said the proposal had been great news – news that she set aside, figuring it could be dealt with at a later time.

More important to my parents was that I was about to head into my second surgery. After Kennett and my dad returned from their brief chapel excursion, the surgeon came out to visit my family. He went over the details of what surgeries would be performed, including the plan to wire my jaw shut so the bones could heal. After the surgeon turned to walk away, my dad caught up to him and said, 'Doc, I'll be praying for you.'

Once I woke up without brain damage or paralysis, my parents were able to relax a little. Both thought highly of Kennett before the crash, and the timing of his proposal furthered their confidence that he would take good care of me into the future. I was the one who finally dialed up their excitement. It would have been hard for them to have *not* become wrapped up in my elation and my cheerful demands for the blue sapphire ring.

Kennett and I aren't the type of couple to purchase an expensive engagement ring. In fact, Kennett isn't one to go buy a ring at all. At the time, our money was going to new bikes, buying a friend's 1995 camper van, and traveling to races. However, in the hospital I wanted Kennett to go home immediately to get a ring in my jewelry box. It was one that my parents had bought me in high school with a dark sapphire stone inlaid into a gold band. I didn't mind if the ring wasn't a designated engagement ring; it would serve the purpose. When everyone else thought I was being ridiculous for requesting expedited service on a ring that I already owned at home, I had to explain, 'I want the nurses to know you are my fiancé.'

When the nurses walked into the room, I would hold out my black-and-blue hand with the pulse oximeter attached and, with my eyes smiling, point to my ring finger. Little did I know as I laid propped upright in bed, beaming with joy, that many of the staff knew I was engaged before I did.

Even when I was in the room alone, the ring was an important visual. Kennett had always told me he wasn't going to leave me over a bad bipolar episode, but I didn't fully trust him because I knew how stressful my mood shifts could be. Now, there was a scenario much worse than bipolar and he vowed to stay by my side forever, even with the potential for lifelong facial disfigurement. The ring reminded me that I would get better, that Kennett would be here for me until I did, and that there would be a celebration at some point. When I wanted to escape the pain, my immobility, and the white walls of my hospital room, I pictured where we would get married.

There was no delay in planning our wedding, especially when my sister came to visit. Lydia and Jeff got engaged that prior summer while the two of them were on Ride the Rockies, a week-long bike tour through the mountain towns of Colorado. She was already deep into wedding planning herself.

Sitting on a bench near the window, Lydia said, 'Jeff and I talked it over, and we would love for you to do a double wedding with us if you want. I mean, you already know that we are getting married at the Gold Hill Inn up Sunshine Canyon. We already have it reserved for Memorial Day, so it would be a case of you liking the venue too. You and I share family and lots of the same friends, so it wouldn't be too many more people. The space seats 150, and we won't have that many on our own. Just think it over and talk to Kennett about it.'

It was clear that Lydia and Jeff had discussed it and put a considerable amount of thought into the idea of a double wedding before suggesting one. My mom, who was also sitting in the room, was impressed. 'Lydia, that is so sweet. I can't believe how special it is that you even thought of it!'

Next time Kennett was at the hospital we used my pad of paper for making lists of who we thought would come to our wedding. During these times I drifted out of the hospital in spirit. I was just another girl getting excited while creating a party list.

Ultimately, we decided it would be best to do separate weddings. I look back on it now and sometimes wish I had shared my wedding day with Lydia, but I have to remember what the circumstances at the time were. We didn't know what my recovery would be like. I pictured all the stunning wedding photos I'd seen throughout the years. Like the brides in all the photos, I wanted to be beautiful on my wedding day, and at the same time, I didn't know when, if ever, I would feel attractive again. Turning down the idea of a double wedding wasn't just about me; it also didn't seem fair to my sister.

My injuries had drawn attention to me. The concern and communication between family and friends was still about how I was doing. Lydia was in the hospital every day taking care of me and making sure I was upbeat. I wanted her to be the center of attention for her wedding. Lydia and I weren't going to be any closer as friends by sharing a ceremony. What matters is that, for a little while, we both seriously considered how fun it would be.

After I returned home from the hospital, Kennett and I scoped out venues with a vague idea of doing a fall wedding. Later, when I was drained from a long winter and wanted to have a sense of calm and life-as-normal, we took our attention away from a wedding and focused on finding a place to call home.

We scrapped all wedding plans in February when I saw a new condo listing in North Boulder, exactly where we were hoping to remain located. Because I had been in the Coast Guard, we were going to get a VA loan, which has special requirements. One is that in order for both individuals' incomes to be considered, they have to be married. If we wanted a loan big enough to cover a condo in Boulder, it would have to include both of our incomes.

Property in the area goes overnight. There are bidding wars, cash offers for tens of thousands over the listing price, and no seller is going to wait for a couple to get married for the loan to get approved. When Kennett came home from work, he mentioned the same condo listing and had separately come to the conclusion that I had: we should get married before the weekend's open house.

My parents happened to be in town visiting and we explained our new wedding plans over dinner that evening. We'd leave work for a lunch date and head over to the Boulder County Clerks and Recorder's office to sign marriage documents. Both of us worked at the same company, so coordinating the whole event would be easy.

Kennett and I got married on Friday 13th, 2015. We told our office that we were headed out for a quick lunch. It took ten minutes to sign the marriage papers, after which we walked outside and found a cement picnic table. My parents brought crackers, cheese, sparkling grape juice, champagne glasses, and a few other snacks. Afterwards, we drove to Whole Foods and bought a cake to surprise our co-workers with. Our boss told us to take the rest of the day off, which we spent riding our bikes downtown and looking at wedding rings, none of which we'd purchase because we were saving for a condo.

We did find a place that weekend. Not the one we expected, but a perfect one-bedroom loft with a garage for all the bikes. Over the course of several weeks we would share the news of our marriage. Unlike my engagement, where everyone knew before me, I got to treasure the secret and surprise people with it during random conversation. It was still important to have a celebration with friends and family who supported us, so we hosted an informal ceremony and party at the local Elk's Club that September.

While weddings are often a grand affair, both our legal marriage and the party were anti-climatic. It was impossible for them to not have been. Ultimately, it wouldn't have mattered how fancy or elegant our wedding could have been, it would always play second fiddle to Kennett's romantic proposal. Those first few days, when I flaunted the ring and told everyone about my engagement, I might as well have been twirling around in a white wedding dress instead of a hospital gown. And, with the stakes so high from the crash, we felt married as soon as Kennett proposed to me anyhow. We immediately adopted each other's family as our own because we needed all the support we could get. We jointly looked forward to a better future together and kept our sights on when it would all feel like a bad dream. By February, our energy was drained and the wedding was merely a brief, but welcome, distraction from the stress we were under from my recovery.

When my parents tell me about Kennett's proposal, they both have the tendency to bring up one other memory. They tell me what a childhood neighbor told her parents after she found out how I had been proposed to. She expressed that she wanted to find a guy who would stand by her in the way Kennett did for me. In her mind it was a fairytale engagement, and I couldn't agree more.

CHAPTER 8
COPING WITH CHANGE

'Leeches are too bloody'
Me in the ICU

In the spring of 2011, at age twenty-four, I finally felt ready to move onto the next phase in my life. It had been over a year since I'd been honorably discharged from the Coast Guard and moved to Colorado. At the time it seemed like I was just fine-tuning what I wanted to do, which is common for many twenty-something-year-olds. In hindsight, the number of jobs I held in that brief period should have been a warning sign of my mental instability. First I nannied, then I took a temporary position teaching math at an alternative high school. Later I was a field instructor for a wilderness therapy program, and I followed that job with a retail position at Title Nine. I didn't understand it at the time, but I was inherently adjusting my life to function with my undiagnosed bipolar. Working part-time kept my stress levels low, which made me more emotionally stable. During a period where I was hovering at a baseline mood, I felt confident that I could manage a career again and decided to apply for graduate school.

While I was applying to grad school, I decided I needed to connect with my inner athlete again. In high school I had the highest self-esteem when I was on the swim team. In college I felt the most attractive and accomplished after I'd raced the Marine Corp Marathon. But I was on the search for more than a boost of confidence. When I sensed instability in my life emotionally, a major achievement would bring me back into control.

One February morning I sat at the kitchen bar in my house. I was already on my second helping of breakfast, and while I wasn't aware of my bipolar diagnosis yet, I inherently knew binge eating was a bad sign. *Not to worry*, I thought. *All I need to do is to sign up for a race. I've got the time to train now. Once I'm training I'll have more reason to eat healthy.* I looked at races on my laptop for the umpteenth time before pulling out my credit card. I chose to sign up for Redman, an iron-distance triathlon taking place mid-September, along with a few shorter races to help me prepare.

I knew from swim training in high school that I'd always be capable of swimming 4,000 yards in the pool, so I figured the equivalent in open water would be manageable. Biking 112 miles was a stretch, but I'd ridden 95 miles one day with my sister while we were bike touring. I'd also completed two stand-alone marathons in the previous years. However, putting all these events together would require a new level of discipline. If I could finish Redman it would be proof that I had both the physical strength and the mental control I was always questioning.

The spring and summer came and went. I was accepted into a one-year master's program in urban education through the University of Denver and would begin in the fall. I completed the shorter triathlons with my eye still on Redman. However, I couldn't seem to put my head down to focus for long. Over the course of my seven-month training period I moved apartment and changed jobs three more times, quitting one of them so I could take a two-week trip to Alaska. So much for developing discipline and consistency ... My emotions and my nutrition were just as shaky as my training regimen, but I didn't know life any differently. I wanted to be an accomplished athlete who held a strict training schedule, but I could never stick with my plans from week to week.

When Redman rolled around, I asked my mom to fly to Denver and drive with me to Oklahoma City. She later told me she was reluctant to join for the trip because she – my own mom – didn't think I would finish the race. She must have been aware of how little I was training. I ended up finishing Redman within my goal time. I recall very little from the swim and bike, but three miles into the run I began to struggle. There was another woman who was maintaining the same pace as I was and we joined forces to motivate each other for the remaining 23 miles. When I crossed the finish line, I entered the circus-like tent to find water, fold-out chairs, food, and my supportive mom waiting nearby. I was physically tired, but I had so much energy from my accomplishment that I had trouble falling asleep that night.

While Redman was an immediate success, it did not fulfill any larger role in my life as I had hoped it would. It did not propel me into becoming a dedicated athlete, and within a few months I had a resurgence of the same fear that I would not have the mental fortitude to get through the rough patches in life. Redman had been a controlled environment that I could prepare for, but what if something horrific happened? Even my master's program was proving to be too much. Midyear into getting my master's degree I found myself in a similarly agitated state as when I was underway in the Coast Guard. I had trouble with my graduate professors because I was stubborn and irrational. It was a struggle to keep my emotions in check when I was student teaching in front of a classroom full of high school students. All my energy was spent at school, which meant I would frequently fall apart when I got home.

I'd call my mom and dad, crying in the fetal position on the floor. Beside me would be the empty four-pack of muffins I had just bought and a plastic bagful of leftover nuts from two pounds of triple-chocolate trail mix. On the other line my mom would be encouraging me to move. Sometimes she would suggest a walk or jumping jacks. A successful conversation would be one where I'd have the focus and control to follow along with her for six deep breaths. Plenty of times I hung up on them, angry because they couldn't help me, scared because I didn't know how to help myself, and convulsing in a fit of tears. My parents would always call back and eventually I would calm down enough to crawl from the floor to my mattress, rarely leaving the room before falling asleep. I took sick days without the slightest sign of a sniffle or fever so that I could catch up on sleep and give myself a chance to regroup.

By the end of my master's program the following July, I spent most days binge eating, watching the same two or three movies on repeat, and sleeping. I'd gained thirty pounds. It was at this low point that I managed to get diagnosed with bipolar II. Life improved after I began taking medication for my mood swings, but the feeling that I might not be strong enough to handle life's normal stresses remained lodged in the back of my mind.

Two years later, just before the crash, I was training for my second iron-distance triathlon. This time around I didn't sink to the same lows I had earlier in my life because I had the additional support of being on bipolar medication and having Kennett as a coach. However, I still struggled to maintain a consistent schedule and there were often a few days each month that my workouts fell through. While I was coming at this race from a more stable place, I was still using the training as a way to ease my mood swings and give myself a sense of control. Because of bipolar, I never thought that I'd be able to cope with a truly traumatic or difficult situation. I couldn't even handle my own mood swings and depression at times. If a master's program was too stressful for me, how could I survive the death of my parents? If I couldn't get out of bed due to bipolar, how would I fare if I ever became paralyzed in an accident? Each interval I pushed through in training made me feel like I was building mental strength for the inevitable day when something tragic would happen. Each workout I completed made me feel one step further away from a mood swing derailing my life.

Of course, when I smashed into the red Fiat, it was without any advance warning. My triathlon training helped me build a tolerance for brief, stressful environments and taught me to dig deep during painful training sessions, but it didn't prepare me for the hospital. Contrary to what I had assumed – that my brain would crumble under extraordinary stresses and that I needed to learn to overcome this disability – I didn't need to control or fight anything in the hospital; I simply had to accept my reality.

Both my mind and body did an incredible job of adapting to my situation. Prior to the crash, someone would have had to pay me a hefty sum to allow a leech near my body. The few times in life when I learned I was swimming in leech-infested water I made immediate progress toward land. Fast-forward to the hospital. A leech costs about $3, but to ship them costs about $500 – fees that would ultimately be added to my hospital bill. Dr. Carter was excited to use leeches to increase the circulation to my upper lip, which had effectively been ripped back to my neck and was at risk of necrotizing. At his direction, nurses began applying them immediately after my second surgery on Tuesday, well before I woke from my sedated coma. The first few hours that I was coherent were still a morphine-induced blur, and by the time I was fully awake, continuing leech treatment seemed to be just another part of my routine. Because the situation necessitated it, I had simply and effortlessly let go of my prior dislike of leeches.

Every four hours a leech was ordered from the pharmacy, unfrozen, and brought into my room. To help control the leech, nurses placed it in the hollow tube of a plastic syringe, which acted as a makeshift container, as it latched onto my lip. Each leech had its own personality. Some were eager to suck up my blood while others were a bit fat and less hungry. They would begin about a half-inch in size and grow to be two or three inches long, and obese with my blood.

The most skilled leech-whisperer, Josh, worked nights. On top of mastering the actual feeding, he quickly devised a way to keep the blood from dripping into my mouth afterwards. It involved wrapping a face mask (like one a person would wear on an airplane to avoid germs) up so it formed a tampon-like tube shape. That sat over my mouth while the face mask loops hooked over my ears to keep it in place. Josh made the procedure more entertaining by drawing a handlebar mustache on the contraption with a black Sharpie. Over the week I had several more masks made because each blood-soaked mustache was, of course, single use.

Personally, I was quite pleased that my eyes couldn't strain far enough down my nose to see a leech sucking at my skin. I felt a tingling when they latched on, but I couldn't even discern where on my lip they had been placed because the whole area would ache from the increased blood flow. The nurses, while excited, had a calm demeanor when they were bringing in the leeches, and this calmness transferred to me.

My mom and sister thought it was fascinating that the medical community had returned to a technique used by Egyptians some 3,500 years ago. Though back then, leeches were thought to cure all sorts of ailments, from headaches to hemorrhoids. The practice of bloodletting continued and became quite popular for Europeans and Americans in the 1800s. Toward the end of the century doctors began to discredit many of the claimed benefits and the use of leeches died down. Leeches are only recently coming back as standard practice in hospitals, meaning that many nurses had never actually seen the use of them in treatment. More than once, my nurse would come to the doorway accompanied by other curious nurses from other floors of the hospital and ask if her colleagues could watch the process. I was happy to let them see. Maybe they've gone on to use the knowledge on other patients. While I found the leeches unpleasant because they caused so much bleeding, I developed other people's appreciation for them. For all the medical technology there is, a large family of leeches was ultimately what saved my lip.

I'm inclined to say that every patient has a breaking point with tolerating leeches. We were slowly reaching my limit when nurse Shannon brought my late afternoon leech into the room. I was relaxed and even had a few visitors. As she placed the leech near my lip, it went wild. It started to crawl up toward my nostril, as I lay helpless in bed. Shannon quickly responded by throwing it back in the petri dish, where it continued to splash water around. We all laughed about it while another leech was ordered from the pharmacy. I cooperated, but I also made a point to ask Dr. Carter if we could stop leech treatment when I saw him next. Aside from the overactive leech, I was worn down from having them administered on such a constant schedule. The bleeding was substantial, leaving my lip sore and my teeth covered in blood clots. Between leeches, the strings of dried blood would tickle between my teeth and my tongue, as though a strand of hair got stuck in my mouth. With Dr. Carter's approval, the treatment stopped shortly thereafter. The leeches had effectively done their job and my lip was healthy enough to heal on its own.

Having leeches on my face was made easier by the fact that I was on a high dose of drugs and that the people surrounding me all thought highly of the treatment. Nevertheless, to this day I am amazed by how calmly I accepted that they were necessary. For years I was skeptical of whether or not I'd be strong enough to handle life's shocks. Yet, when the day came I didn't have a choice, so I just went along with the flow.

Leeches, however, were only a small sign of a much larger problem – that my face had taken the full impact of hitting the car. Thursday, Friday, and Saturday came without me glancing at my reflection because I didn't trust that I could cope with the image staring back at me.

I was mostly sequestered in my room where there was no mirror to begin with, but each day I was venturing further. By Saturday, my dad wheelchaired me to the main hospital's arts and crafts fair. Vendors that displayed handwoven scarves or jewelry also had a small mirror propped up on the table for customers. I managed to get through the entire conference room of wares without a glimpse of myself. I wasn't so lucky the next day.

On Sunday afternoon, day nine, the nurses called a security guard who opened the doors for Kennett and me to go outside. With Kennett's help I was able to walk over to a nearby bench so we could read get-well cards together. Eventually, the cold stone slab we'd been sitting on sucked away all of the heat from my pre-warmed blankets, so we decided to go inside. I steadied myself on Kennett's arm as we rounded the corner past a small tree. As we turned, I saw myself in the large mirrored windows of the hospital. I believe I said, 'Oh, so there's that.' I was solemn but not discouraged.

I had thought about what I'd look like in the days leading up to this, but I couldn't visualize it. The problem was I had never seen a large, fresh wound on someone's face. I'm sure I saw people who had experienced facial damage, because now I'll watch shows like *The Wire* and be hyper-aware of Marlo or Omar's scars. But at the hospital I was at a loss. I knew my face had been peeled off and I had broken almost every bone on the left side of it. It sounded gruesome but my mind wouldn't translate it into an image.

Had I known I was about to look in the mirror that day, I may have spent more concentrated time mulling over the possibilities of what would stare back at me. But I hadn't anticipated seeing my face this soon. Instead, when we turned the corner toward the building, I was reflecting on how nice the get-well cards had been.

When I first saw myself, I was most relieved that, after shattering the entire left side of my face, my cheekbones were level and aligned. The most unsettling detail was the large black gaps in my mouth where teeth should have been. I knew my face was cut but I wasn't prepared for how swollen and puffy it was. I had lost twelve pounds in the hospital, but my face made it look like I had gained thirty. It was such a foreign sight to me that I needed to spend time adjusting and understanding what was what. So I just stood a foot from the window with white woven blankets hanging from my shoulders and Kennett standing patiently to my right-hand side. Kennett had seen me for several days and it was reassuring to have him next to me re-introducing me to my face. He pointed out that the black holes, which looked like gaps in my teeth, were actually dark maroon blood clots that had dried across them. I was missing part of my two front teeth, but none of them had been fully knocked from my jaw. My eye was nearly swollen shut, my nose was covered in a splint, and when I gently twisted my neck I could see the prominent life-threatening laceration, covered with hundreds of black stitches, that went as far back as my ear.

Standing there, Kennett and I made predictions about how it would heal and what would disappear or return to normal. It made me feel like we were in it together. Knowing he planned on loving me regardless of how I looked meant I'd also have to learn to love whatever was to come. When Kennett and I walked back into the building I was met by a few of the nurses. Nurse Shannon had a

contagious smile as she said, 'So you saw yourself, eh?' At first, I
couldn't understand how she knew. Had I really looked that distraught
as I'd come inside?

She explained, 'All of us at the nurses' station saw you examining
yourself through those one-way windows.' So while I had frowned
and pointed at my reflection on one side of the window, the nurses
had watched me analyze my face. My mood was boosted by the
uplifting comments of the nurses, who had already accepted me with
tenderness despite what I looked like.

I wasn't initially as upset about my face for a few of the same reasons
as the leeches – pain medication and the knowledge that I was fortunate
for simply surviving the crash. Furthermore, while my appearance
would never return to pre-crash state, I also knew that what I saw in
the window would improve. The blood clots would be cleaned up, the
swelling would eventually go down, and dental work would be done.
Later, I mourned the changes to my appearance. At that moment,
it was much easier to forget about my face when my family and the
medical team looked at me like I was completely normal.

While all of the major injuries I'd sustained were located above
my shoulder, I still had to cope with the stomach tube. Initially,
the surgeons during my Tuesday operation planned to wire my
mouth shut. In anticipation, they inserted a feeding tube into my
abdomen. When the oral surgeon came into the operating room
later, he changed his mind about what was necessary to stabilize my
jaw. Instead, three metal plates were screwed in to keep the bones
aligned. The result was that the nurses were feeding me smoothies via
a syringe that went into my stomach tube, but I could still open my
mouth slightly to sip on foods like pudding.

To prepare me for my mechanically processed diet, my mom
had already ordered a Vitamix. This increased the variety of foods
I would be able to eat. (Basically anything can be blended in a
Vitamix.) Kennett and I discussed all the ways I could get enough
protein in my diet to aid healing. I assumed that, since I was going
to be able to get sufficient calories in through semi-liquid foods like
soups or smoothies, my stomach tube could go.

On either Sunday or Monday, I spotted Dr. Horn, the intensive care doctor, by the nurses' station. *Oh, I need to catch him! Maybe he can start making arrangements to have the stomach tube removed.* I reached down for a pair of sturdy basketball shoes Kennett had brought for me and tied them as quickly as possible. It was no longer necessary to bring a clipboard because over the weekend I had been able to start talking again. I caught up to Dr. Horn, who reminded me of an upbeat, friendly mad scientist because of his slightly shaggy grey hair. My mouth barely moved, as if I were speaking for a puppet, as I eagerly asked, 'When do I get to have the stomach tube removed?'

Dr. Horn made it seem like the procedure could happen that day, or at least before I left the hospital. He was going to confer with Dr. Walker, who had put the tube in. Later that afternoon I was tucked back into bed. Kennett was keeping me company in the room when Dr. Walker walked in and gave me the news. 'It's going to be another several weeks or so before that stomach tube can come out. Right now, there's a hole in your stomach lining and it will need to seal against your skin before we can take it out. Otherwise there is a gap where your stomach acids could get into your body and the acid would be life threatening.'

Hearing that the stomach tube would remain with me was a huge let-down. I took several deep breaths and told myself it was okay, but I was heartbroken and on the verge of tears. When I was discharged from the hospital after eleven days in intensive care, I left with the stomach tube still in place. In the weeks to come I was repeatedly overwhelmed by the tube. It wasn't an actual injury from the crash, but it turned out to be the most painful aspect of it. I couldn't stand up straight because stretching out my stomach made it hurt. Most of the time the tube laid flush against my body with the help of medical tape, but inevitably it would get bumped or I'd have to clean around it. Moving it also caused an ache deep into my core.

Each week I had an appointment at Dr. Walker's office, a multi-story building across from the hospital. Kennett and I would always be directed back into the same patient room where the only reading material was pamphlets for varicose vein procedures – Dr. Walker's other specialty when he wasn't saving lives in the operating room. We always looked forward to Dr. Walker's cheerful 'hello' upon entering. For the first few minutes of each appointment we would just talk with him about my injuries in general. On a whiteboard he drew a graph to show the trajectory of my recovery. According to him I'd be better by June. Another time we talked about how he also had fake front teeth because he'd had them knocked out by a puck while playing hockey in his younger years. Once my jaw healed enough, I would also have to get crowns across my upper four front teeth. After the small talk we would get down to business and I would ask if the stomach tube was ready to be removed.

For several visits I hated asking the question because I already knew the answer. Each time I was told, 'Not yet', I would leave the appointment extra hunched over, my hopes deflated for another week. However, I still enjoyed going to see Dr. Walker. He was the surgeon who had spoken with my mom the night I'd entered the hospital and told her about his daughter having facial trauma. He was always very honest with me about my recovery, but when he gave me medical updates they were always softened with his compassion. If I couldn't be in control of the situation, at least I trusted the person who was.

Then, on my week five visit, Dr. Walker said it was time. I thought he would have to do an X-ray or some other test to ensure my stomach had indeed sealed against the lining. Nope. Dr. Walker was a seasoned trauma surgeon who was about ready to retire. He just *knew* it was time.

As I leaned back on the medical examination table, I was scared of how painful removing the tube might be, but the fear was eclipsed by my excitement to be one step closer to normal. I lifted my white shirt up to my breastbone. Just like every other shirt I'd worn since the crash, it had a circular stain just to the left of my belly button. It was dried pus that had seeped through from where the tube entered my skin.

Dr. Walker made a snip at one of the strings that held the stomach tube in place. I said, 'Oh gosh, that hurts,' because the tube had been moved in the process of cutting the string. Seconds later he held gauze pads in his left hand and pulled the tube out with his right hand. I sighed, 'Oh, that's it? That wasn't bad.' The berry smoothie I had eaten for breakfast flowed from the half-inch hole, but was quickly covered by the gauze.

I was sent home with a paper lunch bag of gauze and instructed to recline the car seat to get as close as possible to horizontal for the twenty-minute drive home. Over the next twenty-four hours the dime-sized hole in my abdomen would completely seal itself. In the meantime, I had to stay on the couch or in bed to prevent more of my liquid diet from escaping through the opening.

Even before bipolar played a part in my life, I thought the best way to handle fears was to overcome them. Growing up in the suburbs of Pittsburgh, we would go to the local amusement park Kennywood and I would stand anxiously in line for the Pitt Fall, hoping to rid myself of acrophobia. The 251-foot ride featured four open-air seats on each side of the tower, into which riders were strapped with the typical rollercoaster harness. Then we were lifted up via a cable to the top, where legs dangled and I maintained an ever-increasing death-grip on the handles. It was an excruciatingly long eight seconds at the top before it dropped to the ground.

The spring of my junior year in college, I was in good enough academic standing to be chosen to go on exchange to the United States Air Force Academy for a semester. One reason this was a privileged spot to fill was that the exchange students were offered the chance to either get their wings by successfully skydiving five times, or learn to pilot a glider plane. When I was able to choose, I went with skydiving because I wanted wings on my uniform, a rarity in the Coast Guard. When I think back on the weeks of Saturday training and the plane rides up to the jump spot, I feel a sensation similar to heartburn. The thing is, I'm still scared of heights, and I can't foresee a time when I won't be. Similarly, despite my lip being saved by leeches, I know I would still freak out if I found one on me now.

As bipolar became worse in my teenage years, my biggest fear was that my chemically inferior brain would somehow hold me back in a stressful situation. I began setting big goals such as Redman in a futile attempt to test my emotions under duress, hoping to overcome my undiagnosed bipolar. The flaw in this approach was that I assumed I'd have choices. However, when the choices disappeared, my mind didn't have to stress about what the right options were for me and there was a sense of calm about things that typically would have instilled fear. Instead of becoming scared, I simply adapted to my new circumstances and accepted the support from those around me to buoy me when it felt daunting.

CHAPTER 9
GOALS

'No offense to you, but I need to leave here before I learn
your job'
Me, joking with the nursing staff

On the outside, bipolar and my crash may seem complete opposites.
One caused me to gain thirty pounds and the other caused me to
drop twelve. My crash was very external – from the injuries to the
publicity of it – whereas very few people even knew I was dealing
with bipolar. And while there could be a long list of ways they differ,
the challenges of the crash mimicked the challenges of bipolar.
In hindsight, I think having bipolar helped me through the crash
because I had already developed strong self-care habits for pushing
through when life looked grim. Prior to the crash, my biggest injury
was a broken finger. Yet, because of bipolar, I knew what it meant
to be incapacitated. Each time I had a depressive episode I had to
focus on what I could accomplish to get myself back on track.

Self-care was one of my coping mechanisms from long before
the crash. With bipolar, especially before I was diagnosed and
understood what was going on in my body, being depressed would
inevitably make me feel disgusted with myself. It would begin with
the exhaustion, then I would binge eat carbs to find energy. I would
cease to work out and between the carbs and rising cortisol levels I
would gain weight. To calm my nerves, I would pick at my face or my
cuticles. It wasn't a pretty picture on the outside and inside I was often
floundering to stay true to any part of my identity. During some of

my worst times with bipolar, when my face became oily and was puffy from crying multiple times in the span of a few short days, I would schedule a facial. If I could feel clean and fresh, it seemed to provide temporary relief. Facials or manicures wouldn't solve my fatigue, binge eating, mood reactivity, and paranoia. What they did help do was ease one of my symptoms, which was picking at my skin in an attempt to calm my nervous system. Making small improvements made me feel more capable of handling life. I took this knowledge with me into the hospital.

On Saturday night, day eight, Kennett left around 10 pm and I was on my own with the night shift. One younger woman on the staff, whom I'd never met, walked past my room a time or two. She was taking care of other patients before stopping by to check on me. When she walked in, I wrote, 'Hi, could we baby wipe my face and put new ointment on?'

I had been waiting to ask this question until nighttime hit, which was the best time to ask for favors because it tended to be quieter in the hospital. Over the past week my face had become a canvas for nurses to paint with bacitracin, a triple antibiotic cream that had to be smeared on with a Q-tip several times daily. One of the nurses must have thought the thicker the layer of cream, the more protection it offered. With each generous layer added upon the previous, none of which were wiped off, an outer crust to my skin began to form. Getting cleaned up may not have improved my appearance, but I at least wanted to feel a bit more put together.

When I asked if my face could be cleaned, the nurse replied, 'That sounds like it would be fine.'

Behind her, Nurse Josh walked into the room.

'She wants to have her face cleaned up with some baby wipes. That would be fine, right?'

'We'll have to use sterilized water, not baby wipes, but sure.'

'This is going to feel awesome!' I wrote.

The female nurse began to wipe gently around my mouth and down my neck with a soft cloth. Nurse Josh took a baby wipe and reached for my right hand. I'd been writing so much during the day to communicate that I had pen marks all over my fingers, just like an elementary schooler. He smiled as he worked off the ink and said, 'These pen marks on your hands have been driving me nuts. We need to get them off.' I smiled a crooked smile but couldn't participate in any more of a conversation since my writing hand was being washed.

This spa experience was unlike any other I've had – instead of calming music and low lighting, this cleansing took place under bright fluorescents with loud beeping machines crammed around beside me. Yet, I hardly noticed any of it. And because this all occurred before I saw myself in the window, I was able to ignore the actual damage and focus strictly on how I felt. Having my pores exposed to air again was refreshing, and despite the hospital gown and catheter, I felt presentable.

I understood how important it was when I was depressed to tackle small tasks and acknowledge my successes. Setting realistic markers when I'm low on energy focuses my mind for the next hour, afternoon, or day. If I accomplish a goal and I get positive feedback, it cancels out negative self-image loops that might be playing in my head. Depending on my mental state, a realistic expectation of myself could be as small as finishing a puzzle, walking downstairs for a hug, or having a conversation with a neighbor. Though my mental outlook was surprisingly upbeat in the hospital, my physical condition required me to stick to small, short-term goals – something that I had been unintentionally preparing for since I became bipolar.

I was seeing quick progress, so every day that I was in the intensive care unit I set out to do more than the day before. Every day I also slept less, a common problem for patients in intensive care because of medications, lights, and machines. While the lack of sleep had the potential to trigger a bipolar episode, it also gave me extra time to plan where I could create little successes in my day. And that is why, at five-something in the morning, I rang for the nurse with a fantastic idea – I wanted to wear my own clothes. I had taken stock of each wire attached to my body. There was a PICC (peripherally inserted central catheter) extending from my left arm just above the elbow. This allowed them to deliver medicines intravenously without continually stabbing me with needles. Clipped over my finger was a blood pressure monitor that also attached to a cord. After assessing the current set-up, I decided that I could probably dress in loungewear if it was allowed. Kris, the night nurse, came in soon after I rang the bell because the ICU tends to be fairly calm at that time of day.

I wrote, 'Ok, I know it's early but I am on pain meds and feel good SO let's start the day. #1) My sister brought lounge clothes from home. Could I wear them here? Tank top & pants?' I had forgotten about one thing sticking out of my body until Kris reminded me – I still had the catheter. This was going to make it tricky, but I wasn't about to give up. 'Tank top & new gown at least? We could cut a hole in the pants?'

Kris would answer each question as I scribbled and brainstorm alongside me. The two of us decided that shorts would work better than pants. I quickly turned to the possibility that my mom could bring some shorts from my sister's house where she was staying. My parents were the morning crowd; they always got to the hospital early and would be my first visitors of the day. I asked Kris to call my mom for me. I joked on paper, 'My vocal cords aren't good on the phone.'

While she was upbeat, Kris was also slightly more in tune with the situation. She pointed out that it was five in the morning, and perhaps my mom might not be ready for a phone call, especially one from the hospital.

'My mom wakes up really early.'

Wow, even Kris thinks it's possible! I could be dressed before the new staff takes over for the day. I knew that to make this happen we needed to get ahold of my mom before my parents drove to the hospital. I also thought about attempting to walk later that day. *I won't have to worry about my butt hanging out of the gown like a caricature of a hospital patient. What a great start to the day!*

From my standpoint this seemed like a slam-dunk, but I didn't want to be too pushy, so I conceded to Kris that she could take her time making the phone call; it was still early. I did manage to change into a royal blue tank top, and then I stared at the clock in front of me. Of all days, my parents took forever to arrive at the hospital. My sister didn't have shorts readily accessible to pass off to my parents. Instead they waited for Target to open so they could buy a pair of ugly salmon-colored basketball shorts from the clearance aisle. It didn't matter; I was in my own outfit. Being dressed added to my confidence. My dad was equally pleased with this development because I was one step closer to being the daughter he visually knew me as. He couldn't stop smiling. 'Addie, this is great. Walking in the room today I didn't expect you to be in your own clothes. And then the lights were on for the first time! Where did you get this shirt?' During moments where conversation went dead later in the day, he would bring up how thrilled he was to see me dressed.

As someone who never, ever let my mom dress me as a child and who fought my dad to wear leggings instead of OshKosh overalls, I didn't exactly feel put together wearing an outfit I hadn't chosen and that didn't even match. However, everything in the hospital was on a scale. I wasn't exposed to the outdoor world where I would have seen other women dressed nicely to go to work, or even work out. Instead my scale was based on how much improvement I had made. So what if I didn't like what I was wearing? I had succeeded in my efforts to get into clothes and it seemed to uplift everyone around me too.

There were two mindsets I could have had after the crash. One would have been to focus on how much had been taken away from me and how much worse my life had become. The other way to view my recovery was to recognize that I had already experienced the very worst of it and everything was about healing and improvement from that point on. I'm human and I experienced both of these emotions over the entire recovery, but my initial accomplishments and the recognition of how well I was doing helped me maintain the mindset that I was on the upswing.

My desire to get out of bed and walk brought other changes. It meant in the future I could get up to use the bathroom, so I graduated from the catheter that morning. As the day continued, I kept checking off the rest of my goals:

1 Dress normal
2 Write to a few people
3 Try the talking thing later
4 Wheelchair outside with Lydia
5 Walk a few steps down the hall
6 Paint nails (someone can do it for me)

Trying the 'talking thing' was my quick way of referencing a Passy-Muir valve, because I didn't know its name. Previously I'd been on a ventilator, which meant there was a smoker's hole in my throat. Now that I was off the ventilator, air escaped through the hole instead of passing by my vocal cords. The valve, which looked like the top circular part of a kazoo, would enable me to speak again by allowing the air I exhaled to pass through my upper airway and past the vocal cords.

I was rolling through my goals that day. Before noon I was not only fully dressed but I had already explored the hallway. When I was lying back in my hospital bed, Dr. Turner arrived with the Passy-Muir valve. When he came to the side of my bed, he didn't clearly announce what was going to happen. It should have been a simple transition – I imagine like replacing a cap on a soda bottle. However, they weren't sure if the valve size was correct to fit in the hole. While they were trying to size the valve and fiddling with my airway, I became upset. Once a valve was in place, they instructed me I could talk.

My voice didn't sound like me; it was higher pitched than I recalled. When they determined they should switch the valve size because it wasn't fitting comfortably into the hole, I asked that they not bother. I didn't like the sound of my voice and figured I could adjust to that surprise at a later date. I decided I'd rather continue writing instead of talking and we agreed to try again the next day. At this stage it was more important that I felt comfortable with the changes to my body and that I was given the leeway to make decisions like this. Besides, there wasn't time to dwell on one specific task; I had other activities written down to accomplish.

In the evening, my sister painted my toenails. It was as good as a sleepover in my room. As I laid there picking out a dark blue sparkly polish, Jeff and Kennett decided to join in on the fun. While Lydia was painting my toes, Jeff was painting Kennett's nails, and my dad was complaining about the terrible nail polish fumes. On my dad's insistence, we left painting my fingernails for when we could do it outside. And so, 'painting fingernails' made it back onto the next day's goals – along with talking.

Many of my goals, such as a clean face or getting dressed, required the approval or attention of the staff. Knowing this, when they walked in my room many nurses would look at my wall where I made Kennett post my daily list, or they would ask me directly what I had planned. During a quiet moment Nurse Kris asked me about how I learned to create such defined goals and if I felt they were helping my recovery. She had seen my steady progress and was curious about how I thought my methods might help other patients.

I wrote to her, 'I normally have goals. Not always for one day, those are often just to-do lists, but more long-term goals. Given the state of my world in the hospital, one-day goals seemed more appropriate and manageable. I do try to always have a direction I'm headed in my life and my dad says I've been that way since I was young. Before the crash my main goal was the triathlon I was training for … I believe goals for ICU patients are really important. Even a three-goals-for-the-day list.'

I explained that for me, 'If things are bad, well at least I checked off a goal. Realistic/fun are both key … breaks the day into chunks.' What I didn't tell her was just how accustomed I was to using very short-term goals to get through a challenging day of bipolar. While regaining my speech had never been on my list of goals in the past, getting dressed nicely or putting on nail polish were two of my go-to things if bipolar made a day too challenging to do much else.

For as much as I enjoy accomplishing goals, I am also habit-driven and don't enjoy quick, unpredictable changes. The next day, the ICU doctor came into my room and we agreed to try the Passy-Muir valve again. This time I was prepared for my voice to sound unfamiliar, so it went more smoothly. Within a few moments the correctly sized valve was placed in the hole of my throat and as a result I was able to talk. Shortly thereafter, when my room filled with family and friends, I ignored my foreign voice and chattered non-stop.

Worried about my energy, the nurses still cautioned me to rest my voice at the end of each day. I reverted to writing when necessary and my hands continued to be covered in pen marks. I had actually come to enjoy writing down my end of conversations. I'd got so good at writing since the first day that I could scribble out sentences with my eyes barely open. What really mattered wasn't whether I was talking or writing, but the fact that I now had control over how I chose to communicate.

By Monday, my tenth day in the ICU, I created an ambitious goal list of six tasks that ranged from attending the hospital craft fair to writing a blog. My goals were becoming larger than the boundaries of the ICU. I had come a long way from writing on my notepad to see if someone could wash my face. My next question for the nurses was: when could I leave? Various staff told me it was typical protocol for an ICU patient to be released into the general hospital before being discharged. 'You'll probably be sent to the general hospital area tomorrow and then, maybe, you'll be headed home by Thursday.'

I repeatedly heard all the benefits of moving out of the ICU to another wing of the hospital. The nurses were upbeat when they told me that I'd have my own door that closed for privacy. I don't know who thought this was a selling point, because in my mind it sounded like isolation. If I left the ICU for the general hospital I'd have to say goodbye to the staff who had quickly become family to me, which meant nobody would come in and say hello when I was bored. I'd be trapped. The only way I wanted to be discharged from the ICU was if I could go home to my own family.

Just like I had assessed all of the cords that had been extending from my body when I wanted to get dressed, I took stock of my physical and mental state to determine whether I felt ready to return home. I wasn't sleeping, which made me think of the time I spent getting up for watch in the middle of the night when I was in the Coast Guard. It gave me yet another reason to fear a mood swing. I was walking on my own and I had mastered feeding myself via a syringe that pumped food through my stomach tube. As far as I was concerned, I'd be fine sitting in my living room. Secretly, I added another goal to my list – to be home the next day, Tuesday. That night I sat up writing out a full list of reasons why I deserved to be discharged.

In my list I talked about how I wanted to be in my own bed because my neck was sore, that I needed to have a full night's sleep without interruptions from staff, and that I wanted more natural light instead of hospital fluorescent lights. I figured I had plenty of support at home with Kennett, Jos, Galen, and my mom all being around to help. When I needed more treatment, I could always come back for an outpatient visit. I also made notes about how it would be easier to eat with Kennett cooking meals at home and how I hadn't pooped in the hospital, which was concerning to me.

All I had to do was convince the staff and my mom. I didn't need to worry about what my dad thought because he had flown home on Sunday. The plan was that he would get back to Pittsburgh, make longer-term arrangements for the dog and work, and then drive the car back to Boulder. When my dad left, he was also under the assumption I would still be in the general hospital when he returned. Those were everyone else's plans, but they weren't mine.

Despite my late night on Monday, I woke early on Tuesday and waited for the rest of the unit to get busy. At 6 am I put on my sneakers and wobbled to the nurses' station to meet Dr. Turner, who had just arrived for the day. I made my case for why I should be allowed to go home. He agreed to talk to my surgeons and come to a decision later in the morning. I retreated across the hallway, and through the glass door into my room. Instead of sitting back in bed, I moved to the left and proceeded to take down close to thirty family photos that were taped to the wall. I had to stand on my tip toes and shuffle sideways. More proof that I could take care of myself if left alone. Plus, I figured if I started packing my own bags, surely they'd let me go.

Over the course of the morning I got cleared from the facial surgeon, Dr. Carter, and the trauma surgeon, Dr. Walker. Then it was just a case of waiting for the discharge papers to be put together. My mom sat with me and as we flipped through a *Competitor* magazine we talked about getting RoadIDs for Kennett and me. If I had been wearing a RoadID at the time of my crash, the emergency personnel would have known my name, that I had low blood pressure, and a low heart rate. Most importantly, they would have had contact numbers to call on my behalf. In the early hours of the morning I had been worried that my mom would feel I was rushing to leave the hospital before I should be. Instead, we were talking about ways to improve my safety when I would return to riding.

By the time I had all my instructions and appointments had been made for future outpatient visits, it was lunchtime. The final requirement was that I order cafeteria food to the room and finish a meal before leaving. With my broken jaw I enjoyed sipping tapioca pudding off a spoon and looked forward to seeing Kennett at home later that day. My mom left to drive the car to the main hospital entrance. Nurse Shannon pushed me out in a wheelchair, which was protocol for any patient being discharged. As she wheeled me down the hallway to the hospital entrance, I looked around and took in my surroundings. I'd never actually seen this part of the hospital before. With the wide sliding doors to the parking lot and the large canopy, it reminded me of a fancy hotel. Except instead of a valet standing by to help me get into a limo, it was Nurse Shannon pushing me toward the rental car my mom had pulled up.

On the drive home we stopped by King Soopers, a large chain grocery store, for medicine. I realized I couldn't go in with my mom based on my appearance. It wasn't necessarily that I was embarrassed about how I looked, although I'm sure that played a part. The reason I sat in the car and waited was because I didn't want to scare anyone. I looked like a monster with a nose cast, an eye so swollen it was halfway closed, black and blue marks on my cheeks, broken teeth coated with dried blood, and a massive bandage covering the trach hole on my neck. I could no longer feel presentable with just my own clothes and a freshly washed face.

While I thought I was regaining control of my world by getting discharged from the ICU and being sent home at midday on Tuesday, I had no idea how hard re-entering the world would be. The worst aspect was that I was forced to witness other people living their lives when I got released from the hospital. Instead of seeing how far I had come since the crash, I started to see how far I was from being fully recovered. It got harder and harder to think of little things I could do to feel better. I started having to describe my crash to people who asked, and, in doing so, I had a chance to reflect on what had happened. The emotions that I'd been able to shut out in the hospital began flooding in.

CHAPTER 10
PUBLIC APPEARANCE

*'.75 hours riding, really slow and easy. Barely managed to
get out there and not turn around. It's really hard to ride
now with Adelaide hurt at home and both of us depressed. I
need the endorphins though.'*
Kennett's November 4th training journal

On the afternoon of October 28th, the day I was released from
the hospital, Kennett was waiting outside when my mom and I
arrived at the apartment. He came over to the passenger-side door
and helped walk me up the stairwell into our apartment, while my
mom went out to fill my script for pain medication. Once inside,
I summoned my energy to climb the narrow, carpeted stairs to
our bedroom and bathroom. The first thing I did was soak in the
bathtub with only a few inches of water because I wasn't allowed to
get my stomach tube wet. Kennett came up and sat on the closed
toilet lid to keep me company.

In my ongoing attempt to cleanse myself from the hospital,
I asked Kennett to find our neighbor who was a hair stylist to see
if she could make a house call. I hadn't known until I was released
from the hospital, but my hair had been chopped off on the left side
of my face. This had been necessary to access the lacerations created
from the car glass. Meanwhile, my hair was still shoulder length on
the right side, giving me a lopsided appearance. Kennett was worried
about leaving me alone, but I assured him I wasn't getting out of the
bathtub without him and that I needed a symmetrical haircut to feel

balanced. When Kennett left, I sat there, dismayed that I couldn't fill the bathtub higher with water, and prayed that he would be able to find our neighbor at home.

Within a few minutes Kennett returned and told me that our neighbor would be able to stop by that evening with her hairstyling shears. After helping me balance to get out of the tub, he went downstairs to make a smoothie for me. I sat on our bed and stared out the window toward the street below. Kennett came back upstairs with a pint glass filled to the top with a berry smoothie. It was important I eat because, despite my only strenuous activities being coming home, walking upstairs, and taking a bath, it was significantly more than I had been accustomed to doing the previous days. Not to mention, my body was exhausted from trying to heal. When I got dressed, I put on a new pair of sweatpants that had come in the mail while I was gone. Normally, I eagerly check the mailbox for packages I'm expecting. In the midst of my crash I had completely forgotten about the sweatpants purchase. I had also lost twelve pounds in the hospital, making them extremely baggy. Still, a new pair of sweats that I had chosen for myself was a significant wardrobe upgrade from the hospital gown or the basketball shorts my parents had brought in for me. Happy, I hobbled back downstairs to park myself on the futon for the rest of the afternoon.

Those first few days it was enough to simply sit in the sunlit living room and say hello to an occasional visitor. I could walk around the neighborhood with Maybellene as long as someone else held on to her leash, but my biggest outings were the almost-daily appointments with the surgeons at their outpatient clinics near the hospital. Kennett and my mom took turns driving me since I was on a steady amount of pain medication. After returning from an appointment or after the door shut behind a visitor, my mom would encourage me to take a nap. It didn't take much for me to go from sitting upright on the futon to curling on my side and closing my eyes as conversation quieted around me.

It is generally accepted that patients heal better at home if they are healthy enough to manage themselves when left alone for a couple of hours. For the most part, I could function by myself as long as I wasn't ambitious. However, tasks like applying ointments took twice as long without help. By the evening I would give up and, for efficiency's sake, ask Kennett to tape my stomach tube in place, clean around the stitches, and reapply bandages.

I couldn't do much to speed up my recovery, but there came a point when life had to start again. As we reached mid-November, I had fewer visitors and fewer appointments. Kennett returned to his part-time job as a barista and began training for the upcoming bike-racing season. My energy was returning enough for me to be bored and frustrated by how little I could do, but my mom was still pushing naps on me. At our request, she returned to Pittsburgh so that we could settle into our own routine. She hadn't been home for a long time and also needed a rest. This meant that Kennett, in addition to being a barista and bike racer, was also my primary caregiver.

So if I had a panic attack in the middle of the night because I couldn't sleep soundly like I had before the crash, Kennett had to be up to console me as we ate blended apple pie with ice cream. A few times, because he was a light sleeper, he'd simply spend the night on the futon. Even that wasn't a guaranteed good night of rest. Once I got up in the middle of the night, thinking I could walk the few feet to the bathroom, only to fall and make a huge crashing noise. When he ran upstairs, he found me on the ground crying – another night fixed with pie, ice cream, and a warm bath.

Previously in my life it was the lethargy I experienced from bipolar that held me back from participating in the world around me. In those situations I would do everything in my power to fight my low energy and come out of it. Friends, exercise, a few healthy, high-protein meals, and a good night's sleep were usually enough to turn the corner for a mild depressive state. For more major episodes it took longer to balance out my brain chemicals, but it was still possible to take measures that would shorten the timeline.

This was different. My exhaustion was physical, not emotional. During the last two months of 2014, when I tried to return to work, exercise, or be social, I'd become exhausted in ways I couldn't easily recover from. I had to be careful, because putting myself in an energy deficit meant I was more prone to the negative emotions and patterns that come from bipolar depression, such as a feeling of helplessness. And an all-encompassing belief that *nothing* will *ever* get better. Meanwhile, every time I relied on Kennett to help me because I was too tired, I drained his finite energy reserves too.

The opposite tactic was to stay home and rest like my mom recommended. However, when left to my own devices I had time to dwell on how sorry I felt for myself. I'd been left behind – others were doing activities that *I* wanted to participate in. Being in a community of athletes, I would consistently see people out on their Saturday ride, Sunday run, or a bike commute across town. Those were all activities that made up my life, up until the crash.

The worst was when Kennett told me he was going for a training ride. I'd become frantic. I was being left alone to do what? The hospital had asked if I could physically function on my own before they released me, but nobody questioned if I could emotionally manage to be in my own company. When he left I lost my primary companion and I'd be alone with my negative, self-indulgent thoughts and FOMO (fear of missing out). As I wrote in my journal on November 18th, 'Kennett is going for a 5-hour ride tomorrow, which means I'll sit home until the dentist. That I'll be in charge of taking care of Maybellene. It sucks because I'd rather be out running or cycling. I don't necessarily want to be working, but I am sick of sitting at home. Everything at home is a fucking mess, even after it gets clean. I realize I am lucky. I really do, but I am really bored.'

As Kennett got ready to leave, I'd sit on the couch, trying to ignore him until he left. He spent time getting dressed for the chilly weather and I could only pretend to ignore him for so long. I'd walk upstairs and plead for a hug. Then I'd start crying. By the time he'd left for his ride he would have given me multiple more hugs, even one by the door as I wept with puffy eyes, 'I'll be okay …'

Time after time Kennett would head out on his ride still focused on whether or not I was okay. His mood would be dragging, just like his legs, and often he would cut his ride short and return home.

Another wasted workout that put him one step further back from being in racing shape. A good day would be when he came home to me crouched on the ground with my back against the tan couch, consoling myself, trying to relax for long enough to come up with a plan for entertaining myself.

Bad days were the ones where I had enough energy that my self-pity turned to anger. One winter day it looked like snow would drift over the foothills by afternoon, but at that moment it was a mild temperature. Kennett left for a ride. I was frustrated at being left alone, annoyed that I couldn't also get endorphins from a workout. In a fit of rage, I ran upstairs and began throwing anything near me. I limited myself to our bathroom and bedroom, so the mess wasn't as blatant when Galen and Jos returned home. Maybellene ran into a corner to get away from me and then escaped downstairs.

In our bathroom we had window markers to write on the mirror. Most recently Kennett had written 'A+K' inside a heart. Like a toddler, I scribbled blue, red, yellow, and green lines across the entire mirror until they all smeared together over the top of his heart. Not intentionally; it was just a casualty of my temper. After throwing the markers down I swiped the counter clean of all the lotions, deodorant, and sterile scar-treatment ointments. I walked out of the bathroom and saw the hairdryer plugged into an outlet on my left by the doorway. It became my next target. As I mentioned earlier, the condition of my hair was a sore subject. I screamed and let the hairdryer fly across the room, the plastic cracking as it hit the ground.

I felt momentary remorse. I had damaged my personal property in the past, mostly before being on medicine for bipolar. In college I broke the 'R' and 'I' keys on my laptop when I slammed my hands down on the keypad in response to something my boyfriend had written in an email to me. Once, as an adult, I threw my phone after I hung up on a disagreement with my sister. I was in a parked car at the time and while my phone survived because of the Otter case, the windshield didn't fare so well. Over time I learned to contain my emotional outbursts enough to avoid throwing possessions that break.

My brief awareness of the chaos I was causing didn't calm me down enough. The adrenaline coursing through my body made my stomach ache. As I glanced out the window, I focused again on how trapped I felt. I took the flimsy cart full of miscellaneous items like scissors and scarves from the corner and flung it to the ground. The drawers flew from their slots and the contents spilled across the carpet. Turning to my left, I ripped clothes from the closet and threw them on top of the mess.

I was interrupted by my phone ringing. Climbing over the pile to reach it, I saw that Krista was calling to go for a walk. I was done. I left the ravaged room behind and went downstairs to retrieve a tucked-tail Maybellene, who was fried from being anxious. She and I met Krista at a nearby park. Walking along the concrete bike path toward the foothills, I told Krista, 'Kennett is going to be mad. But I lost it and I just had to get out.' Then, so I could actually go into detail about the situation, I backtracked and explained my bipolar II diagnosis to Krista for the first time. She listened without any judgement, which gave me confidence to turn to her in the future when I needed emotional support.

Sure enough, Kennett came home and found everything. He came searching for us and when he found us I felt bad he couldn't show how infuriated he was with me because Krista was there. When we parted ways with Krista back at the park, Kennett and I just held hands the rest of the way home. He was angry, but we were still in this together, and it was tough enough that neither of us wanted to go through the pain without the other person nearby.

Over time we got better at handling days like this. I began asking Kennett to give me at least one day's warning if he was planning a five-hour ride. The advance notice gave me ample time to find a friend to spend time with or schedule my own activity. Eventually, my ability to go exercise or use the car to get to my own doctor's appointments freed Kennett up. If I cared for myself emotionally, it gave Kennett space to take care of himself. The more I allowed Kennett his personal time, the more he was able to show up and help me for the rest of the day. The tricky part was, we were actually experiencing the crash from very different perspectives, so we didn't always know how to help one another.

One repeated disagreement Kennett and I had during this November and December timeframe revolved around how we discussed the crash with others. Part of this simply stemmed from what people could assess just by being nearby one of us. Sight unseen, I was slurring my 'P's and 'T's while trying to speak with a broken jaw, bitten tongue, and chipped front teeth. It was even easier for someone to ascertain that I'd been hurt if they saw me. As my downstairs neighbor recalled three years after the crash, 'When I saw you for the first time I thought, *Don't look at her face, don't look at her face, oh my God — look at her face!*' I didn't have any reason to tell people that I was having a rough go of it. They could discern that on their own. Meanwhile, if Kennett was in public solo, there was no visual clue for people to decipher why he looked haggard. For people to understand why he was so worn down, Kennett had to share what we were struggling with at home.

My response to people I ran into was almost always positive. Tripping over my words, I'd say, 'I know it looks bad, but you won't believe how lucky I was. The *best* myofascial surgeon in Colorado just happened to be on call that night. Even though I broke my eye-socket, I never lost my sight. My sunglasses must have protected me to some degree.' There were so many ways to spin how I was lucky. If I didn't bring up my surgeons and eyesight I'd share that my legs miraculously didn't get injured, that I'd avoided bleeding in my brain, or that Kennett had proposed to me. I think it calmed down people around me to hear me be upbeat, which in turn improved my mood. What I failed to do was provide an accurate depiction of what Kennett and I were dealing with behind closed doors. Friends and acquaintances could still see that I was hurt, but this approach failed to recognize the impact my crash had on Kennett.

Kennett may not have showed it, but he was having some of the worst days of his life — repeatedly, back to back. As a coffee shop barista, he would stand behind the white marble counter top and greet people. Actually, he'd just look up and wait for the customer to speak. The exchange either started with their drink order – 'Hi, I'd like a two-shot, one-pump, half-caff, extra-foam, soy latte ... with whipped cream' – or with, 'Hi, how are you doing today?' At which point Kennett was expected to say the pleasantries – 'I'm doing good, you?' or 'It's a nice day, can't complain' – or, at worst, 'It's been a rough morning, didn't sleep well. Luckily I can just grab some more coffee as I work.'

It wouldn't have been acceptable for Kennett to respond honestly, in which case he would have said: 'I'm really depressed actually. I'm worried that my fiancée is at home losing her mind, or that she hasn't eaten because she's sick of the current choice of soup. I don't want to go home to witness a breakdown and I'm worried because I can't take away the pain she's experiencing since some asshole drove into her lane of traffic and almost killed her.'

The result was that Kennett had few places to let his guard down. At the coffee shop he grew exhausted from faking his responses to customers and at home he had to put up with me. When we did have the opportunity to get out, relax, and socialize, Kennett desperately wanted someone to empathize with about the strain my crash was causing on daily life and his training.

I would hop into a conversation, share how amazing it was to have my stomach tube removed, and overshare that my blueberry smoothie had seeped out of the hole afterwards. Later he'd be talking to the same group who already had the impression I was doing stellar. I'd inadvertently controlled the course of his conversation by talking so positively. It was no longer possible for Kennett to follow up my story with how he decided to turn around fifteen minutes into his ride because he was concerned I was emotionally unstable. He would have preferred it if I mentioned how often I cried, how little we slept, and how hard it was for me to look in the mirror and accept my new appearance, especially if I was tired. Kennett felt it belittled our situation to partake in social niceties. He didn't think it helped anyone to tell people we were doing better than we actually were. Most of all, Kennett was mad because everyone else got to see the perky me, but he had to deal with the depressed, crying version of me when I was tired and at home.

I tried to stay ahead of my bipolar depression. Three weeks after the crash I was able to ride my bike a mile down the road to participate in Krista's strength training class. I'd only do a quarter of the workouts, but it provided structure to one day of the week. I also tried to entertain myself by going back to work and being around my co-workers. November 12th, three and a half weeks after the crash, I went back to the office. I lasted three hours. My brain couldn't focus on the computer screen and my shoulder hurt just resting it on my desk. I sat in my boss' sunlit office with my supervisor and told them I thought I could be back to working full-time by the end of the year, just two and a half months after the crash. They looked at me and essentially told me not to rush it, that my job would be there when I got back. While I was happy to have the flexibility with work, I was also frustrated that I couldn't even manage a desk job.

Initially, I thought the biggest barrier between myself and my normal life was the stomach tube. For five weeks the tube prevented me from reaching up high, taking baths, and working out. None of which I was happy about. To exacerbate my impatience, I couldn't drive while I was on pain medication. I never liked driving, and after the crash I liked it even less, but no driving meant I was confined to being near the apartment when I was alone. When I got the stomach tube out on November 22nd, I was able to put the alligator medicine spoon and pain medication into a closet drawer. It was around the same time that I was given the okay to eat solid food. In a matter of forty-eight hours huge progress had been made. Without the need for drugs I came out of my foggy existence. However, my energy levels were still extremely low because my body was healing. I had lost a lot of strength that would take months to regain. Even a 35-minute ride took up a fair chunk of the day because it would be followed up with a two-hour nap. By early December I went for my first 1.37-mile run/walk until the seizing in my stomach became unbearable. My muscles were too weak from the incisions that had been made into my core during the surgery to insert the stomach tube.

Removing the stomach tube did improve my physical condition, but my moods did not follow the same upward trajectory. There were never-ending new triggers that would upset me. The crash caused so much more than the physical trauma. My injuries were due to another person's negligent behavior. Someone had taken my plans, like racing the triathlon in November, away from me. Sure, I could return to running and build my endurance and regain speed, but riding would be forever changed for me. So while in conversation I liked to share how amazing it was that my legs weren't injured and I'd be able to return to normal activities, it wasn't quite that simple.

My emotional experience was harder to explain. I only opened up about my bipolar to people I was already close with, like Krista. It was challenging to tell someone how poorly I was handling my injuries because I wasn't sure what emotions were crash-induced craziness and how much was based on irrational bipolar thoughts. I would become worn down quickly throughout the day, and once I was drained I became increasing irrational about my reality. I would fall apart from the smallest trigger, such as having Maybellene accidentally bump my nose while it was still in the final phases of healing.

On January 5th, Kennett and I wrote a blog as an interview of each other. I asked Kennett how he was doing. He said, 'Today mediocre. Until the anesthesiologist's office called for bill collection, which reminded you of how fucked up things have been and you started throwing things and screaming. *Then* I was doing bad. But then I went on a ride and felt a little better. It's been hard to train these past few months. Really difficult, actually. For some people exercise is a distraction or therapeutic. It melts away stress. For me it brings out all the negative emotions that I have and I simply cannot carry on so I have to turn back early.'

Ultimately, the challenge was that there were physical limitations *and* emotional upsets. Sometimes they mirrored each other, like when I couldn't go ride. Other times they were completely unrelated, like when I would throw a fit over a medical bill. Both Kennett and I were operating on limited energy reserves. Socializing kept me from wallowing; it also put me in the danger zone for having a meltdown. My emotions drained Kennett and prevented him from finding the necessary energy to complete his workouts. If Kennett missed training, his tolerance for being around me dropped and we would get in fights. It was a vicious cycle. We could hold hands when we were angry with each other because we knew we weren't trying to hurt each other. We also understood each other in a way most others couldn't at the time and depended heavily on each other for support. On top of all of this, I wanted to pay attention to the legal ramifications for Rush, who had caused the crash. This added another layer of stress. It drove me mad that Kennett and I were struggling all winter and Rush would likely suffer no consequences.

In an outpatient appointment, the trauma surgeon reminded me that I wouldn't be fully back to physical strength until June. Surely that wasn't true, I thought, because I was more athletic than other patients. In the end, that turned out to be almost irrelevant because that didn't take into account the emotional recovery. Leaving the hospital had not meant the worst was over; it simply indicated that I was healthy enough to be thrown back into the world.

CHAPTER 11
THE VALUE OF SUPPORT

*'Holy cow, I know Adelaide! We were at the Coast Guard
Academy together. Best wishes for her recovery.'*
Comment from DrunkCyclist.com

During periods of my recovery, it didn't seem like I'd ever come
out the other side. Would I have the strength to ride again? Would
I be comfortable with how my face healed? Given that Kennett
had proposed to me, I was pretty sure my relationship would last,
but how much would it change if I could no longer enjoy riding?
Cycling was part of my identity. Would I lose a sense of self until
something filled the void?

I was lucky to be surrounded by people who believed I was strong
enough to overcome what lay ahead of me. These same people
understood I was a victim, which became important later when
I grew frustrated by tough interactions with the police and court
system. Even when I felt I had to prove I was a victim to the outside
world, I had a core group who supported me.

While I had family and close friends to offer encouragement, I don't
recall knowing anyone who had gone through injuries similar to mine.
Everything, from the hospital experiences to facing my own mortality,
was uncharted territory for me. I knew one of Kennett's friends had
been in a life-threatening crash, but I'd only ever met him once,
weeks before his crash. I lacked a full comprehension of how long
physical and emotional recovery could take and what they would look
like along the way. Still, people with all different backgrounds came

out of the woodwork to console and buoy me up. It turns out that there are universal aspects of trauma, and even though they didn't all have a bike crash experience like me, their support made me feel less alone.

The reason I had such an outpouring of support was because my crash had been widely publicized. It seemed every person who shed tears while reading Kennett's blog passed it along to another person they knew. Within Boulder, the *Daily Camera* newspaper made its rounds. The larger cycling industry heard news of my crash through my co-workers. I wasn't aware that my story had gone viral for days after I woke up.

The first exposure I had to how publicized my crash had been was through the cards I began to receive at the hospital. To this day I've held onto the ninety-seven cards by storing them in an Amazon box that was once used to ship a novel or two. Occasionally, I'll take them off the shelf in the garage and bring them to the couch where I can reread the notes and place them neatly on the coffee table as I go. Each card brings back the memory of the first time I read it.

I remember smiling at the tilted head of a zebra with a grin of pearly whites that took up the front of one card. Pastel flowers and animals made up several cards with heartwarming notes. Papyrus designs a card of a pink cruiser bike with flowers overflowing from the wicker handlebar basket. It is impossible to associate this type of bike with a horrific crash and it reminded me of the beauty of riding. For each of these cards someone had diverted down a different aisle in the store with me in mind. That alone made them special.

Many times I was surprised at who the sender was, either because I hadn't seen the person for years or because, like the cards sent from my parents' friends and co-workers, I had never met them. Other times it was a friend who sent the card and I could immediately recognize them based on their handwriting. Some of the most important cards were the ones where I was told, 'Everything I know
·† you tells me that you're a fighter and a very strong woman';
a wonderful circle of loving support and the strength and
·ner hero. We do not know each other, yet I am so

very proud of you'; 'I know you will pull through this with grace and resilience'; 'You are an extremely strong, resilient, and positive person ...'; 'From the day I met you I was impressed with your energy and kindness.'

The words written to me said little of the actual crash. They didn't talk about the pain I was enduring or the power of the body to heal quickly; each writer simply told me what kind of person they saw me to be. Sitting in intensive care, I feared losing my identity as a cyclist, and I was pretty certain that at some point I would lose my confidence with a depressive episode of bipolar. The notecards helped me realize that I could be myself just through the attitude I kept. Even now, when I pull the cards from their storage box, I am reminded to see myself in a positive light.

Hearing from the outside world in the hospital also kept me from feeling isolated and helped me stay upbeat through the most painful days. The cards showed me that I could lean on the support of others around me, which I desperately needed once I was out of the hospital and no longer had nurses by my side.

As an emotional person, I become easily attached to others, whether it's seeing the same person at the gym's front desk or a familiar face at work. Since I'm sensitive, I always assumed that other people meant more to me than I necessarily meant to them. Post-crash, as I had friends write how much they missed seeing me, I became aware of how much my presence mattered to others. This made me more willing to reach out to friends when I began to experience depression. I saw this most clearly with my friend Krista, who was my Sunday running buddy.

Before the crash I had a routine that included training with some variation of a two- to four-hour bike ride on Saturday and a long run on Sunday. At the time, Sunday was typically my favorite day because I got the best of two worlds; I'd have at least an hour to hang out with Krista and at the same time I'd get a solid workout in too. Our routine was to meet Sunday morning at a small park down the street that was equidistant to both of our houses and then plan our route based on how we felt. The weekend prior to my being hit, we decided to run to the Boulder Reservoir. It was the perfectly executed 13-mile run that we negative split because we both pushed the pace on the false flat uphill returning back to the neighborhood. Our conversation died off during the last 3 miles as our breathing became more labored and our eyes watery. Every mile our watches would ding with our average speed for that mile – encouragement to keep the pace up for just a little longer.

That run, among others with Krista, is etched in my brain. Krista and I had discussed how great it felt to get a workout in with a friend and how lucky we were to be the same pace running, but again, I always assumed I was 'lucky enough to get to hang out with Krista', as opposed to the other way around. When I crashed, Krista wrote me a get-well card that said, 'You have been such a wonderful friend and I feel such sadness and depression without being able to call or text you for a workout, coffee, or just to hang out …'

I remember thinking, *Wow, she misses me just as much as I miss her. She not only misses our runs, but just the ability to hang out with me.* It took me almost being killed for Krista and me to really acknowledge the importance of our friendship. Hearing how much she valued me as a friend gave me more confidence to call her later when I was doing bad. It is why I went for a walk with her after I destroyed my room in a rage when Kennett went riding. It is why I finally opened up to her about my bipolar II. I'm not sure our relationship would have gotten to the point it is now without the crash. To this day we still support each other with personal struggles that we can't share with the world at large.

Krista wasn't the only person I became more connected with. I also grew closer to my co-workers after the crash. The first glimpse I got of this was when I heard my boss had visited the hospital while I was in a coma. Then I got two cards full of notes written from all of my co-workers. It wasn't simply signatures next to the Hallmark 'get well'; each person had taken the time to write a personalized note and many addressed me by one of my nicknames from the office. I had only been at my job for nine months and up until the crash I hadn't been sure how I fit in.

My office desk had previously been Kennett's. When he left the position in anticipation of racing in Sweden, I told him I wanted his job. The position was as a content writer for bike shops' websites. Content writers were the ones who wrote the prices, specifications, and the peppy description for each bike-related item that could be purchased online.

I knew very little about writing content for bike shops and I knew even less about the bike components themselves. To get the job I spent several weeks in December 2013 writing practice descriptions of bikes that Kennett would proof and correct. For part of the job interview I had to complete test descriptions of various products and after all of my studying I felt like I was going into the SATs.

This was the same winter I was promoting a bike race in attempts to distract myself from Kennett's departure to Sweden come spring. While promoting the bike race, which happened at the end of February, I got the call that I had got the job. I began working immediately following the race. My studying wasn't over after I began working. I was constantly reading magazines and blogs to keep up with what I should already have known about bikes.

As a result, I spent a large chunk of my time at work in front my computer wondering if I was a fraud. In the desks surrounding me were people I thought very highly of. They were talented writers, witty conversationalists, and excellent bike riders. Like I had assumed with Krista, I figured that my co-workers meant more to me than I did to them. To make up for my lack of knowledge, I worked on my ability to contribute to the witty office banter. The problem was that, while I could come up with jokes, I often didn't spit them out in time because I think slowly on my feet (and in an office chair). I also tried to fit into the office culture by riding with my co-workers at every chance I got. Just weeks before my crash I purchased a dirt jump bike to ride the local pump track before work. Anything to help build rapport within the office and have fun on bikes.

After the crash there was a constant concern that came mostly from my family members of whether or not I'd ride again. While nobody in my office discussed it in front of me, I'm sure it popped into their heads too. Instead of pushing away from me because I represented a fear that every person working there held in some capacity or another, they rallied around me. Indirectly, they also encouraged me to ride again by connecting me to the widespread cycling community.

One of the contributors for a website called Drunk Cyclist wrote a post while I was in the hospital: 'Biker Down: Adelaide Perr'. In the blog he included links to two other sites. The first one was a link to Kennett's blog of the day I was hit. The second was to a GoFundMe account that was begun on my behalf. Kennett's blog was so compelling that strangers could emotionally connect to the severity of my crash. In addition to the financial assistance, which helped me pay for my surgeries and dental work, people took the time to write me notes of encouragement.

'Believe it or not, you will look back at this unexpected journey someday and it will somehow make sense. There will be some important life changes that come into play because of all this. I know because I too survived a serious accident by a neglectful driver on September 19, 1988. My injuries weren't as bad as yours, but I'll never be able forget that day. A few surgeries to put together my bones and I was up on crutches a few days later with stitches across my head.

But here's why I'm writing to you. I want to share some of the psychological recovery process I learned on my own. Don't be afraid to ask for help, any help. PTSD is to be expected and can be managed. With some help, your recovery will be much quicker and less painful than mine.

The most important single thing I learned was how to transform myself from a victim into a survivor. From a limited, broken patient into a functional, useful human being again. I made goals to get healthy. To become strong again. To endeavor in life with my second chance. By six weeks I was back on the bike again even though I still had a pin sticking out of one thumb and one leg was slightly longer than the other. Six months later I rode my first MS 150 and continued to train. The racing bug took me to new heights of physical and emotional recovery and I even won a state track championship in 1990.

Over time, my PTSD shrunk into an occasional flash that quickly dissolved. Nothing in the world can hold us back once we take charge of our lives again. With determination and building confidence, you too will take charge of your life and conquer fears, inhibition, and anxiety that may have appeared due to the accident. You will be a survivor!'

Every note that I read (and I read them all) introduced me to a person who had taken time to console me. Some notes made me try harder. Some writers reminded me that Kennett was the most upstanding guy. More often than not, a note would include some background of the person writing it. They'd tell me about being hit by a car like the post above or they'd share another event in their life that triggered PTSD, such as being bitten by a dog. These anecdotes were included as a way of saying, 'You are not alone.' Without ever questioning if I wanted to ride again, people would write, 'We will ride someday' or some variation of wanting to see me back on two wheels. With all these other cyclists cheering me on, how could I *not* get back on the bike? In my mind, if I had decided to never ride again then it meant I was deciding to extricate myself from this supportive, funny, caring community; I couldn't picture that.

The international support I received made me realize that my impact on the world is larger than I previously thought. I am part of a cycling community that extends well beyond Boulder. If there is a cyclist in another city, I now acknowledge that we are bonded through the sport. If someone has been in a crash, I realize that we share experiences that go beyond which bones were broken and extend to the deep emotions that go hand-in-hand with recovering.

Encouragement and support poured in from around the world, but it was the people in Boulder who gave me something to look forward to and the confidence to be in public. For instance, while I was busy with a schedule of doctor's appointments, my co-workers were busy organizing a silent auction on my behalf. Those same talented writers, witty conversationalists, and skilled bike riders were also capable of securing gifts from companies to auction off and throwing a blowout party in their spare time.

Posters went up everywhere, including a Starbucks I visited in Longmont after my oral surgeon's office appointment. I looked up at the corkboard to see a photo of me riding with co-workers for a photo shoot that had taken place the previous spring. I was a bit uncomfortable that a whole event was being thrown on my behalf, but once I got there I realized the evening was also a chance to heal the community.

The fundraiser was hosted on Wednesday, November 19th at Rocky Mounts, a local company that designs and installs bike, ski, and gear racks for vehicles. When people arrived, they opened the two glass doors into Rocky Mounts' front display room. Bike jerseys lined the top of every wall. Car-top carriers were displayed along one side and racks along another. Bikes themselves hung from the ceiling. The bar was fully stocked with beer that had been donated. Black leather couches gave people a place to sit although most people were mingling in small groups. The back warehouse had been cleared to make room for the silent auction items, which were arranged on two long workspace tables. A baby-blue Surly fat bike was clamped onto a work stand for those who wanted to bid on the big-ticket item. Around thirty people gathered in each room, many sporting a down puffy jacket, typical for the active Boulder crowd. I even fit the dress code with my black puffy vest and leggings. Kennett and I rocked matching black T-shirts that said 'Pay Attention' on the front.

At one point during the evening I found myself on the black couch with two guys named Dave, one on either side. I'm not sure that they knew each other before that night but either way, they got to talking. I was listening to their conversation, glad to take a break from talking myself. Both had serious leg damage due to crashes on their bikes. At least one of their crashes had involved a car. It was really interesting to listen as they compared injuries, surgeries, and what pins had been stuck into their legs. It wasn't a sad conversation; their laughter surrounded me, yet it was apparent that the discussion allowed them to connect with someone who understood.

Another person came up to me between the auction tables and the tall warehouse shelves. He said, 'I wanted to talk to you about your crash. Not many people know this about me, but I was in a bike crash years ago and had extensive trauma to my face as well. Sometime I'd like to talk with you and share what I can to help you.' Indeed, at a later date, we sat and talked about the ups and downs of recovery and the medical procedures required. This was personal enough of a topic for him that I don't ever mention his injuries to other people. His story was not one he wanted to tell, but he had a purpose when he shared his experience with me. If he could have a positive impact on my emotional healing by opening up, it was worth giving up details of his life that he normally kept private.

When I mingled, I heard several people mention that they didn't want to get back on their road bikes after hearing of my crash. My friend Dan said, 'This is my nightmare. Kennett and Adelaide are living it. We all know the risks and we all know we might be next, but it's never real until it happens to someone you love.' My boss shared a similar sentiment when he told me, 'My nightmare is that my wife or my kids will end up dead or in the hospital because of a lifestyle or hobby I introduced them to.' It is a version of hell if you are the victim, but it is equally awful to be the one who has to watch someone you love be hurt.

There seemed to be a general sense of relief when people like Dan and Will talked to me and heard I was doing much better. After all, most people who showed up that night enjoyed riding a bike in some capacity or another. My crash had made their fears very concrete and they needed to see I was recovering and that the story would end up being okay.

Those were the deeper results from the silent auction evening, but on the surface, it was simply fun. With little daylight and cold November weather, people weren't riding as much. It was a great excuse to bring the community together. People got to win some new bike gear and other local gifts. Kennett and I had spent days looking forward to the event because it was our first big outing. Kennett had a few beers and enjoyed time socializing without me. I drove home on the quiet street and, because we hadn't owned a car prior to the crash, it was the first time I'd been behind the wheel in months.

That evening was a momentary glimpse of what life would be like soon enough. It was encouraging to have so much social time again, even if the laughs only lasted a few hours. At some point past midnight my physical pain took over. I woke up crying because my stomach tube hurt and my teeth ached. Kennett grabbed me some pain medication from its semi-permanent place on the bathroom counter. There were moments that evening when I felt normal, which provided me with a wonderful escape from reality. However, I couldn't replicate that kind of social evening often. I spent the next several days mostly napping at home to regain my energy.

Just when I felt like the world was an evil place full of painful experiences, I had a community pull together around me – a community in which I had previously believed myself to be an outsider. All of the gestures, from the auction to the cards and everything in between, reminded me that the love people have for each other overpowers the hardships we encounter. While I was struggling to stay positive throughout each day, I had friends and strangers reassuring me that I was stronger than I felt. Currently, I'd say I'm more inclined to open up to friends. I make a greater effort to tell them they are important to me. When I can, I put the cycling community above myself and try to be an advocate. I have more empathy and understanding of what pain feels like. It took me being completely helpless from my injuries to realize the impact each individual can have on another's life.

CHAPTER 12
TRAFFIC CASE PART I

'Be skeptical of crash reports in local newspapers'
My blog

In the spring of 2017, I was working at a local bike shop for their women's night. Mostly women, and a few men who represented companies in the bike industry, had gathered on this rainy Tuesday for door prizes, a bike clothing fashion show, and shopping. After I had done a catwalk in the store to show off a new bike kit, I began socializing with others over appetizers.

I wasn't in the mood to socialize with people I didn't know, so I was relieved when I saw an acquaintance nearby. I had met him once or twice previously during industry events, but I couldn't even remember his name. He and I began a conversation over a small plate of chips and guacamole. Somehow, the topic of conversation became about my crash, which was not unusual. Since my name is not common and I still have scars, people are quick to recognize that I am the girl who got hit back in 2014 and make mention of the crash while talking to me. What I was flabbergasted by was how misinformed this person was. I learned that the extent of his knowledge had been gleaned from what he'd read of my crash in Boulder's newspaper.

The *Daily Camera* quoted a Public Affairs Officer from the Colorado State Patrol, who said, 'The driver had come to a complete stop and yielded appropriately, when they were hit by the bicycle. The driver had started from a stop sign, but stopped for a turning vehicle. That's when they were hit by the bicyclist.'

It didn't make sense to my acquaintance how I had simply run straight into a car of my own accord. However, that is what the police had implied and, like most people reading the newspaper, he assumed the police thoroughly understood the sequence of events. So, three-and-a-half years after my crash, I was having to explain what actually happened to someone who reported on bike stories all the time – someone I assumed knew how biased police, media, and society-at-large are against cyclists.

I was no longer worried about having to make conversation with other women in the store; I had to set the facts of my crash straight with the person in front of me. This wasn't a conversation I could table for later, because I didn't see this person regularly. Nor was it a discussion I was willing to let slide. As someone with influence in the cycling community, he needed to know that the newspaper story was wrong. It wasn't until he politely excused himself from the conversation five minutes later that it dawned on me: *I may have embarrassed myself. I don't think he cared that much and he probably didn't want to hear about all the injustices of being hit by a car.* I looked around the room, still stunned from the encounter, and wondered how long I could get away with revisiting the appetizer stations before I had to talk with another person. *Stupid Daily Camera article. I guess I shouldn't have laughed it off at first.*

The newspaper article had been written on the day of my crash, and I learned about it from Kennett in the hospital. He prefaced it by telling me that the paper had got the facts wrong. I didn't really care at the time. You could say I had bigger fish to fry, but I think I just didn't understand the long-lasting impact a local newspaper article could have on people's perceptions. And, at that moment, I was like the *Daily Camera* in the sense that I also lacked many of the details about what had occurred after the Fiat pulled past the stop sign.

It was only when I learned more about my case that I felt mistreated. It was only when I pushed to have my questions answered that I recognized the story was larger than my own. In the years between my crash and when I had this conversation in the bike shop,

I learned of several other cyclists who had been injured or killed. These stories, which blame the cyclist, leave drivers with a sour taste in their mouth when it comes to bikes on the road. They begin to feel that anger toward anyone on two wheels is justified, which increases the driver's animosity. Even cyclists disown one another if they read in a newspaper that the cyclist is presumed to be at fault. This means that the injured person becomes re-victimized by their peers instead of receiving much-needed support in their recovery. However, I know several other high-profile cases that were also misreported like mine. What many people don't realize when they read a news article about a bike crash is that the reporter is getting their primary information and quotes from a Public Affairs Officer sitting in a chair 50 miles away from the scene. This officer lacks crucial information, because a full investigation has not yet been completed. Of course, it took me a while to learn this, and my journey began with my own police report.

Jeff Malin, my brother-in-law, had requested the Boulder County Sheriff's police report for our family. I first saw it in an email on Halloween, two weeks after the crash. I was sitting on the futon in our living room with the laptop on my legs.

The email contained two attachments. The first document initially looked like a job application because of its neatly formatted boxes, labeled date, time, name, witness eye color, etc. This was the official report from the Boulder County Sheriff's Office, and I was interested to learn about what had happened at the scene after my memory failed me. Included were narratives each officer had written about conversations they'd had with witnesses. One officer wrote details that sounded an awful lot like the *Daily Camera* article.

'I learned that Mr. Rush was driving eastbound on Hygiene Road and had approached the stop sign at North Foothills Highway. He told me he got to the stop sign and he stopped.'

There was no way the driver stopped! I saw him roll up so quickly in front of me. I kept reading.

'He looked to his right, which was facing northbound, and saw there were two black vehicles of an unknown make or model traveling southbound on North Foothills Highway. Those two vehicles were in the southbound lane of travel and as they approached Hygiene Road, the second black vehicle decided to turn into the turn lane for eastbound Hygiene Road at the last minute. Mr. Rush told me he had started to creep out after being at a complete stop because he saw the traffic for northbound North Foothills was clear and he just had to wait for these two cars to pass. He told me he had seen a handful of bicycles, but they were quite a ways up the hill from where the stop sign was at and he felt he had enough time to pull out. When the unknown black SUV decided to turn onto Hygiene Road at the last minute, it forced him to stop so that he didn't get into a vehicle accident at that point ...'*

Black vehicles? I got a tight chest and felt sick to my stomach. It's hard to understand without looking at a diagram, but it would have been physically impossible for either of those cars to have turned as described. If a vehicle had been turning, it would have been between the red Fiat and myself. If a driver had decided to turn onto Hygiene Road, I would have hit the side of their vehicle instead. I also would have an image burned into my brain of a black vehicle. I would not have been able to see a bright red Fiat in those final moments as I skidded toward the worst afternoon of my life.

Rush made up a story for the police. How could such a blatant fabrication of the events make it into the official police report?

I needed to read that his story had been discounted in another part of the document. This was just the narrative of what the police officer had heard in conversation, but surely they knew it was false. I continued to scroll down the page, but I never found what I was looking for. Nowhere in the police report did it discredit Rush's claims of the black cars.

I read another account from one of Rush's passengers, which stated, 'Ms. Perr was traveling at a very fast rate of speed.' *What the FUCK!?* I wanted to get into this guy's face to ask, 'What constitutes a "very fast rate of speed?"' I knew I hadn't been going above 40 mph and most likely I had been under 35 mph. I was confident in this assessment because when I had been a new cyclist, I went above 40 mph with poor bike-handling skills and my bike shook underneath me to the point where I thought I would crash. That experience scared me enough that even though I had improved my descending abilities, my hands always instinctively squeezed the brakes before I could get up to those speeds. Never mind that the speed limit for cars is 65 mph on that section of road.

The nauseating sensation grew into anger, which shook through my frail, injured body. How could my speed be used against me? The car traffic had been going 30 to 40 mph faster than me.

I opened the second attachment, which consisted of six sheets of college-ruled paper that had been scanned into the computer. These were the witness statements, but at a quick glance they could have been mistaken for a high schooler's scribbled class notes. Each statement included an account of what they had seen, along with their name, address, phone number, signature and an officer's signature. Witnesses included two of Rush's passengers, Scott the cyclist, and two people who had been traveling in their respective cars when they saw the event unravel.

Reading these statements was a little less stressful because Scott and the car drivers stated that the Fiat had pulled out into the intersection in a sudden manner, that no other vehicle impeded its movement, and that I had no way of altering what happened. Yet, there were still two witness statements from the passengers of the Fiat, who, sticking to a variation of the two black vehicles, mentioned a turning truck that prevented the Fiat from moving. I thought, *How come nobody bothered to ask ME what happened?*

I expressed my shock to Kennett, who sat down next to me. 'They lied! There was no black car in the way. How come nobody got my witness statement? Obviously the police couldn't ask me what happened at the scene, but I was awake five days later. They still haven't contacted me to ask what I remember. They aren't going to either – this is it. This is their entire police report in front of me.'

To help me take action, Kennett opened his computer and forwarded me the email address of James Wise, a Colorado State

Patrol officer. He was the officer who had arrived at the scene after I had been taken away in the ambulance. My fingers scrambled across the keyboard as I wrote an email to Officer Henderson introducing myself and pointing out the fallacies throughout the current police report. After hitting the send button, I closed my computer and grabbed my purse, which was made of old bike inner tubes. We were off to yet another doctor's appointment.

The previous day I'd had another, more positive, experience with the Colorado State Patrol. Officer Mark Vaughn, a victim's advocate, called my cell phone while Kennett, my mom, and I were in the car outside of the grocery store in Longmont after a doctor's appointment. Sitting in the parking lot, I listened as either Kennett or my mom spoke to Officer Vaughn. I couldn't pronounce my words enough to talk on the phone. He told us that he had reported the crash to Rush's insurance company. This was not part of his job description, but he said he had felt particularly angry when he had heard of my injuries and figured Rush had never called Farmer's Insurance himself. Officer Vaughn's hunch was correct – Farmer's hadn't known about the crash prior to his call.

Officer Vaughn's actions offered me insight into what power the law enforcement had to help me, or ignore me. Granted, he was a victim's advocate, so he understood how to emotionally support a victim and be a resource when they have questions. Still, I wasn't his responsibility. He just stepped up and continued to look out for me. On my behalf, he investigated what traffic ticket Rush had been written – a detail that the newspaper had also not reported. A month after the crash, I learned from him that Rush had been ticketed with Careless Driving Causing Injury.

To learn more about what the implications of a Careless Driving Causing Injury traffic ticket were, I went back to Officer Henderson. Over several weeks, Officer Henderson and I had exchanged several emails, attempted to meet in person, and finally, once my jaw had healed enough that I could enunciate my words, we spoke on the phone.

Even though I could speak, I didn't feel that I was being heard. I brought up the lies in the police report and asked to put together my own witness statement. Officer Henderson didn't think a witness statement from me was necessary. I repeated that I wanted to submit a witness statement and asked if emailing it to him would be preferable.

Next, I asked why, as the person who had written the ticket, he didn't charge Rush with the more serious offense of Reckless Driving Causing Serious Bodily Injury (SBI). After several minutes on the phone trying to explain the traffic law to me, Wise simply said that the District Attorney (DA) wouldn't accept 'reckless driving' as a charge and they'd just change it to 'careless', no matter what he said. In all my email interactions up to the call with Officer Henderson, I had felt like I was pulling teeth. During the call itself, I felt like I was just being placated. The last email I received from Officer Henderson was later in the day, after I provided him with my witness statement. He gave me the contact information for the Victim's Advocate at the Boulder County District Attorney's Office.

With my lack of understanding and my strong desire for Rush to be handed a more serious charge, I felt I had to contact the DA directly. I drove to the courthouse on January 20th to meet with the Deputy DA, Lisa, who was in charge of the traffic case, *The People of the State of Colorado vs. Larry Rush*. (I wasn't actually part of the case, and, in a lot of ways, I was butting in. The DA works for society at large, not for the individual victim.)

Also included in the conversation was a victim's advocate for Boulder County. The room that we met in resembled an elementary school room. I recall thin brown carpeting, a literature stand about the law, and a circular table where we sat down to talk.

I walked into the room already defensive. 'I'm not going to back down on this. He should be charged with reckless driving. It doesn't make sense and I don't know why you wouldn't even *try* to charge him higher. In fact, it's situations such as this one that allow drivers to get away with killing cyclists.'

Lisa said, 'I have to be able to prove beyond a reasonable doubt that he committed the violation. If I cannot prove each bullet point of what Reckless Driving is, he'll get off scot-free. However, if I charge him with Careless Driving Causing Injury, he'll definitely be guilty and have some repercussions. I want to make sure he gets sentenced. I think you do, too.'

That news didn't sit well with me, emotionally. I was still charged up, but I finally understood the dilemma. The victim's advocate and Lisa calmed me down by telling me that they were truly on my side. For evidence, they showed me that my case was being held in a yellow manila folder, which were only supposed to be used for cases that required a victim's rights advocate. Being seriously injured by a vehicle in traffic doesn't fall under the Victim's Rights Act of Colorado like burglary or assault. Even so, Lisa told me that they understood that I was a victim regardless of Colorado law and, as such, I should still be informed about the progress of the case.

It also helped that Lisa agreed with me that the charge didn't match what had happened. We discussed what counts as careless driving versus reckless. A differentiating point between the two charges is that for a DA to prove reckless driving, they have to show that the driver acted in 'such a manner as to indicate either a wanton or a willful disregard for the safety of persons or property.' And it was that simple addition that meant she wouldn't be able to walk into a courtroom and claim that Rush should be charged with reckless driving. What does wanton or willful disregard look like? Of all the examples she gave me, I'll never forget when Lisa said, 'Driving donuts is considered reckless.'

Doing donuts? I had an image of being a passenger in a truck in college at the U.S. Air Force Academy as we did donuts in an empty dirt parking lot at night. The only people at risk were those of us who had willingly got in the car. Rush, however, had put multiple people who he didn't know at risk. 'So you're telling me a person in an empty parking lot who puts skid marks on the pavement doing donuts is going to get a higher traffic infraction than the guy who put my life and several other people's lives at risk? I'm sorry, Lisa, but this still isn't making sense to me.'

Before I left, Lisa drew a chart of different charges on a yellow notepad. She listed all the types of charges one could receive in

Colorado, with the most serious being a Class 1 felony – think life imprisonment. It gets less severe from there. Felonies are divided into six classes and then there are three classes of misdemeanors. Traffic infractions are treated slightly differently and there are only Class 1 and Class 2 misdemeanors for these cases.

What Lisa was trying to explain was that there is a massive gap between the charges of Reckless Driving causing SBI, a Class 5 felony, and Careless Driving causing SBI, a Class 1 misdemeanor. The maximum punishment Rush could possibly ever see with his charges was a $1,000 fine and a year in jail. Had he been charged with reckless driving, the sentencing could have been up to three years in prison and up to a $100,000 fine. 'Shouldn't there at least be an in-between?' I asked.

'Yes, I completely agree. But that requires changing the law. I'm on your side as a Deputy District Attorney, but there is nothing I can do that would change how the system currently is. Keep fighting; I support you.'

When our meeting was over, I told Lisa I would get her everything she needed to put up a good fight during the sentencing. Once I returned home, I sent her all the police documentation and hospital photos I had on hand. The meeting had shifted my perspective. I had gone in trying to prove that I was the victim and I walked out realizing that there were more people like Officer Vaughn – people who were actually going above and beyond their job description to support me. I couldn't change the outcome of how Rush was charged, but maybe if I advocated for new laws, I could prevent others from going through the same experience.

I didn't know what it meant to change the law except that I wasn't prepared to do that. So instead, I digested what I was being told and I repeated it to anyone who would listen. I shared my disbelief that nobody asked me for my witness statement. I recited the definition of wanton and willful disregard. I drew the diagram that Lisa had sketched down for me about the different levels of crime in Colorado. If people weren't going to learn these things from the *Daily Camera*, they would learn them from me. Each time I was hoping that whoever was listening was as outraged as I was. I didn't feel empowered myself, but I figured maybe by being a squeaky wheel I'd build momentum or at least get to share my story with someone who had more influence than me.

Before the crash, I hadn't owned a car. Biking was not only my sport; it had become my primary means of transportation. However, with my injuries, not to mention the PTSD I sustained, a car became a necessity to get to the doctor's appointments. I was left with no other choice but to spend thousands of dollars to invest in a car again. To me, it seems reasonable for someone who causes harm with their vehicle to lose the convenience of a car and have to turn to other means of transportation. As I've met more bike-crash survivors, I've learned that I'm not alone in my opinion.

If my meeting with Lisa was a crash course in how the legal process would work in my traffic case, I got a one-day intensive when I showed up at a courtroom to support a Fort Collins family. The father, Jeff, had been hit a few months prior to me while training for Boulder Ironman. His injuries were more extensive than mine and the scenario was more egregious. The 72-year-old woman who hit Jeff drove away, leaving him bleeding to death on the side of the road. She then turned around and drove past the scene again, at which point someone followed her and called the police. These are not the caring actions of your typical grandmother.

I hadn't known the family before my crash, but shortly after, I got a Facebook message from Jeff's wife. She told me to lean their way if I needed anything and wished me a speedy recovery.

A few days later, I also received a message from Jeff. They lived just an hour north of us. It resonated with me that he knew exactly where I had been hit. While I couldn't say the same, I knew the type of road he was riding on when the woman had hit him. It was a quiet, country road that wasn't well traveled. With Jeff's facial and brain injuries, he was still recovering like me. What's more, he was one step ahead of me in the legal process.

With the proximity to each other, our families kept in touch enough that I was aware when the date rolled around in January 2015 for the sentencing of the woman who'd hit Jeff. The family wanted a court packed with cyclists, so we drove up to the courthouse in Fort Collins. We took in our helmets even though we hadn't ridden there and joined a room full of bike commuters and racers. We hugged Jeff and his wife for the first time. Jeff was still missing part of his front tooth and reminded me of what I currently looked like to others, better than any mirror could. The courtroom itself was various shades of brown with seven or so rows of hardwood pews for us to sit on. We slid in about three rows back from the table that the driver sat at with her lawyer.

Jeff and his wife both stepped up to speak to the judge and courtroom. With pages of notes in front of them, they spoke of the trauma they had endured. Listening to his wife's testimony was even more emotional for Kennett than me. It was probably the first time someone had shared the horror he had experienced in such detail.

She addressed the judge but spoke to the whole courtroom when she recalled waking up, eating breakfast, and receiving a phone call from the hospital that her husband was in a critical condition. It had taken her unfathomable strength to sit near Jeff in the ICU when his body was destroyed. Not many people can relate to Kennett's first moments beside me after he had been told I was in a critical condition. He was the only person who saw me in the emergency room before being wheeled into surgery.

Because Jeff's crash was even worse than my own and the driver did a hit-and-run, Kennett and I knew that whatever the outcome of the sentencing, it was more than we could expect for Rush. However, Jeff and his family asked the judge not to impose jail time. They said they forgave the woman because they didn't want to hold a grudge. Their request was that her community service be related to speaking in front of other drivers. When the driver's daughter spoke, she declared her mother was too shy and it would be unfair to force her into a specific type of community service. My fists clenched, my eyes shut, and my newly healed jaw tightened. I screamed inside my head but kept my mouth shut. It was audacious that the daughter should complain that a few hours of community service would be too much for her mother to cope with. Behind her sat Jeff, a father himself, who had been unfairly punished with injuries that would last a lifetime.

The worst part of that day in court was walking out after hearing the sentencing passed down by the judge. Four years of supervised probation was complemented with 320 hours of community service (80 hours per year) and a $3,000 fine outside of restitution. She lost her license for an undetermined amount of time. Because she had left the scene, her traffic violation resulted in a Class 4 felony, which I knew, thanks to DA Lisa, was a much higher charge than Rush was ticketed with.

If that was all she received, Kennett and I felt sick at the idea that Rush would get an even lighter sentence. Afterwards, we sat for coffee at a local shop because lattes have always been a special treat for me. Kennett took his bike off the car rack and pedaled out his anger for the 45 miles back to Boulder, while I drove myself home and lost my emotions in a bag of chocolate chips.

I asked Jeff over Facebook if he felt the sentence was enough. He replied, 'I am glad that it is over. It was great that you guys came up. After I got out of the hospital, I read about your accident and I was torn up about it. I think of us as an accident family. Initially, I was glad that the judge increased the sentence from 200 hours to 320 of community service, but after reflecting on it more, it isn't enough.'

We both agreed that an increase of community service hours doesn't send a big enough message to the public. Currently, there is no stigma against driving carelessly like there is with driving drunk. We both want much stiffer license-suspension laws. Jeff and I agreed that Colorado needed to impose sentences that take away licenses for years, not months.

As demoralizing as the sentencing was, it showed me that I had some control on a smaller level. There were decisions I could make. Did I want to invite family and friends to pack the courtroom when Rush's sentencing came around? Did I want to forgive Rush? Several local news outlets updated the Fort Collins community about the sentence that was handed down. Could I get the *Daily Camera* to update the public about the outcome of my crash? Would reading about a light sentence deter people from driving irresponsibly or would it reinforce their belief that they were untouchable in the eyes of the law? The legal system takes a while, and I still had more time than I wanted to ponder how to handle myself when Rush's court date arrived. I desperately wanted it to be over with, and after seeing the outcome of Jeff's hit-and-run, I couldn't see anything good coming out of the traffic case for my crash.

CHAPTER 13
BACK TO THE BIKE

'My motivation for training is almost back to normal, which is a huge relief. After the intervals I went up Flagstaff, where I got punched.'
Kennett's blog, February 2nd, 2015

Three years after the crash, another Boulder cyclist was sitting in the hospital with life-threatening injuries after being hit by a speeding driver. After hearing about this incident, I had a physical therapy appointment. Lying on the table to get dry-needled, I got so worked up that I didn't even notice the needle go into my extremely tight glute muscle. I started spewing out facts from my own crash to the physical therapist.

'The *Daily Camera* misreported my crash and said I was at fault. The police officers that are quoted in these bike crash newspaper articles are sitting in an office miles away. The woman who was hit recently was another experienced triathlete. I bet you anything she wasn't at fault, but that is what the newspaper implied. It makes cyclists look reckless when they report these types of stories.'

Life becomes more difficult when I hear about other crashes, because my mind wanders to how I can help keep the public from blaming the cyclist, who is clearly a victim in my opinion. I know if they have to fight with the reporters and police it will be frustrating at best, and insulting and debilitating at worst. I want to protect them from this experience because there are so many other problems they will need to address. In the timeline of my recovery, I was simultaneously pushing to correct the facts in public records and also trying to ride in traffic again.

I have often been asked some version of, 'Are you afraid to ride now?' and my answer is always 'No'. One reason I wasn't afraid to return to the bike after the crash was because I felt confident with my own riding ability. It wasn't my fault that I hit the pavement that day. I also didn't have to get back on a triathlon bike immediately. Instead, I started on my road bike, which had a more upright position and allowed me to see traffic easier.

Physically, the only restrictions I had after the crash were my stomach tube, a stiff neck, and a jaw that I was warned, should I crash again, had not fully healed yet and would re-break. Beyond that I was free to start riding whenever I felt ready.

On Sunday November 23rd, Kennett went for an early ride and I cried and cried after he left. Once my face had dried, I walked over to my road bike, which was sitting on the trainer in the dining room. Perhaps I would feel more accomplished and less left behind if I also got to ride. Propped up against the wall next to the bike was my co-worker's Powertap wheel. Power meters measure how many watts a cyclist is generating when pedaling. When I first learned to train, using a power meter was a huge motivator. On the day of my crash, my power meter was on my bike, which then came to be held in evidence by the police. I couldn't access any of the parts on my bike, such as the power meter or Garmin computer.

Before even returning full-time to work, I borrowed this wheel with the idea that I could begin measuring my new baseline fitness and see progress. Somehow it made sense to me that I would begin adding a thirty-minute trainer ride into my daily schedule, right between applying ointment across my face and working on my other exhausting activity: completing a large puzzle.

The power meter never made it onto my road bike, and instead of being a way to see progress, seeing it sit there beside my bike was a visual reminder of my weakened body. I'd overestimated my physical abilities. Before I could even worry about power numbers, I needed to be capable of pedaling casually for thirty minutes without using up my entire energy allotment for the day. If I really needed a challenge, all I had to do was carry my bike downstairs and onto the street.

When I walked over to the bike that Sunday, it all seemed so futile and I grew angry. I threw a shoe at the puzzle in the living room and knocked a few other items to the ground. I left the mess and went for a walk with Krista. I just wanted my anger to be out in the open for a while. When Kennett left for those rides, I felt such as sense of loss. There used to be so much in us getting dressed and ready to ride together. It was after Kennett returned from his ride that Sunday that I must have made him agree to ride with me the following day.

So, five weeks after the crash, my destination was a gym about half a mile from our apartment, and the plan was for me to attend the women's strength class Krista coached. Kennett rode along as my second set of eyes, or, as I liked to think of it, bodyguard.

The gym was around the corner from our apartment, but it had been so long since I'd ridden that I couldn't even get my directions straight and we missed the turn. The detour we took brought us to the slight uphill of US 36 before it heads out of town. I was especially aware of the headwind because I didn't have much extra energy to push through it. The hood on my gray puffy jacket got in my vision as I turned my head to look behind, before making a left. It didn't matter much because I couldn't turn my head enough to see traffic due to my injured left shoulder. So Kennett told me when to cross and made the move first, so I was confident enough to follow. He rode me all the way to the front door, just like a loving father dropping off his toddler at preschool.

The class itself was similar to preschool in the sense that it kept me occupied and allowed me to socialize. It wasn't difficult because I could barely do any of the moves. I still had my stomach tube in, so for most of the class I was simply stretching my legs while other women lifted weights and did jumps.

I wasn't scared to be back on the bike when I rode to Krista's class, because I knew Kennett was watching out for me. On the way home, I felt safe enough to ride by myself because I was traveling through residential streets with a maximum speed limit of 30 mph and a designated bike lane. If anything, I was proud for being so independent and for embracing the bike when so many people doubted I would ever ride again. Even without a power meter to tell me as much, I knew I was making progress.

I think this must have been the first day that I could see my life was returning to normal. In addition to the morning ride, I drove the car for the second time so that I could get to a massage, which left my body feeling relaxed and pliable. I only had four milliliters of pain medication during the day, and I was more alert.

My energy continued to trend upward after my first ride. The next day, I was given permission to start chewing soft things again. Dr. Knight's requirements were that I stay away from carrots, steak, and toasted bagels. We went straight from that appointment with Dr. Knight to see Dr. Walker, who finally decided my stomach tube could be removed. Within a day or two, I was completely off pain medication.

I was on an emotional high from all the gains I had made in a short period of time and confused this progress with being better. In my excitement, I got a membership to the gym. When I tried running on the treadmill, the pounding hurt my face, so I moved to the elliptical and briefly tried the erg (rowing machine). However, my desire to be on my bike took precedence over the gym.

Within a few weeks of my first outdoor ride, I headed out behind Kennett and our friend Matt to climb Flagstaff Road. I was really content as I followed them up 6th Street, until I grew thirsty. I reached down to my water bottle with my right hand, but as I put it to my mouth, I realized I couldn't drink from it. I couldn't pull the top open with my teeth and my lips couldn't create suction. I had to stop, unclip my shoes from the pedals, and pull the water bottle open with my left hand. I was pissed off. *How in the world can I ride hard if I can't drink water on the bike? This is stupid. It isn't even hot out this time of year. Is this really something that I'm going to have to adjust to?* I got back on the bike and continued to ride because, more often than not, pedaling helped me work through the tough emotions and made me feel empowered.

Days before, I learned at Dr. Carter's office that I had severed a nerve that pulls the lip up to smile. Hopefully it would regenerate, but there was no guarantee, and even if it did, it could take up to a year. I thought I could get away from these challenging realities when riding, but there were moments like the water bottle incident when it would all catch up to me. Rides like the one up Flagstaff were less than ninety minutes, but they would wear me out enough that I would later sit in the bathtub for an equally long time. The downside to being tired meant I was more prone to getting upset and crying.

I rode this seesaw for months. One day I would be riding my bike outside, cleaning the house for three hours, or driving myself to appointments. Another day, I'd catch a glance of myself wearing sweats in the mirror and I'd melt down at what I saw looking back at me. My lopsided haircut framed a pink-scarred face with a fat, deformed lip and chipped teeth. I felt so ugly. Once, I tossed the bathroom trash can aside, along with a few other items that stood between our closet and me. I pulled out my nicest outfit, a knee-length purple dress and a black leather motorcycle-style jacket. My guttural screams and accompanying tears were enough to make Kennett miss his ride. Eventually, I cried myself to sleep while still wearing the dress.

Some emotions I'd attribute to bipolar and others were very obviously related to the PTSD I was unwilling to fully acknowledge. When I did get the energy to ride, I was naive to think that the biggest hindrance I'd experience would be pursing my lips to drink from a water bottle.

I had my first bad encounter with a driver in December. I'd ridden around the neighborhood a bunch at this point, but I'd only kitted up in my green-and-white cycling bibs and jersey once or twice prior to that morning. I was excited to be back outside and while I don't remember the exact route I took, I recall holding my chest high with pride even though my shoulders were hunched over from the exhaustion that I knew would stay with me for the rest of the day. In the final mile, I headed into the north end of town, coasting the slight downhill within the bike lane. I reached the intersection by Amante

Coffee Shop and looked behind me to make sure the road was clear before I merged left into the turn lane.

I stopped and put my right foot on the ground while I looked for a gap in oncoming traffic so that I could make my move. All of a sudden, there was a vehicle out of place and before I could even come up with a rational answer as to what was happening, a familiar 'oh shit' feeling erupted in my stomach. It was the same visceral reaction I'd had when I hit the brakes on October 18th. The silver grill of a white F-150 was headed straight toward me. The driver had crossed the double yellow lines in an attempt to speed around another vehicle and he was headed into my lane of traffic. Fortunately, he was able to stop in time and move back to his lane. I decided to turn around and began to follow him. Luckily, he was headed only 100 yards up the road to a storage unit. As he passed, I saw that he wasn't just driving a truck, he was also towing a large white trailer. At the storage unit, he stopped and got out of the truck with his wife and kids in the parking lot.

I nervously said, 'You almost hit me. You need to be careful. You were completely over the yellow line. I was recently hit and it was by a driver who wasn't paying attention. What were you thinking?' I left when he refused to apologize and rode back to my apartment. I stood in the kitchen, still in my kit, and tried to calm my shaking body and rattled nerves. I stared at the cabinets because I needed food, but I couldn't get my muscles to move toward making a smoothie. I thought, *Kennett would never let them off that easy. For fuck's sake, the guy didn't even apologize.*

So I slid my running shoes on and headed back outside, jogging slightly to reach the storage units in time. The guy was inside talking with the manager, so I leaned my butt against the window ledge and waited. Occasionally I got up and paced for a few moments, before waiting it out on the ledge again. It seemed to take forever for them to rent their unit.

When the four of them got outside, I spoke with a little more authority. I wanted an apology. Instead, I got excuses. 'I'm from out of town ... I was following my brother-in-law ... I didn't see you.'

From out of town? Are you kidding me? Double yellow lines exist everywhere. And his brother-in-law wasn't headed straight at me.

It was obvious by his impatience when speaking to me that he had no remorse for his actions. His discomfort stemmed from being called out for his illegal driving. He wouldn't look me in the eye. He was evasive when he spoke. I threatened to take their license plate number if they didn't listen to me. His wife, a stout woman with a Midwestern-style haircut, seemed to think I was going to harm her. 'Don't touch us. Leave us alone.' The guy looked to be around 210 pounds, and was wearing a purple football sweatshirt.

'Are you serious? Look at me, I'm barely out of the hospital, I weigh 120 pounds, and I don't even want to get near you! I *just* want an apology. Some sort of recognition that what you did put my life in danger. That maybe you'll go away from this experience shaken up, because you should be. Instead of giving me excuses, you should be upset.'

I showed them photos from my phone of me lying unconscious in the hospital, hoping it would invoke a reaction in them. It didn't matter; they showed no empathy and there wasn't much that would make me feel better at that point. I left and walked to Amante Coffee Shop, where Galen was working a barista shift. I asked him for a hug and began crying. Then, my day continued as it was supposed to. I walked the final block home, ate food, sat in the bathtub, and tried to relax. Kennett came home, which helped me feel safe again, but that December day never sat right with me and has since stuck as a vivid memory.

I felt like a victim all over again that day. Why, after someone acted carelessly and put my life at risk, was I the only one who walked away from the intersection distraught? I realized that while I had followed the rules of the road, I had done something wrong in how I handled the situation afterwards. I spent most of the spring trying to come up with my own pre-planned strategy, so that when other instances such as the F-150 happened, I'd be ready and confident enough to handle the situation without becoming a victim.

Kennett also had to learn how to handle traffic given his own PTSD from my crash. His learning curve was figuring out how to tame his anger toward drivers, which he'd had even before my crash. I actually had a co-worker, Tim, pull me aside one day. I looked up at Tim as he said, 'I'm really worried that Kennett is going to harm a driver if he gets into the wrong situation. When he used to work in the office before your crash, he would come back from a lunchtime ride and talk about how he had yelled at multiple drivers on the road. Is he going to therapy now? I don't want to see him get in trouble and I know he is already prone to being aggressive to people who drive like assholes.'

Tim's concern worried me because I knew he was right, and as much as I tried, I couldn't get Kennett to go to more than one intro session of therapy. I was relieved after I saw how Kennett handled his first major post-crash confrontation with a driver. He was climbing up Flagstaff when a driver pulled around him and then proceeded to back up into Kennett a minute later around a blind corner. When Kennett came around to the driver's window, the driver began yelling at him for being on the road and accused him of 'riding like an idiot', even though Kennett was riding solo on the far shoulder of the road. The driver was possibly drunk and likely confusing Kennett with another rider. They quickly got into an argument that ended with the driver reaching out his window to punch Kennett in the chest. At that point, Kennett told the driver he'd been filming him, and the driver quickly sped off. Kennett called the police and filed a report because, as he later mentioned in a blog post, 'Backing into someone on purpose is the act of a maniac.'

Kennett was able to film the driver punching him, along with the Subaru's license plate, because he bought RideEye cameras for our bikes after my crash. The cameras attached to the bike like a flashing light and recorded looped video for two hours at a time. I only used them sporadically because I had to charge them, wipe the lens of dirt kicked up by my tire while riding, and download the video occasionally to make sure it worked. Plus, I was skeptical that the camera's footage would capture a careless driver because of the speed at which a driver can make a fatal error.

When Kennett returned from his ride up Flagstaff, I was equally relieved and impressed. First, Kennett could have easily escalated the interaction by fighting back, but he chose to call the cops. The fear Tim had instilled in me subsided. I was also surprised that the cameras had been helpful. So much so that, as a result, the district attorney's office pursued the case and the driver was actually charged with harassment – a third-degree misdemeanor.

Ironically, while Kennett was completely uninjured from the event, the fact that it was harassment meant he was considered a victim based on Colorado's Victim's Rights Act. For the most part, I was really pleased with how Kennett's interaction with the Subaru driver played out. The only niggle I had was that I hadn't been seen as a victim in my crash while Kennett *had* been in his incident. It was just another example of the law's shortcomings. I couldn't help but think, *What the fuck?*

After this, I desperately wished I had video footage of the F-150 in December. Yet, my hesitation to use the cameras persisted. After some soul-searching, I realized that one of the reasons I was still able to continue getting on the bike was because I didn't go out each time thinking about the worst-case scenario. I wore my RoadID, a bracelet with contact information in case of emergency, but taking the time to set up cameras reminded me of the reality that something awful could happen again. Instead, I wanted to go out thinking I was going to have an enjoyable, exhausting training ride. In fact, within six months of buying them, both Kennett and I put the cameras away for good. Kennett makes sure we stay visible on the road with high-vis neon booties and brightly colored clothing instead.

As time went on, it occurred to me that there was another distinction between my encounter with the F-150 and Kennett's incident with the Subaru. I had never called the police on the driver of the truck. Initially, my thinking was, *Shouldn't the driver have cared about my life without involving the police? The police don't need to be involved because there was no crash. What can they do?*

By summer's end, Kennett and I had been exposed to enough situations with careless or aggressive drivers that I'd found the most appropriate way to handle such incidents: dial the non-emergency police number. But first, I started distinguishing between an inattentive but benign driver and a person who actually put my life in danger. It wasn't healthy for me to continually say, 'I almost got hit again' after returning from a ride. So, I reserved those words for the more blatant, egregious interactions. My telltale sign to distinguish whether a person actually came close enough to hitting me was if I got chills and my nerves immediately became activated, enough so that I became exhausted shortly after the experience.

To this day, when a car doesn't endanger my life, but still poses a risk, I'll consider calling the police. I immediately look at the license plate number. If I have a chance to talk to the driver, my first request is for an apology. It offers humanity to the situation and acknowledges that their actions were unsettling to me. If I'm told my perception is wrong or that my feelings aren't valid, I'll take a second look at the car's license plate number to make sure I've got it memorized for the police. I never know if calling the police has any impact beyond making me feel better, but that is enough of a reason to call. Every action I have on the bike is a balance between being careful while still being aggressive enough to navigate traffic. I need to be aware of traffic, but I don't need to be hyper-focused on how each driver treats me. It took time, but my comfort increased drastically when I learned exactly how I wanted to react toward distracted or aggressive drivers.

My approach may seem like overkill. Neither Kennett nor I have been hurt since my crash, yet I've reported several drivers during that time. Before the crash, I'd continue on my ride after a bad interaction. I'd curse, but I always managed to let it go. I'd tell myself, *Nobody actually got hurt.*

Now I look at it like this – reporting these incidents is a way of tracking someone's driving patterns, which is no different than tracking an employee's work behavior so that there is justification for firing them. If the driver does hit or kill someone later, the court will have an accurate record of their poor driving. The driver may even rack up enough points on their license to have it revoked. It isn't just that I'm pissed at a distracted driver who cuts me off or fails to stop at a stop sign; it is about protecting other people who are out riding the same roads as me.

Since I began working on this chapter alone, I learned of three other cyclists in the area who had been hit by a driver and sustained serious injuries that sent them to the hospital. And how did I manage after hearing about all the recent crashes? Just like I did when I first rode to Krista's class after my crash, I made sure to have an enjoyable experience on the bike. After doing some writing, I made plans to ride with my 75-year-old neighbor. We took a few gravel trails and connected them with quieter roads. The skies were blue, the lilacs made the spring air fragrant, and we both kept marveling at how lucky we were to be out riding on such a gorgeous day.

CHAPTER 14
CRASH SITE

'I know people that have been hit by cars multiple times over their years of cycling. Recently someone told me he'd been hit 4 times already. If I ever get hit and killed by a car, I want a white bike to go up.'
Draft email to my parents

One spring day in 2015 I had a neurologist's appointment, which was located in a bland office park building about twenty minutes away in Louisville, Colorado. It was a one-off appointment where I had to do multiple tests to ensure my brain hadn't sustained any previously undetected damage as a result of the crash. Any findings would be documented for the civil case. A few weeks later, I got a call from the neurologist. My brain function was deemed within normal ranges for someone of my age and education, but she did mention that the test for post-traumatic stress disorder (PTSD) had come back as positive.

I began debating with the neurologist over the phone, 'I wouldn't really say I have PTSD.'

'Your test came back positive.'

'But I'm riding my bike now. Yeah, I have a heightened sense of traffic around me, but I wouldn't qualify it as PTSD.'

'We were able to assess that you do have it. The test is clear-cut.'

I thought through all of the tests I had done in the room that morning. Some had been administered on the computer, while others had required me to recite things back to a proctor. I tried to remember which test might have been for diagnosing PTSD. *I had been asked to recall that list of words several minutes after they had initially been said … but that would have tested my short-term memory, not my stress response. One thing is for sure – my memory isn't good enough to remember all of the various tests.* I was more upset that I couldn't recall the specific tests I had taken than learning I had PTSD. I didn't understand what PTSD meant in the context of my crash. I wasn't experiencing flashbacks. I was able to continue riding. How exactly did I exhibit symptoms of PTSD that so clearly showed up in a test taken sitting still in an office?

I was more fascinated by the fact that PTSD could be tested for in absolute terms than I was by the diagnosis I had personally received. Given that I had almost no memory of the crash because of the state of shock I had been in, it was difficult of me to comprehend the severity of it. PTSD, therefore, seemed like an extreme condition that didn't apply. While I didn't understand it at the time, I had dissociated from the crash, which is a clear sign of PTSD. I considered the person who had been hit as 'her'. 'She' had lost a lot and had to be taken care of with love. I, on the other hand, was taking control of the situation. I had already been riding and was focused on regaining my physical strength.

As part of my recovery, I knew I had to confront the crash site if I were to fully return to the bike. Given that it was on a major road that cyclists ride, it wasn't whether I would pass by the site again, it was just a case of when. Even if I went out of my way to avoid the area, it would only be a matter of time until I joined a group ride whose planned route went past the intersection.

I planned an intentional visit to the crash site and asked Kennett to ride with me for support. To a fault, I consider him a safe zone while I'm riding. On January 10th, almost three months after the crash, we rode the 10 miles to the crash site. It was a grey Saturday, just before ten o'clock in the morning. As we began the ride on US 36, we talked, but within the first 3 miles I shifted from riding beside Kennett to drafting behind him. Tears rolled from underneath my sunglasses.

We crested the hill above Hygiene Road and I immediately slowed to a stop, 50 feet before the intersection. There was a reflector pole on the right-hand side of the road that stood out to me. I knew it was where I had begun breaking on October 18th. I unclipped and stood over the top tube of my bike, my head bent down between my arms as I sobbed. Kennett, who had already ridden down to the intersection, turned around and rode back to me. He also unclipped so that he could give me a big hug. Through my heaving breaths, I said, 'This is where I started to skid.'

Once I collected myself, we coasted down to the intersection. Kennett gave me a play-by-play of how far the car was out into the intersection and where my skid marks and blood had been visible on the road in the days that followed the crash. Then, I took a right turn and went down Hygiene Road to below the stop sign. I flipped my bike around to the other side of the road and stopped at the same stop sign that Rush, the driver, should have stopped at to watch for cyclists and cars approaching. I checked the line of vision from the stop sign itself. I could see the entire way up the hill on US 36. I told Kennett what he already knew. 'There was absolutely no way he could have missed seeing me if he had stopped at the sign.' It wasn't one of those intersections that require that a driver creep forward past the stop sign to see around a bend or a bush before they go.

Kennett and I spent several minutes at the intersection. After taking in the scene, we continued down the hill. I told Kennett he should try to catch up to the group ride he wanted to be on. There was no need to stick with me. I was going to ride home slowly and hop on the trainer instead. I didn't want to replay the crash in my head anymore for the day. Instead, I rode my second hour inside while watching *Gilmore Girls* reruns on my computer.

Riding to where I almost lost my life and verifying that it was indeed just another wide-open intersection gave me a sense of relief. It was like being scared of someone breaking into the house and then walking downstairs, turning on the lights, and finding the kitchen empty like it is supposed to be. I was proud that I had taken time to properly mourn my prior self and checked it off as another step toward my full recovery. I knew I'd be okay riding past there again in the future.

The next evening, Kennett and I drove down to Denver to visit our friend Travis, who had been hit by a car south of Boulder the day before. While he was okay, he had some pretty swollen bruises on his legs and a trashed bike. He was in such a state of shock from being hit that he never called the cops and accepted a simple apology from the woman. I thought to myself, *I wonder if I hadn't been in such a serious crash if I would have also taken an apology. I probably would have somehow managed to apologize in return. Women are generally less aggressive and I have a tendency to be overly compassionate to people.*

Overall, the weekend was both physically and emotionally draining. Still, I couldn't identify it as PTSD. I emailed my dad to say, 'Today was hard but I think it was just bipolar. I know it was. It was a little extra hard because I rode to the crash site for the first time. It is a little weird – like riding to your graveyard. Except it wasn't, which is good.' What I didn't tell my dad was how many times throughout those months I focused on an alternate reality – the one in which I died. I couldn't escape it popping into my head at unexpected times throughout each day.

I knew from crash scene photos that someone had propped my bike up against the stop sign. This got it out of the way so that the police and EMTs could attend to my injuries. The fact that my triathlon bike could have later been replaced with a white, spray-painted ghost bike resting against that same stop sign didn't escape me. Ghost bikes are similar to roadside crosses used to mark driving fatalities. Flowers are stuck in the wheel spokes, notes attached to the frame, and mementos left behind by loved ones. Not only do ghost bikes act as a memorial, but they also raise awareness of cycling deaths.

Ghost bikes began in 2003 after a cyclist was killed in St. Louis. Now they are a common symbol used around the world. Sometimes, family members are the ones to lock a white bike near the crash site; other times it is a friend or cycling advocate within the community. I remember the first time I learned about ghost bikes. It was before I had met Kennett and before I was riding frequently. My friend Kim pointed one out to me on Violet and 28th Street, about half a mile from where I live now in North Boulder. She told me that the man killed had been engaged. My heart sank for his fiancée at the time. It was extra sad to me because I would think about how she was planning to start her life with this guy and hadn't even had the chance to do so. Years later, I still think of this man and his fiancée, both unknown to me, every time I pass by. The white bike is no longer looking over the intersection, but it is forever etched in my mind.

A white bike was never placed at the intersection where I was hit because I survived, but I pictured it being there nonetheless. My mind often went to ugly places like this. I knew what my family had been doing on the day of my crash and I could see myself looking down from overhead as they found out I had been killed. I'd imagine everything I would have missed if I hadn't survived. For one, Kennett would have never proposed to me. However, the most concrete event I held on to ended up being my sister's wedding. Jeff and Lydia were getting married on Memorial Day weekend in 2015. Thinking about lying in a coffin, instead of standing by my sister's side, regularly brought me to tears.

By visiting the crash scene and by continuing to expose myself to traffic, I thought I had overcome what little PTSD I might have had. I didn't realize it at the time, but I had friends who recognized that exposure therapy wasn't going to fix the problem. They were extra sensitive to what routes they chose when we rode together. I don't remember the ride, but years later, a friend, Bill, told me about the time we had stopped for a snack and water refill at the Hygiene market with a few other friends. Bill suggested we go back home via Hygiene Road, which would have taken us through the crash intersection. Since I don't recall the ride, I'm not sure if I was upset by the suggestion, but our friend Nora was looking out for me. She stood behind me and started shaking her head 'NO' to Bill. The plan was amended and we went back via a quieter road.

Within half a year of the crash, I started writing this book. In the process I had to interview people about their experiences and learn more about the facts of my crash. This probably encouraged me to continue dissociating from my emotions. Even years later, when I'd learn a new detail, I would actually get excited. It would add more to the descriptions in my writing. This was the case when Kennett and I became friends with Chris, another triathlete, two years after my crash. At one point, Chris realized I had been the girl hit that day and told Kennett he had been riding the same roads as me on October 18th, 2014. He was only minutes behind me, so he had seen me leaned up against the tire when he rode by. In fact, Chris was the one who told me I had been propped up against the driver's side wheel in the first place. Until meeting him, I had assumed that, post-impact, I had been laid out across the pavement.

I didn't talk about the crash with Chris because, after two years, it was no longer in the forefront of my mind. Then, one day in 2016, we were both on a group training ride that took us past the intersection. The group of eight rode two by two, with Kennett and Chris at the front. I was positioned directly behind Chris. On the way out, Kennett was showing Chris how to get his position more aerodynamic by dropping his head. I laughed because from behind I could see their heads bobbing up and down as Kennett demonstrated to Chris how low it was possible to get.

When we crested the hill to descend into Lyons, Chris, who was still directly in front of me, rolled through the crash site intersection in his aero bars like it was no big deal. Meanwhile, I pushed myself even more upright and coasted through, letting the six or so people behind me come around.

Kennett waited for me at the bottom of the hill. When we were side by side, I said, 'I just didn't want to rush through.'

'I know.'

'I don't know why Chris felt it was necessary to go past the intersection in his aero bars.'

'He was safe. There weren't any cars.'

'He should have known I was right behind him. I'm surprised he wasn't more impacted by the crash scene.'

Kennett listened to me express my annoyance and then we pushed a little harder to catch up to the rest of the group. I slipped back behind his rear wheel so I could get his draft when the pace increased.

When I started writing this chapter, I had a conversation with Kennett and explained to him why I felt Chris shouldn't have rolled through the intersection in his aero bars. Kennett proceeded to say, 'You are wrong about blaming Chris. I go through the intersection in my aero bars all the time. He has told me that he thinks about your crash every time he goes by it.'

It was really frustrating to hear Kennett stick up for someone other than me, and this topic led to a small spat. I tried to hold my position by saying, 'I think very highly of Chris. However, I still feel like he should have known better with me right on his wheel. He could have just popped up. I never said he was going too fast … just that he could have taken a moment to make himself more visible on the road because I was in the group.'

'He looks out for you all the time. When you tag along on rides with us, he routes us away from Hygiene Road.'

Kennett didn't budge on his stance and initially I didn't either. I think I went upstairs to do laundry to avoid further conversation. However, I thought about it more throughout the day, and Kennett was correct to say that the intersection isn't dangerous. Just like I confirmed the first time I visited the crash scene; the area is wide open, and it is easy to see what is going on. It is a safe intersection to roll through in the aero bars (if there are no cars present) because, as a cyclist, you can track traffic coming up from Hygiene Road. Similarly, any remotely attentive driver approaching the stop sign would easily be able to spot cyclists picking up speed on the downhill toward them. I also had to consider that it was Chris I was complaining about. Over time, he had become a good friend of Kennett's. Even though he is barely older than me, I think of him as a big brother because I know he would do anything to take care of me if I were hurt on the road. Chris is a safe rider, who I trust. It dawned on me that I was blaming Chris for what was strictly an internal conflict. Before the end of the day, I apologized to Kennett for attacking his friend's behavior and I agreed it was another instance of PTSD.

It has taken years and another crash for me to realize that, just because I don't stop and bawl over my handlebars when I pass the crash site, it doesn't mean I don't experience an elevated stress response. Now I feel like I pass the intersection less often. For one, I don't go on as many group rides. Also, US 36 has become so busy that many riders don't go that far out before they turn east or west off the highway. However, when I do get close on a group ride, I interrupt the conversation I'm having with the person beside me. I'll explain my history and tell them I plan to just go quiet once we come up on the hill that dips down past Hygiene Road. There is no ghost bike there because I didn't die, but I still like to acknowledge my previous self when I roll downhill. The 'her' that had lost so much at this location. It has transformed from a gravesite to a memorial for me. It is a place where I'm reminded I'm lucky to be alive – where this other reality didn't happen. But, at the same time, it is where I lost a large part of myself, where my world changed forever.

CHAPTER 15
TRAFFIC CASE PART II

'I do drug treatment court every Wednesday afternoon, and one of the things that I deal with, some of the foundations of treatment court are the foundations of accountability and honesty. And I got to be honest with you all. I mean, I read these memorandums, I saw the pictures of Adelaide, and it brought tears to my eyes.'
Judge handling Rush's traffic case

The bipolar depression I feared so much from the first days in the hospital came in the spring. Even though I had healed nicely over the winter and had returned to work, life didn't go back to normal. Because of PTSD, I would become excessively exhausted after riding in traffic. Even if I wasn't physically drained, chances were I was emotionally worn out. In moments of quiet, I would have time to reflect on my disfigurement. Then, of course, there was the biggest trigger – Rush's traffic case.

After seeing how Peggy Brown was sentenced, I knew I would be unhappy with the outcome, but I held onto a sliver of hope that justice would be served and remained invested in the court case anyway. Meeting with Lisa at the District Attorney's office in January was the first of many times I poured emotional energy into what would happen to Rush in court.

After visiting Lisa in person to discuss Rush's charges, she and I would email back and forth. I sent her police reports, photos, and a HIPPA release form so that she could get my medical records.

She would send me updates each time there was a meeting. When she walked into the pre-trial conference with Rush's attorney in February of 2015, she knew my wish was for Rush to get the harshest punishment possible. She told Rush's lawyer she wouldn't offer a plea deal and that Rush's sentencing would have to be left up to the court.

After the pre-trial conference, she told me that, according to his lawyer, Rush wanted to plead guilty but he was worried about restitution. This spurred what would become an almost continuous outrage within me throughout the spring. *What the hell! Are you kidding me? He isn't pleading guilty because he did something awful – he is pleading guilty to save his ass. He is bargaining so he doesn't have any long-term repercussions.*

Restitution is a court-ordered payment that the offender must pay to the victim. It is calculated to cover costs such as medical bills, lost wages, therapy, and property damage, but the defendant's finances are also taken into account. It is often a trivial amount when compared to the cost incurred by the injured party. Restitution does not account for pain and suffering, which is only considered when damages are sought in a civil case. Because restitution is minimal, it is only awarded when the defendant doesn't have enough insurance for the victim to recoup their financial losses in a civil court. If the DA's office stipulated that restitution wouldn't be sought, then it was implied I would pursue financial compensation from Rush in the civil court and that he would plead guilty in the criminal proceedings. First, my lawyer, Brad, needed to research the insurance policies to determine if they were large enough to cover my damages. After discussions with him, I replied to Lisa's email:

> *'There is enough insurance money that I shouldn't have any need to request restitution. Rush can plead guilty, everyone else can walk away from the case and feel good because it is all over with except me, who will have to deal with it for the rest of my life. He can pay his ticket and go on driving with a minimum coverage policy and continue to be a jerk on the road.'*

At this point, I knew Rush held an insurance policy of $150,000. My hospital expenses alone exceeded $250,000. The only reason that restitution wouldn't be necessary was because he was driving a rental car that his friend, Brian Clifford, had rented from Hertz. As such, Rush wouldn't be the only person liable. By handing over the car keys when they went to look for real estate together, Clifford would also be legally involved in the civil suit. In legal terms, this is called joint venture. Rush's request to have restitution taken off the table was exponentially more offensive to me because he was being saved by his friend's insurance policies, not his own. Rush was a deadbeat in my mind and, with time, my opinion of him only dropped.

Next, there was a case management conference scheduled for March 12th. This conference between Rush, his lawyer, the DA, and the judge was when Rush was expected to sign plea papers admitting guilt, after which the judge would set a sentencing date. Lisa invited me to come but I declined because it dawned on me that I had no memory of Larry Rush.

In my mind, he had long grey hair pulled back into a ponytail. He was lanky and perhaps a smoker. I assumed he was wearing a pair of jeans and a casual short-sleeve button-down shirt as he stood on the roadside, watching emergency personnel kneeling next to me. Kennett verified that the image I'd created of Rush was completely wrong and I realized that this was a good thing. Allowing him to remain an imaginary figure lessened my anger toward him. It's hard to hate someone when you don't know what they look like. I figured that if I met him again at legal proceedings, it would be like adding kerosene to the slow-burning contempt within me.

While I wasn't at the case management conference, I knew what was supposed to happen. The day before, Lisa emailed to inform me that she had talked to Rush's lawyer and Rush planned to plead guilty. Lisa emailed a few days later to tell me that Rush got 'cold feet'. His lawyer had been handed the plea papers and returned thirty minutes later with them unsigned. Rush still claimed he was going to plead guilty, but he wanted more time. Another case management conference was set for April 9th, 2015.

When I asked Lisa what Rush's strategy was for delaying his court case, she told me she was frustrated. She had no explanation for how extra time could benefit Rush. I was absolutely livid. The only thing I could think was, *He had five months, FIVE MONTHS, to figure out how he wanted to plead. In the meantime, I have had the worst five months of my life.* I took it personally that he avoided signing the plea papers, because delaying the court proceedings meant he was drawing out my emotional pain. I couldn't work through the emotions of his sentencing if he wouldn't even plead guilty.

Even when there wasn't a pending update for the criminal case, I was emailing Lisa. I emailed her about a book I'd read in March called *A Deadly Wandering*. It was about a young driver in Utah who drifted over into another lane and caused an eighteen-wheeler truck to swerve into a car. The crash killed two fathers carpooling to work. In this case, the police had a high suspicion that the young driver was texting when he drifted across lanes, so they subpoenaed his cell phone record to prove their suspicions. I considered my own crash. It had never made sense to me how Rush hadn't seen me – unless he was looking at his phone or he was on drugs – so I asked Lisa why nobody had checked out if Rush was using his phone. She told me that to get Rush's cell phone records, an officer would have to sign an affidavit stating grounds for getting a warrant. The warrant would go to a judge who would determine if there was probable cause to order the cell phone company to produce the records.

I responded, 'I am not looking at the crash scene photos now, but I believe when Kennett and I looked at the images, a cell phone was in the center console. Grounds for getting a warrant should be that he wasn't paying attention to where he was stopping. It is quite simple. If nobody asks and looks into it, he gets away with it. I don't care about the punishment on this, if he was on the phone – he needs to be charged with it as well. Simple – no? I realize it requires more work from others. At least people are getting paid to do this work. I sat in the hospital recovering from this for days upon days because of this. This should be a simple thing that is done after every crash.

'I am still stuck with insurance claims and doctor's appointments that upset me SO much and I really don't think it is fair that he gets to choose when he pleads and that everyone lets him off easy because it requires more work or there is a chance it would fail. Sometimes, you have to fight for something to turn out.'

I pushed this point until Lisa explained to me that even if Rush got charged with misuse of a wireless device while driving, the fine would only be $50. The District Attorney's office could not justify using all the resources it would require to get the cell phone records when it was a mere $50 on the line.

My frustrations with the pending criminal case for Rush bled over into daily life. Throughout the entire spring, Kennett and I were in couples therapy with a sports psychologist. We thought it would help make me more comfortable with riding and with watching Kennett head out the door to train. With each evening therapy session, it became more and more apparent that my issues went well beyond riding. Most of the time I spent crying on the loveseat was because I felt like a victim of the legal proceedings. With the additional stress of the pending court case, I grew depressed. My bipolar symptoms also flared up, which drove a wedge between Kennett and me. Our first months as a married couple were far from blissful.

I also became consumed by a sense of loss over missing our trip to Mexico, which had been planned for the prior November but had been cancelled when I ended up in the hospital. In my journal, I wrote, 'Sunday of this weekend was great but I am really struggling. I came home from work early today. Kennett and I watched *Arrested Development* tonight and for a brief instance it showed a tropical beach island. I am so sad and angry that we lost our trip to Mexico. I'm unhappy more than happy these days.' Kennett and I had talked about going to the beach since we first started dating, so I had spent over a year and a half looking forward to Mexico before it was ripped out from under me.'

Finally, after a therapy session at the end of March, Kennett and I sat on the stairs outside the office and talked over what actions we could take so that I would feel better. Therapy itself wasn't getting me anywhere. He was supposed to fly to Redlands Bicycle Classic in California to race the following week, but I didn't want him to leave. My ups and downs with bipolar are always easier to handle when there is someone nearby. Kennett, in particular, knows to cook balanced meals and keep me away from the chocolate aisle at the grocery store. He is great at motivating me to get a workout in, he helps maintain the house when I fall apart, and, in general, his presence keeps me from going too deeply into an emotional hole. It was a double-punch: Kennett would be away and he'd also be in sunny southern California – not quite Mexico, but it was substantially warmer than the Colorado snow.

The desire to travel to the beach went beyond just wanting to relax in the sun. I desperately wanted to hit an imaginary reset button. Before I knew I had bipolar, I made several escapes to start anew. In high school, I was sure my mood swings were caused by the terrible cloudy weather of Pittsburgh, so I graduated early and moved out. I enjoyed each new semester start in college because it meant moving into a new room in the barracks and having a different schedule. I was always sure the next job, the next home I lived in, the next trip would set me straight.

With my diagnosis, I've learned I'll never be able to fully escape the ups and downs of my mental disorder. My struggle has been to not get up and escape anytime something goes wrong. However, there are times where escaping is still a great coping mechanism. A change of scenery can do anyone good because it allows the current worries to dissipate. I had been through enough in the past several months and I knew I wasn't strong enough to bring my brain back to a consistently positive state of mind in Boulder.

Earlier in the spring, we had brainstormed a lot of ideas. One was for me to attend a training camp in Tucson with an ex-professional triathlete. I emailed her three days before the camp was supposed to start and Kennett bought me plane tickets on Southwest, but shortly after I cancelled because I didn't have the energy to travel alone, let alone train hours on end.

Next month, Lydia took over the challenge to get me out of my slump. She suggested going to Princeton Hot Springs and to the quaint Colorado town of Salida. Princeton Hot Springs is upscale and Salida has been one of my favorite escapes nearby. However, they weren't going to cancel out the emotional trauma I'd been experiencing. My response was, 'I really like that area but I don't want to go somewhere cold.'

Sitting on the steps outside the therapist's office, we continued to brainstorm and then rearranged our plans for the following week. I would drive out to California with Kennett. We decided to leave a few days earlier and go to the beach in Dana Point before his race. It wasn't Mexico, but it was an escape. I brought my bike on the trip and we did several rides through Dana Point. Later in the week, when Kennett raced, I rode to the course so I could watch.

While we were gone on this trip, Rush finally turned in his signed plea papers. It took him a total of 169 days after the crash, twenty-four days after he was supposed to plead guilty the first time, to finally admit guilt. I have little recollection of reading Lisa's email with the update. I think that is because I was out of town and focused on enjoying the trip instead. In the same email, Lisa told me that she would no longer be handling the case because she had been moved to a different office. She introduced the new Deputy DA who would replace her. Up to this point, I'd had to fight to get my witness statement included in the police report, to find out what Rush's ticket was for, and to understand why Rush wasn't charged with reckless driving causing serious bodily injury. I had grown to trust that Lisa would do a good job and take my wishes into account, but this guy Michael? I wasn't so sure.

One early evening in the midst of all this, I went over to my sister's house. The sun was just ducking behind the mountains and the temperature was warm enough to wear my capri tights, a long-sleeve shirt, and a vest. We walked through her neighborhood in South Boulder. As we passed the parking lot of an elementary school, she brought up the point that maybe I should forgive the driver.

'Just the other night, Jeff and I were driving and a person riding a bike came out in front of us from almost nowhere. We could have hit him. The situation was terrible, but sometimes accidents happen. It seems like a lot of energy for you to not forgive Rush.'

'Lydia, this wasn't a dark night where I didn't have lights on my bike. It was a beautiful blue-sky day, perfect visibility, no obstructions. And to forgive someone, I think there needs to be an apology. He never apologized.'

'He did show up to the hospital on Thursday after the crash. He couldn't see you and thankfully security kicked him out, but he did try.'

Lydia was correct – Rush did attempt to visit me in the hospital, although I had no clue at the time. He showed up, sobbing and accompanied by a friend. Kennett immediately recognized him when Rush and his buddy walked into the ICU waiting room. To avoid starting a fight, Kennett rushed out of the waiting room to calm down. My dad realized who Rush was somehow, possibly picking up a cue from Kennett's unease, and left the room as well. Thirty seconds later, Kennett came back, somewhat calmed down at this point, and said, 'You need to leave.' Rush's face was beet red from tears. He wanted to get into the ICU to see me, but, in Kennett's mind, the time for an apology had long since passed. Someone called security before any type of altercation happened, and Rush was escorted out of the hospital.

As I talked with Lydia, I sided with Kennett. 'Thursday was six days after the crash. It wasn't even an appropriate time to see how I was doing. It upset you guys. Kennett was ready to attack him.'

'Well, I just think you should think on it …'

I did consider what my sister had said. I wondered if I was hurting myself more by refusing to forgive Rush. There were just so many reasons not to offer forgiveness. One major reason being that by refusing to plead guilty in March, he had just postponed a piece of closure for me, which delayed my psychological recovery.

The court date was a big event in my mind. Contrary to what I had originally wanted, which was to have the courtroom filled with cyclists when the sentencing date came around, I decided I didn't want anyone to show up. I wasn't going to either. I knew he'd offer his apologies in front of the judge – he'd have to be a sociopath not to. I didn't want him to have the relief of apologizing to me directly.

Instead of showing up to court, I asked friends and family to write statements for the judge to read in their absence.

In my own letter to the judge, I expressed that whatever Rush's punishment was, he would be getting off easy. It was uncomfortable for me to see how vindictive I could be. I wrote, 'People ask me about forgiveness. I don't care to forgive Mr. Rush because he hasn't even bothered to apologize to me. I received dozens and dozens of cards telling me to get well, but he never even bothered to say he was sorry through a letter or flowers. I am not going to be here today to listen to any apologies because they won't be sincere. They'll be in self-interest – to save himself from any harsh punishment.'

I forwarded along fifteen letters to the judge before the May 12th sentencing date. These statements of support gave me a sense of peace that, regardless of how the DA approached the case, at least some of my side of the story would be told. Up until this point, I had been skeptical, because within hours of my crash a police officer was quoted in the local newspaper as saying, 'The driver had come to a complete stop and yielded appropriately, when they were hit by the bicycle. The driver had started from a stop sign, but stopped for a turning vehicle. That's when they were hit by the bicyclist.'

That version of events was completely false, both because of his alleged stop at the stop sign, and because of the imaginary turning cars that impeded Rush's forward progress onto US 36. However, that was the story that made the newspaper, and it was what remained in the police report, too. I wanted to make sure that wasn't the narrative that was heard in the courtroom during Rush's sentencing.

Initially, I feared that Michael, the new Deputy DA, wouldn't understand the importance of my case like Lisa had. In an email, I asked, 'Have you read Kennett's blog?' He didn't answer my question when he replied with other updates on the sentencing, so I kept on asking him. 'Did you read Kennett's blog yet?'

After being pushed with the second email, he said he'd get on it. In the next email, he told me he was 'up to speed'. I was wary and wanted Lisa back. I copied her on many of my emails. I'm not sure at what point Michael truly began caring about my case. It is possible that he immediately took it on with the same passion as Lisa and I was just too stubborn to recognize it. Regardless, at some point, he began to really back me up. This became apparent when I read the sentencing memorandum, which was a document Michael had to prepare for the judge ahead of the sentencing.

On May 12th, two days before the sentencing, I sat behind my computer at work. Looking for a moment of distraction, I checked my personal email account and saw I had received a new message from my lawyer, Brad. The email contained both the sentencing memorandum and a personal note to me, which read, 'It's quite compelling.' After reading through the first few pages of the attached memorandum, I called to Kennett, who was working at his desk off to my left. 'I just got the sentencing memorandum. Get this – Michael did an amazing job! He told the judge that I was following the traffic laws to "a T" when I moved left to take up the entire turn lane. He even included the relevant statute as evidence!'

I was eager to take in the entire document and couldn't read fast enough. When I got to section six, where it stated that I couldn't have avoided the crash, my lips curled upward. Michael had pulled quotes from witness statements to explain that others also felt the crash had been unavoidable. My eyes lit up when I got to section eight. In response to the black cars that Rush had claimed responsible for his stop, Michael wrote, 'And, if that [black] car did abruptly decide to turn left into the defendant's path, it is difficult to imagine how that car would not have also been involved in the accident.' A subtle way of saying that Rush and his passenger had lied.

I'd spent several months crying, screaming, and throwing punches at pillows in response to the traffic case. I had not smiled over the matter – at least not until I was reading an official document saying the crash wasn't my fault. I had known all along that it hadn't been, but in quiet moments I would still question whether or not I could have swerved last minute behind the Fiat. Reading that I couldn't have done any better was a relief.

Spread between page four and five of the seven-page document was the most shocking part. The DA had done his research and had access to Rush's driving record, which I'd tried finding, to no avail, months earlier.

'HOLY SHIT! Get this. He has four ... five ... eight ... seventeen ... NO ... *eighteen* prior traffic infractions! His license was suspended for seven years in the eighties. I gotta print this. You have to read it yourself,' I excitedly told Kennett.

Our office had ten desks, each of which could be raised into a standing position. About half of my co-workers were standing, the others sitting. The desks lined the walls while a faux wood conference table took up the center of the room. One of the perks of the office was that we had a Razor scooter. I have no idea whose it was or how it came to be there, but scooting around the conference table usually made a nice midday break. I went to the printer, grabbed the scooter, and quickly made my way around the office, sharing the news with everyone. I was astonished as I read the words on the page. *Speeding, weaving, improper passing on the left*, and more. Rush was a habitual traffic offender in the eighties, but his behavior had turned around for the better – until recently, of course. In the past ten years, he'd only been caught twice. Michael threw in a snide comment, questioning whether Rush's driving had actually improved or not, saying it was also possible Rush had moved away and they simply lacked his out-of-state driving record.

To this day, I become energized as I reread the DA's memorandum. Looking at it, I'll often get the same urge to share the contents with someone and express my disbelief. It shouldn't be that shocking, especially now that I've read it multiple times, but I am still in awe of how different the narrative is from what was initially reported by the local newspaper. Rush was not some saint who got hit randomly by a cyclist and stuck around afterwards to make sure she was okay. Instead, he is someone with a track record of driving recklessly. He watched from the shoulder of the road while his passenger, and later the emergency personnel, saved my life. Later, when interviewed by the police, he lied to protect himself. With that in mind, I stuck with my decision to avoid the courtroom and meeting him again.

The day of the sentencing was fairly anti-climactic in comparison with reading the memorandum. Brad offered to attend on my behalf so that I didn't have to see Rush. I spent the afternoon with my co-workers on a mountain bike photoshoot. It was a blue-sky day that warranted short sleeves and sunscreen over my scars. I felt a rush of energy because I had chosen to ride instead of being brought down by the court proceedings. My depression was lifting.

After work, I spoke to Brad on the phone to get a summary of what had happened. The judge had expressed on two separate occasions that reading the letters by friends and family on my behalf had brought tears to his eyes. Brad said this was very unusual for a judge to admit. Rush received the maximum fine of $1,000 but avoided jail time, which could have been up to a year. He was also ordered to complete 200 hours of community service, received four points on his license, and earned himself a seat at a level-three responsible driving class.

I was calm about the outcome because, after seeing Peggy Brown's sentencing, it was what I had come to expect. I was just relieved it was over and proud that I had been able to evoke an emotional response from the judge. This doesn't mean I'm satisfied with how the criminal case ended. I had wanted the maximum possible punishment for Rush, which would have included one year in jail, but even that would have been a consolation prize. Jail wasn't the right punishment for what he did; I had simply wanted him off the road. Unfortunately, the judge had no authority to revoke a driver's license. The regulations for driver's licenses are dictated by the Department of Motor Vehicles and the points system. Rush would have had to accumulate twelve points for the DMV to revoke his license.

At one point, I went online to see what the ordered driving course entailed. I learned it was a weekend class. The topics of this class included stress management, staying in control, and – my favorite – personal goals.

I told Kennett, 'I've never had personal goals for driving but I guess now that I think about it, it would be having the ideal radio station with no commercial breaks for my trip, and making sure the back of the seat isn't tilted too far back from when you were last driving. My long-term goals include having a car with seat warmers. Oh wait … and not putting someone in a coma. That's on my list, too.'

I never forgave Rush, but I have ceased to care about him. To this day, I remain cynical on a larger level. From the initial reporting done by newspapers to the final sentencing, I can see flaws in our system. It angers me when I read a newspaper that states the driver stayed on the scene and cooperated with investigators. By acknowledging facts like this, it reads as though the public should be congratulating the driver. It isn't just that sticking around after a crash is the responsible thing to do. In fact, it is the only legal option there is; leaving the scene is its own crime. The problem is that driving is treated as a right instead of a privilege. As such, drivers are given a lot of leeway with their behavior.

I understand why the decisions were made about the charges, not getting a subpoena for the cell phone records, and not seeking the maximum punishment for Rush. Within the confines of how the system currently works, it all makes sense. I just think as a society we can do better. We got to the point where it is socially unacceptable to drink and drive. I've watched an entire community become outraged when a drunk driver killed a cyclist, because they felt it was easy to place blame. Yet people are much more hesitant to place that same blame on a driver who isn't listed as intoxicated. For me, it's a public safety concern. It's not a cyclists-versus-cars issue, although a lot of people treat it that way. We shouldn't allow distracted or aggressive drivers to treat their actions as mere 'accidents'. If it is illegal to text and drive, there should be a high punishment to deter people from doing it, not a $50 fine. If a person causes a crash with bodily injury, the judge should have the option to revoke their license. They should not be allowed to delay the court proceedings and plead guilty only when they feel emotionally prepared to, because that inevitably puts further stress on the victim. Of course, based on the Colorado Victim's Rights Act, I wasn't legally a victim of the traffic incident in the first place. My opportunity to seek justice was left for the civil court system.

CHAPTER 16
CIVIL SETTLEMENT

'The insurance companies will try to be sneaky from the get-go. Protect her, call Brad. He will keep her safe from all shenanigans ...'
Legal advice sent to Kennett in the days after my crash

When I left the Coast Guard back in 2009, Lydia and I had a game we'd play daily. She had left a finance job in New York City and moved to be with me in Charleston, South Carolina, prior to our bike tour. The game went like this: 'What do you want to be today? A lawyer, a teacher, or a nurse?' Each day she'd come up with new options, but many days I returned to the idea of being a lawyer. So much so, that when we traveled to visit a friend in Philadelphia, we made a side trip to walk around the University of Pennsylvania. While we didn't see much more than the beautiful architecture and squirrels gorging on pizza boxes left near a trash can on the campus, I left visualizing myself in law school.

During the civil case for my crash, there were moments when I felt like I was getting a free legal education. But then it all depends how 'free' is defined. While I made money from the civil case, it took a huge emotional toll on me. The moments when I was enamored by the law were eclipsed by how often I felt beat down. The very fact that I was a victim in the case seemed to be casually ignored by the insurance adjusters and their lawyers, who did their best to delay settling the case in the hope of wearing me down.

The first lesson I learned about the law is that victims always need a lawyer to ensure they are fairly compensated by insurance companies. Even when the injuries are grave and blatant, such as mine were, it isn't easy to convince an insurance company to pay the medical costs, let alone damages for pain and suffering. That I would need legal representation hadn't crossed my mind. In fact, Jeff was the one who recommended to the rest of my family that they should interview lawyers. I think this is because, as my sister's fiancé, he was just one step far enough removed to think rationally after the crash.

Several days into my hospital stay, Kennett told me I had a lawyer. Then, he backed up to say, 'Well, your parents and I met with three lawyers in the hospital on Tuesday when you were sedated. You'll have to sign the documents to hire him, but I think we picked out the best one of the three. One was a little sleazy, the other one less experienced, but this guy, Brad Tucker, seems really qualified.'

'Wow – I have a lawyer! Only important people have lawyers. Watch out, Kennett.' Then, in an uppity voice, I repeated, 'I have a lawyer.'

On one of the first days home from the hospital, Brad came to our apartment to meet me. I hired him and he said he would begin investigating the driver's insurance policy. In the meantime, I was told to write down everything I had owned on the bike and the prices. He would submit a property claim as soon as I gave him all the information.

The good news, he explained, was that normally the insurance companies look at how old the property was and take into account depreciation when managing property claims. For bikes, it is too hard to get another used bike in the specific size as a replacement, so the insurance companies typically pay out the value of a new bike. As a cyclist himself, Brad told us that he would waive his legal fees for the property claim so I could put all the money toward a new bike.

Initially, in November, I was excited to get new gear. However, by early December, I emailed Brad, 'My new theory on property damage is that they should pay to replace a chunk of my wardrobe in general. My cycling bibs, after not eating for five days at the hospital, no longer fit.' I couldn't even open the closet without feeling a sense of injustice.

Getting money for my damaged property was the easiest part of the civil suit because a number could be attached to all the bike parts. I think I received a check for my bike and accessories by the end of the year. However, I was realizing how all-encompassing the crash was and why it is so difficult to put a price tag on a civil suit.

Cases involving bodily injury often take years to settle. Personal injury lawyers don't want to rush to a settlement before all of the injuries, pain and suffering, emotional distress, and other damages are accounted for. It isn't always clear what the cost of a lingering injury will be for the victim in the long term, and it is only with time that a lawyer can present an accurate estimate of future medical needs. On the other side, insurance adjusters use delay tactics to entice victims to settle for a lower amount than their case is worth, hoping that mounting bills will force them to give in.

Despite the severity of my injuries, Brad was able to submit a claim by August 2015. My future surgeries could be predicted, the permanent scarring and disfigurement was known, and the crash spoke for itself when it came to pain and suffering. As Brad put it, 'Most people don't survive what you went through. Your case is one where I easily could have been representing your family instead of you.' Because there were few undefined variables on our side, things were set in place faster than normal.

My own car insurance company immediately offered the policy limits on my non-owner auto policy. This was a nice little bonus because, in the hospital, none of my family realized that I had even owned auto insurance. They assumed I got rid of it when I gave my car to Goodwill and became a bike-only commuter. Luckily, when I called to cancel my insurance a year before, the woman I spoke to put up a fight and persuaded me to keep my insurance at a lower premium.

As a result, USAA, my insurance provider, wrote me a check for $25,000 right away. Normally, that would be a shocking amount of money in my world, but as a result of the crash, my view of money was drastically shifting. My own insurance policy limits were the equivalent to the cost of spending just thirty hours in the intensive care unit. My hospital bill for the eleven-day stay was in excess of $251,000, which my healthcare insurance from work was mostly covering. However, each outpatient appointment I went to meant more co-pays and more surgeons' and doctors' fees.

Then, Brad emailed me with the unfortunate news that Rush held only a $100,000 bodily injury liability coverage, the Colorado state minimum, with Farmer's Insurance Group. I had a phone conversation with my dad about this. He was adamant that Rush should be sued personally if it came to it. It was December and I was still adjusting to the fact that I deserved compensation for what I had been going through. At this point, Rush hadn't delayed court proceedings, so my anger hadn't fully peaked. I was too busy worrying about my own recovery to concern myself with my financial future. I emailed Brad to ask, if it became necessary, whether or not we could go after Rush's future income, property, and savings. I wrote, 'I am not sure how far I'd want to pursue this. I guess it depends on where he stands financially.'

Had Rush been driving his own car, this conversation might have gone further, but he was in a rental car. The passenger, Clifford, had traveled from Pennsylvania to visit Rush. On the day of the crash, while they were checking out real estate properties, Clifford handed the keys of his Hertz rental car over to Rush because he had a headache. This meant that Hertz had liability as well, although that coverage was even less than my own personal auto policy. There were now three insurance policies involved, and it was still like counting coins in hopes of collecting enough money for the mortgage. However, because Clifford had handed over the keys to Rush, he could also be held liable.

It was a very unconventional approach, but Brad argued that Colorado joint-venture law applied in this case. They were in a joint venture because Rush was taking Clifford to look at property. With this claim, Clifford was liable, so his personal insurance would kick in. Looking back on the case, Brad has told me that introducing the joint-venture claim was some of the best lawyering he has ever done.

Clifford held an umbrella policy, along with his own auto insurance policy with Safeco Insurance. Because Clifford's policies were now involved, the potential money available was enough to tell Lisa that the District Attorney's office didn't need to go after restitution. It also made the entire case more complex. Not including my own policy, there were four other insurance policies and three parties involved. Until we settled with Safeco, Clifford's insurance, we could not settle with the policies held by Hertz or Rush.

After the traffic case was over in May 2015, I wanted to purge the crash and any legal repercussions from my mind in the hope that it would help me come out of my season-long depression. My interest in the civil case was, for the time being, completely wiped out. In a cry of despair, I asked Brad over the phone to end the civil case as soon as possible. Brad worked hard on my behalf, but he still had to gather what he felt my case was worth. I'd occasionally get an email asking about what future surgeries I might need, or he would copy me on a message to the Safeco Insurance adjuster. Besides that, with the criminal case over, I was able to let the civil case fall into the background as Brad worked. It was summertime, so Kennett and I traveled, raced, and began to put the crash behind us.

On August 14th, Brad submitted a settlement demand to all of the insurance adjusters involved, giving them until 5 pm on Friday, September 18th to respond. In the document, Brad told them that I would settle if all of the policy limits were offered. He pointed out that my case was probably worth upwards of two million dollars, which was substantially more than what all the policy limits added up to. He stressed to the insurance adjusters in the letter that it was in their best interest to settle immediately, because after a year I would start accumulating interest on top of the total amount.

I got really excited about the settlement package because it seemed like another stepping-stone in my recovery. Perhaps naively, I thought they would settle quickly, and it seemed serendipitous that the deadline for them to respond was exactly 11 months after the crash. While I wanted the case to be over for my personal sanity, my interest in the legal proceedings was piqued once again. The conversations I had with Brad were often lengthy because I would ask him to explain each possible scenario.

I was on the phone with Brad several times in the days before and after September 18th. SafeCo Insurance Co., which had the biggest chunk of compensation possible, wanted an extension of two weeks. The insurance adjusters were struggling to understand Brad's claim that Clifford and Rush were in a joint venture at the time of the crash. As Brad later told me, 'Insurance companies are devoid of creativity. There was no box for them to check in this case and it threw them. I have no doubt the case went up and down their legal chain.'

I was also shocked that one adjuster had the audacity to admit that his request for an extension was partially because he was behind on his workload. He'd had over a month to respond to our offer and, given the amount of money on the line, I felt it shouldn't have been a case that got ignored. Brad wrote back that I wasn't going to waiver on the initial deadline and pointed out the good news: they still had three days until the deadline to respond.

Then, on the day of the deadline, Friday 18th, Brad called me. He said, 'I got a call from Christy at SafeCo. She asked for an extension over the weekend.'

'Are you serious? I already told them no.'

'They thought you might be willing to wait through the weekend. What do you want to do? It is entirely up to you. If you want, we can hold firm on the deadline and they will still have until 5 pm tonight to respond.'

'If they don't respond?'

'If they don't respond with what you want, we will file lawsuits against Rush and Clifford next week.'

'Are you kidding me? I am not giving them an extension. They have had more than enough time to figure out what they want to do. I can't believe they are asking! They had an entire month. Isn't a month for a case worth this much enough time?'

Saying no to the extensions was incredibly empowering. For as frustrating as the requests were, it felt good to have the upper hand. And filing a lawsuit? I admitted to myself that it sounded a bit exciting.

At 4:56 pm, Brad received an email response from the SafeCo. adjuster, who offered Clifford's umbrella policy but not his bodily injury coverage because they didn't agree that joint venture applied to the case. Brad was flummoxed, and when he explained their reasoning, I joined him in realizing that the bizarre offer made no sense. SafeCo. was acknowledging the magnitude of my case by offering the umbrella policy, but failed to offer the bodily injury policy, which amounted to just over $250,000 – a much smaller figure than the umbrella policy. This meant that SafeCo. was willing to allow their insured, Clifford, to be sued for a quarter of a million dollars, a relatively small number given the total amount involved in the case, yet an extremely large amount for an individual to cover.

Additionally, SafeCo. requested that I release both Clifford and Rush from further legal action, and that I sign documents absolving Clifford from liability. If they were denying that joint venture didn't apply, thus their refusal to offer the bodily injury policy, why would they add on top of that a demand that I also agree to it?

I was frustrated because SafeCo.' s offer showed me that they didn't have their shit together, and, while I had hoped to settle early, I was getting to learn even more about the law. I'd sit on our porch chair, put my feet onto the railing, and talk through the process of filing a lawsuit with Brad over the phone.

'What happens when we file the lawsuit with Rush and Clifford?'

'They will get served the lawsuit in person.'

'No way. So someone just knocks on their door with the documents?'

'Yes, but their insurance companies are still the ones who will hire lawyers on their behalf. Rush has twenty-one days to respond, but since Clifford is out of state he has a few extra days.'

After the lawsuits were filed, there was another multi-month lull in the case. A judge created another deadline, December 18th, for a second chance to settle. That day came and went, which meant that the next step was court-ordered mediation as the final attempt to settle the case outside of the courtroom. Taking the lawsuit to court would drag on for another year or more.

The date for mediation was set for January 12ᵗʰ, 2016, which immediately set me into an emotional whirlwind. I was scheduled to have surgery on December 22ⁿᵈ. Why couldn't the insurance companies have just settled the case on December 18ᵗʰ by offering the policy limits? Now I'd have to go through the physical trauma of post-surgery recovery, followed closely by the emotional trauma of the legal case. I was a mix of feeling livid and completely deflated. I looked for what I could do to make mediation a little less stressful, such as specifically requesting not to be in the same room as the adjusters and insurance company lawyers. I wrote to Brad, 'I thought I'd totally gotten past that hopeless feeling but it's coming back. The fact that they've drawn the settlement out and in such poor fashion makes me want to blow up at people – not you of course. I really don't want to have to see any of these people in January.'

What made it more insulting to me was when SafeCo. contacted Brad a week before mediation and offered me the same sum of money we had asked for in September. With it just being five days away from mediation, we declined their offer to see what would happen if they were pushed. The last-minute agreement to settle after putting it off for months felt like when Rush got 'cold feet' about pleading guilty and then tried to save his ass with an apology in the courtroom.

The night before mediation, I dreamt about what the day would be like. In the dream, I became so enraged that I hoisted a table off the ground and threw it across the room. Pencils, pens, and notepads rained onto the floor. The table banged against the white textured wall because there wasn't enough room to flip it entirely.

Real life turned out to be oddly similar. It was a long day that started with driving down to the Denver Tech Center on the south end of the city. To beat rush-hour traffic, Kennett and I left the house early and stopped for coffee before walking into the office building.

The mediator, Joe, met us at the office lobby at 8:30 am and guided us into a room where Brad sat, waiting. Inside was a long conference table, similar to the table I'd flipped in my dream the night before. Brad was at the far end, while Kennett and I sat side-by-side.

Joe talked to us first because we had planned a staggered start so I didn't run into anyone from the other parties. Representatives for the other side didn't arrive until 9:30 am. After hearing our side of the case, Joe spent the morning going back and forth between our room and the room of insurance adjusters. Each time he came in, he would tell us what the other side was offering and ask for our response.

I recall little of this process until Brad said, 'Joe, I've held some information back from Adelaide to protect her, but I really feel you need to hear this.'

Brad explained that one of the insurance adjusters had actually asked him in an email for Kennett not to be present at the mediation. I think Brad told Joe this to provide him with an explanation of how low the other party was stooping to ensure I settled.

Learning of that request opened up the floodgates. I began talking, my voice rising with each sentence until I was yelling. 'He requested that the sole person who has stood by me every hour of the day since the crash, through every upset, and nearly every tear, shouldn't be here to support me? Who is he to say that this didn't impact Kennett? Kennett, who, in addition to being my husband, also suffered in traumatic ways due to the crash! The pain and suffering money should be jacked up from this moment alone!' Except it wasn't just that moment – it was the hundreds upon hundreds of other painful moments I'd endured over the past year and a half.

As I was yelling, I glanced down at the table. I considered throwing it, but realized that I didn't want to cause that big of a mess and that the conference table was actually too heavy. Those thoughts all occurred in a split second as I walked around the table. In the process, I hit the back of Kennett's chair (accidentally hitting Kennett as well) and slammed my fists on the table multiple times. My hands began throbbing so I stomped my feet instead and, before calming down, let out a piercing scream. I fell to the floor and tried to regain control over my shaking body.

The last time Joe came back in the room after talking with the insurance adjusters, he told us that they wanted to use my blog against me if we went to trial, arguing that, according to my blog posts, I was recovering just fine. Early on after the crash, Brad had told me to be careful about what I wrote. To some extent, I censored my blogs. But I also tried to stay honest and share with people that I was, in fact, recovering, that I got back on the bike and eventually began racing and training again. Kennett's initial blog about the crash had over 100,000 readers and I knew people were continuing to follow the outcome of my crash. I was doing the right thing by sharing my recovery process. I had people leave comments on my blog about how reading it helped them feel less alone after their own crash. Now, during mediation, the adjusters were threatening to use what I'd written against me.

Brad, Kennett, and I had decided in advance of the mediation talks that I would settle today, regardless of whether the other side offered any more than they had five days prior – the full policy limits that we had requested months earlier. I needed the freedom to enjoy my spring. The first settlement discussions had been in September and it could easily be another four months or longer if we held out in hopes of more money. Deposition and the preparations both sides would make for trial would be devastating to me and I knew it. As much as I would have loved to learn about the trial process, I didn't want to continue putting myself through trauma up until the trial date, which had been previously set by the judge for October 16th, 2016 – two days before the second anniversary of my crash. My outburst during the mediation showed that we had made the right decision. With that, we settled and walked back out into the cold, sunny January air.

When I look back on the civil case, I often wish I had refused to settle in January 2016 and had gone to trial later in the year. Yet, no one, including Kennett and my family, thought it would be in my best interest. At one point, Joe took Brad out of the mediation room and told him, 'She needs to settle the case because she can't handle a deposition. It will be too hard.' Deposition is an intense interview conducted under oath before a trial. They both knew being deposed for a trial is orders of magnitude worse than mediation. I couldn't even sit calmly in my seat while being physically separated from the other parties involved.

My health was actually on the line when I made the decision to settle. I couldn't possibly drag the case out because the stress would bring about a bipolar depression. Just like the year before with the criminal case, I wanted to refocus my energy on training and enjoying time with family.

When Brad reflects back on the case, he tells me that we would have been playing with dynamite if we had gone to trial, as in we would have blown them out of the water. He is certain I could have walked away with a lot more compensation. While that would have been nice to have years later, it isn't the main reason I regret not having the strength to go through a trial.

In hindsight, going to court would have been a great hands-on legal experience. I enjoyed the education I received through talking to Brad and reading his communications with the insurance companies. Unfortunately, what I initially thought would be a free course on personal injury law actually had a huge emotional price tag attached to it.

Because I didn't feel vindicated by the court's decision in the traffic case, I hoped that justice would be served in the civil case. 'Getting even' by dragging insurance companies into the courtroom by the collar may sound satisfying to me now, years later, but that winter I was continuously on the brink of emotional collapse. I felt like a victim after being hit, a victim of our legal system's laws that fail to protect vulnerable road users, and a victim of uncaring insurance adjusters who got to forget about the whole thing every evening when they clocked out.

I may not have felt like a winner in the weeks and months that followed, but I was slowly able to rid myself of that 'victim' title. That was the most important aspect of the civil case finally coming to a close.

CHAPTER 17
NEW NORMAL

*'My mom is really polite in telling me that it is in my head,
that I'm imagining people staring. I don't at ALL blame
people for looking twice. My co-worker asked whether or
not I've tried to hide my scars with makeup. I can hide them
fairly well. I tried once.'*
My blog

During the entire spring of 2018, I had a next-door neighbor who
I saw frequently because we both let our dogs play in the field
in front of our condominium complex. Right before she moved
away, my crash came up in conversation and she mentioned that
she had never noticed my scar. This comment fascinated me. At
first, I thought maybe my scar had really disappeared. On second
thought, I realized this was unlikely. My scar begins at the lower
corner of my nose and crosses diagonally down across my cheek
and neck, ending just above my clavicle. Higher up, the scar is a
relatively faint indention, whereas it becomes thicker and more
discolored further down toward my jawline and neck. I can see how
someone might not notice the damage to my upper lip, which was
saved by the leeches, but to not spot the entire scar that dominates
a third of my face?

I figured my neighbor was simply trying to be kind, assuming I was
self-conscious, and continued wrestling with whether or not to believe
her, until a few days later. I was in conversation with a person whom
I had met a few hours earlier during a bike photo shoot. I brought

up my crash and he immediately asked if that was what my scar was from. He had noticed it from our first introduction.

I understand that people may want to protect me – and themselves – from an awkward conversation by pretending that my scar is invisible. Yet it frustrates me that honesty is such an undervalued characteristic in small-talk conversation, and that people assume I'm not strong enough to talk about or acknowledge my scar. I don't need nor want to be treated like a fragile piece of porcelain. I would rather have someone be honest with me and politely ask the story behind the scar than pretend it doesn't exist.

From time to time, I bring up the scar of my own accord, mostly as an excuse. For instance, I'll forget someone I met at a party. They'll see me in a completely different context, like the pool, and recognize me. Often, I have to admit I have no recollection of them, so I'll say, 'Oh right, I met you at Emily's wedding. It isn't fair; my scar gives me a disadvantage. It doesn't matter if I'm dressed up with blow-dried hair or if I'm wet with a swim cap on, I'm easy to recognize.'

My relationship with the scar has changed over time. Initially, it was simply not a priority. When I sat in the ICU room, I was terrified that, since I'd broken the entire left side of my face, my cheekbone might not be sitting in the same place on my face. I'd be lopsided. Before I first glimpsed at myself in the window, I asked if my face was going to be level and I was promised that everything would look even. Still, I wasn't sure if these promises were truthful, or if family and hospital staff were just trying to keep me from panicking, which I was on the brink of doing. Compared to the fear regarding the symmetry of my cheekbones, scarring was a minor detail.

Nobody could look into a crystal ball and see my future, but I was frequently reassured that there were surgeries to get rid of the scarring. My trauma doctor told me that his daughter, who had sustained similar facial injuries during an accident, had scars that had healed so well that nobody could tell.

The scar didn't make me self-conscious in the days and weeks after I was discharged from the hospital. My scar wasn't why people cautiously tried to sneak a glance at me. There were too many other giveaways, such as the way I hobbled around, my restricted speech, the many bandages, and my broken teeth.

Six weeks after the crash, I walked through the grocery store with my sister and I noticed people were doing double takes. When I first got out of the hospital, people didn't have to look a second time because it was obvious I was critically injured. By the time I was buying groceries alongside Lydia, my stomach tube had been removed, which meant I was standing up straighter. My speech had improved, the splint on my nose had been removed, and I was off pain medication. Although, maybe I hadn't noticed people glancing prior to this because I had been heavily sedated.

I was not self-conscious about these double takes. It meant I was close enough to normal that I could walk in public without people immediately noticing I was seriously injured. It was a sign of the physical progress I was making, and that was more important to me than having a large scar on my face.

By December, the scar was overshadowed by my eye socket. I had finally been given the okay to swim. I put my goggles over my face, and within twenty minutes the pressure from the goggle suction against my upper left eye became too painful to ignore. The area had healed in a jagged fashion and there were, and still are, three small bony bumps just underneath my outer eyebrow. *Will it be this way with all goggles?* I wondered.

It was more than just the pain; it was an overall realization that I'd have to live with certain injuries for my entire life. As I swam, I decided the achy feeling in my eye wouldn't be enough to keep me out of the pool and that I'd just suffer through it. *Plenty of people have suffered through much worse.* Even after reaching this decision, tears began filling my goggles. I was forever changed, and not in a positive way. My face had been a certain way all my life and I was going to be forced to accept these changes, much like a person who loses a finger has to relearn how to write, brush their teeth, and open doors.

The pain in my eye, and the pain in my teeth for that matter, was a reminder that I might not be able to return to what I loved doing. More than that, it was a reminder that death may be prowling around the next bend. If I ever felt like questioning my own mortality, all I needed to do was take a look in the mirror.

A few pool visits later, I lost that pair of goggles. As a result, I did end up finding a pair that sat further into the eye socket and didn't suction on the jagged pieces of bone. Knowing I wouldn't be in pain swimming was a huge relief, and finding a solution on my own, albeit a relatively easy solution, was empowering. I had some control over my destiny, even though it didn't seem like it most of the time. Another decision I'd made recently was to return to triathlon. I wasn't sure when it would be, but I was going to make a comeback. This goal to return to training and racing actually dictated how I chose to manage my scar.

In February, I was scheduled to have laser surgery on my face to reduce the visibility of the scar. The procedure was one that could be done in a doctor's office with some strong pain medication. I needed a driver and Kennett's brother, Galen, stepped up to the plate.

I walked in, checked in at the counter to the left, and sat down in the waiting room, which looked like a sitting area in a gaudy mansion. Before I had a chance to flip through a book about Botox, I was escorted back to an armchair in a small room. I was given liquid pain medication in a small cup and told I could relax until the medication took effect. One of the assistants briefly opened the door to hand me the after-procedure care sheet. Left alone again, I began reading. 'It might feel like sunburn immediately after … You'll need to apply Crisco multiple times a day to keep your skin moist … Sleep in an elevated position … Remain out of the sun.'

When the doctor's assistant returned a few minutes later, I politely asked if there was a timeline on laser surgery or if I could wait to have it done at a later date. After everything I'd been through, I didn't see the need to create a faux sunburn for myself. More importantly, I wouldn't be able to work out as it healed. I bailed on the surgery. At the front, I paid the $35 copay and Galen dutifully came back to collect me. When I got home, the sun poured into the living room where I sat relaxing as the pain medication wore off. I was proud of my decision. I was going to focus on becoming healthy and strong again, not worry about cosmetic defects with my face. More importantly, I had asserted my authority in the situation, which was empowering.

Because I had control over how the scar on my face healed, I wasn't overly upset by it. I knew that, anytime I wanted, I could reschedule the laser surgery. Kennett agreed with me that the best time would be in November. The sun wouldn't be out for as long during the day and it would be off-season for triathlon.

While the scar didn't bother me enough to go through laser surgery, I was still upset with my appearance. Without my knowledge or approval, since I was unconscious, my hair had been chopped off in the emergency room to access the imbedded glass and life-threatening lacerations. As a result, the right side was significantly thicker and longer than my left side. Even after I cut my hair to chin length, I still had a gap by my left ear that made me feel off-center.

I repeatedly said to anyone who would listen, 'If you gave me the chance to fix my scars right now or have my hair back, I'd take the hair.' Then I'd mention a doll I'd owned as a young girl, whose pink and blonde hair grew every time you twisted her arm backwards. With a hint of desperation and resignation, I'd say, 'I wish I could be that doll and grow back all my hair right away.'

Even though I don't take special care to style my hair, I am more attached to it than I ever realized. My hair is blonde, wavy, and rarely blown dry. I wash my hair regularly, but I lack any hair-care routine. Kennett has told me that I wear my hair in a ponytail when I'm not doing well emotionally. I'll wear it down when I feel more energetic. I'll braid it for backpacking trips. Just like a frown or smile, my hair says a lot about my state of mind. Forget fixing my scars; post-crash, I just wanted to *feel* like myself. This included having shoulder-length wavy hair nicely tucked behind my ears. Instead, for a year I had to tell the hair stylist, 'Do the best you can.'

Beyond my hair, the biggest drop in confidence I experienced was from looking at my smile. In the bathroom at work, I would stare in the mirror after I had finished washing my hands. The scar started just below the middle of my nostrils. Beefy scar tissue had formed underneath my left cheek and made my upper lip fat. Nerves had been severed and I couldn't pull my mouth up on the left to smile normally. By December, my upper teeth had been fixed, but it required crowns on my four front teeth, making my own smile foreign to its owner. I was complimented on my new teeth, but they weren't mine and I didn't like them. Each time I stood in front of the mirror, it was like I was introducing myself to … myself. I'd think, *Hello, Adelaide, this is what you look like now. Get used to it.* I didn't need a pep talk every time I looked in the mirror, but it was easy to feel bad for myself and I didn't want to let that feeling stick around for too long and become permanent.

I was equally disturbed by photos from before and after I'd been injured. A week or two before the crash, my sister had held a party at her house. One of the photos taken was of Kennett, our friend Eric, and me standing by the fireplace. All three of us had the biggest smiles. For most of the year post-crash, I would repeatedly open Facebook to that photo and mourn that I would never have that smile back. A combination of nerve damage, smashed teeth, and scar tissue have taken that smile forever.

After the crash, I continued to smile in photos because in the moment I was happy to be around friends. In particular, I remember a picture taken with two friends in June 2015, nine months after the crash. In it, the three of us are shoulder to shoulder, just like the photo of Kennett, Eric, and me. Both the women have beautiful smiles, while I'm on the left with an upper lip that appears increasingly more swollen toward the left. The right side of my face turns upward, but the left lip just hangs down. Of all the photos taken, that one may have been the most devastating. Summer was just beginning, so I knew I would continue to hold off on surgery, but that photo made me long for when I could go back to Dr. Carter's office. I started to wonder if he could do something to fix my lip instead of simply lessening the color of the scar with laser surgery.

Some photos I didn't even want on social media. When Kennett and I got married last minute in the clerk's office, four months after the crash, the only photo that went up was in his blog. My hair was still chin-length and messy. My fat lip was pulled up too far toward my nostril. I wore a pearl necklace as though it would suddenly make me pretty. Instead, it looks completely out of place. Now, when I walk into a couple's house and they display wedding photos, I become jealous – not of the fancy wedding, just the photos. It's a mixed feeling of awe and envy, similar to seeing a gorgeous actress in a $20,000 dress at an awards event, knowing that I'll never own something that nice.

I rescheduled laser surgery for November 2015, a little over a year after my crash. When I called, the surgeon's office manager told me it would be a good idea for me to schedule an appointment prior to surgery to discuss all of the post-operation care ahead of time.

This first appointment was a week before the scheduled surgery, and I got myself psyched up for both. During the appointment, I wanted to ask Dr. Carter about getting rid of the extra skin flaps I had on my stomach and throat from the stomach tube and tracheostomy. They seemed like an easy enough fix.

For the first appointment, I was taken back to a consultation room. For entertainment, I picked up a tri-fold flyer about weight-loss surgery. Dr. Carter walked in and shook my hand while greeting me, 'Hi, Adelaide, how have you been?'

When I began talking, it was like someone had hit the 1.5x speed on my voice. 'Great! I'm looking forward to surgery. Do you think we can we do something to fix my stomach and throat at the same time?'

'Well, those will require that we cut into the skin. If we do that, it will have to be in a completely different surgery.' He looked thoughtfully at my face and said, 'And if we did that, we could also reduce the width of the scar on your face. It won't be like laser surgery where you lessen the color of the scar, but right near your chin your scar is fairly wide and I think we could pull it closer together.'

I was nearly jumping in my seat. 'Can we also do something with my lip?' My excitement was full throttle at this point. Seeing enough disfigured pictures of myself had finally given me the courage and resolve to do something about my smile. Plus, my hair had grown out at this point, so that was no longer a concern.

'Let me take a look. Yes, we should be able to make an incision there,' and he pointed at my left lip underneath my nose. 'We'd be able to release it so it would drop.' He drew a ^ with sharpie on the spot and did the same with the other three spots that he'd work on.

'Can we do this next Tuesday at the same time I already have an appointment?'

'It will take two to two and a half hours for this surgery and I don't think we'd be able to fit it in during the current spot we have allotted.'

'Oh.' My bubble burst.

'Plus, this should probably be done in the hospital. That way we could put you under entirely. You may not be able to handle the emotional toll of staying awake for the surgery.'

'Which one can happen faster? Getting surgery in the hospital or as an outpatient in your office?'

He explained that I'd have to be approved through insurance for surgery in the hospital. I needed a break from dealing with health insurance, so I took that option off the table. Instead, I opted to get the surgery done in his office's procedural room.

Many of Dr. Carter's patients had met their insurance deductible for the year and were trying to get last-minute work done. The office manager promised to call me when they found the soonest opening available. I drove home with the strong urge to get a hug from my dad, who could tell me how strong I was. When I finally had a date for the surgery, I called home to ask if my dad could fly out as extra support after the procedure. This surgery would be more intensive than laser surgery, and the realization that I would be putting myself back in a state of 'victim' had quickly formed. I would soon be on pain meds, unable to train, and stitched up like I was after the crash. I had only just become injury-free, and here I was about to willingly take multiple steps backwards.

My surgery got scheduled for December 22nd and more than once I told people, 'If we suddenly get fluke 70-degree weather after my surgery, you shouldn't talk to me because I'll be pissed. I don't want to miss being outdoors with everyone else.'

Most of December 2015, I felt free from the crash. The closer the surgery date, the more I began questioning it, especially the parts that impacted my face. Altering one's face is disorienting and I wasn't thrilled to go through another adjustment period, especially one that wouldn't immediately be positive.

In the months leading up to this surgery, I'd grown accustomed to the scars in the bathroom mirror. When I put on makeup, I would often skip blending concealer over the scar, but that was by choice. Surgery meant that instead of applying makeup for Christmas while others dressed up, I'd have to smear antibiotic cream over stitches. In my mind, photos taken during Christmas and New Year's were a lesser version of wedding photos – just more visual proof that I wasn't looking my best when others were.

While I had a child-like wish that surgery would reverse all signs of the crash, I knew that wasn't going to be the case. I reminded myself that it didn't matter how skilled Dr. Carter was; my appearance had been permanently changed. No amount of irrational hope would alter that fact, and I didn't want to be disappointed with the results after surgery.

It was difficult to explain my hesitation to get surgery to friends and family. I was repeatedly told that surgery would aid in my emotional recovery, which annoyed me. It felt like people were projecting their own feelings onto me. I knew that removing the visual evidence wasn't going to eliminate the associated trauma. The real problem was when I had to share the road with erratic drivers, when local cyclists were hit, and when politicians considered cutting bike-infrastructure funding. Reading that cities worldwide were banning cars within city limits made me feel more hopeful than the scar reduction ever did.

The week before my surgery, I woke up slowly from a nightmare that the four crowns I had in the front of my mouth had fallen out and all that was left were tooth stubs. When the fake teeth fell out, they had come apart like plastic splitting, as if they were an old ID card.

During the waking hours, I received an email from my lawyer asking when I'd be in town for mediation in January. On top of the surgery, which I knew would be draining, I would have to re-engage with the legal aspects of the crash. Over a year after the crash, I still seemed to lack control over my life.

That night, I just gave up. It wasn't a permanent surrender – just a time-out. This attitude may be a coping skill I picked up through my bipolar, though I'm not saying it is a healthy one. I often, especially at night, just call it. I give up on training, work, keeping the house clean, and whatever else feels overwhelming. Eventually, I come back kicking and ready to tackle life again. As expected, I woke up the next day feeling better, but it would take much longer before I really came back from the trauma of scar reduction surgery.

On December 22nd, my dad, Kennett, and I drove my dad's compact white rental car to Dr. Carter's for my long-awaited surgery. While stopped at a red light, my dad finally figured out how to adjust his seat so he could fit in the car without having to tuck carefully into a ball, before squeezing his legs underneath the steering wheel. I laughed heartily.

At the office, we were told that Kennett and my dad could only be in the procedure room prior to surgery, which wasn't what had been conveyed to me at an earlier date. I remained confident, and the change in plans, which normally would have fazed me, didn't. Sitting in the corner chair, my dad finally thought to ask, 'Are you feeling the pain medication you took before we left the house?'

Kennett responded, 'Are you kidding? You haven't noticed her laughing? She's on a cloud right now.'

Kennett's assessment was accurate, but, just to be sure, the staff gave me some additional valium before leaning my chair back, putting a cold cloth over my eyes, and turning on the bright surgical lights. Contrary to what Dr. Carter and my parents thought, surgery itself wasn't traumatizing at all. I was excited to hear the snipping and requests for different size stitches. I felt strong, tough, and happy that I minimized the surgery to a few hours without having to be admitted to the hospital in a gown. Being able to hear the directions from Dr. Carter made me feel a connection to my previous self, the one who had no memory of the operation room. This minor surgery was allowing me to have a small connection to what I went through in the operating room after the crash, and was oddly calming.

While I was having surgery, my dad and Kennett walked loops around the neighborhood, just as they had during my time in the hospital. In fact, Dr. Carter's office was just a half mile from the hospital, and Kennett and my dad found themselves on familiar roads, though considerably less distraught than they had been a year prior. It wasn't long until Dr. Carter sewed the last few stitches into my face and we all piled into the car for the drive back to Boulder. Pleasantly drugged on hydrocodone and Valium, I was content for the rest of the afternoon and looked forward to my new and improved lip.

In the weeks after the surgery, I plummeted back into the dark pit of despair and anger I had been trapped in after the crash. The weather was miserably cold, I wasn't able to work out, the antibiotics messed with my gut, I had to take pain medication, the incisions hurt, and I still had the civil lawsuit hanging over my head in the background.

The week after surgery, I was back at the Colorado Swim Shop, where I'd been working for the past three months. I left early on New Year's Eve, wanting to run a few errands before I went home. Mostly, I just wanted to spend money on material items to make myself feel better. The streets were extremely busy that day and, as I navigated my way home in the van, I realized I was about to pass the DMV.

I'd forgotten to get my license renewed and it had expired the previous month. I thought about it – New Year's Eve ... nobody was going to be in the DMV. It would be the best time to slip in and out. I was right; my number was called in less than fifteen minutes. As I handed over my license to the woman behind the counter, she asked if I had changed my address.

When I answered yes, she told me I'd have to show proof of where I'd moved to. At this point, I was exhausted and thought I'd just save it for another day. Then the woman told me if I came back the same day, I could skip the line altogether. I had Kennett ride his bike the 2 miles down to me with address documentation and I went back in front of her station. After the vision test and the paperwork, the woman said, 'Just sit in those blue chairs against the wall and they'll call you up to get your photo taken.'

'No, can't I keep my photo?'

'Only if you had renewed online.'

'Please.'

'No.'

'Please?'

Once again, I was powerless. I'd loved my old ID photo, which was taken when I had a great shoulder-length haircut that I'd straightened. I had been wearing my favorite kelly green sweatshirt and my smile was perfect. The new driver's license was going to have fresh stitches on my face – another permanent reminder that I'd lost my smile.

I sat down in a blue chair and texted a sad note to a close friend as a chance to vent. My name was called and I was still wiping tears away from my face moments before the camera light flashed. When I walked down the deserted hall of the old, mostly unused mall, in which the DMV was located, the tears streamed freely down my nose.

I got into our van and was just about to put the car keys in the ignition when my phone rang. It was my mom. I turned off the car and answered. I screamed. I was hysterical. My mom's timing for the phone call was terrible. It was just a reminder that she wasn't nearby when I needed her. It was becoming obvious that, on top of being upset about being injured again, I was suffering from bipolar.

A week earlier, my dad had left town on Christmas Day, and for several nights I called my parents deeply distraught. I'd begged them to come back to Boulder as soon as possible because I was not doing well. 'Not doing well' is my catch-all phrase that means I'm in a depressive bipolar state. They know the symptoms so there's no need to rattle them off between sobs. These calls were made at night and, given the time difference – near midnight for my parents – it was an impossible time for them to make plans.

Nothing had changed now. My mom was still in Pittsburgh and I was still falling to pieces multiple times a day. As I sat in the van with my mom on the phone, my screams were so loud and guttural, and my words so strung together, that I couldn't catch a breath. I'm not sure my mom heard anything I said during the 54-second phone call. After hanging up, I took a few deep breaths and started the ignition.

Once home, I calmed down a little. As I was parking the car, I met a friend who always takes good care of her appearance with nice clothes and styled hair. It was a relief to tell her how I felt, because she validated my emotions by saying how difficult it must be. Kennett, a low-maintenance guy, couldn't relate to why I was in such distress.

My friend, Arianne, and her husband, Sean, came over later that afternoon for dinner and a game of cards. Between the DMV and their arrival, I'd gotten in thirty minutes on the elliptical. The stitches on my stomach still hurt too much to run. We walked through the neighborhood – the three of us and Maybellene. At four o'clock, the sun was behind the mountains and it was bitterly cold. I told Arianne about the DMV experience.

She said, 'You just need to go back in and take a crazy photo. Do something wild and make it fun. Go to Sephora and get them to do your makeup with brightly colored eyes.'

'Yeah, that's a good idea!'

I held on to Arianne's idea because it made me feel like I had a little bit of control, but I hadn't given up my fight. I put her idea as plan B and, in the meantime, I emailed the citizen's advocate for the Department of Revenue to ask if I could have my old license photo back.

My stomach sank when my request got denied. Kennett returned home shortly after and asked me how I was doing. I let a few tears escape. He walked upstairs to avoid conflict and I caught myself from feeling victimized. It was a smack in the face for me that the DMV told me I couldn't keep my old photo, but they let Rush keep his license.

I decided to get pissed, and with all of my angry energy I began cleaning stuff up around the house. Several minutes later, I was done with folding laundry and had moved on to cleaning the cluttered bathroom sink area. We were supposed to have guests for dinner and

I didn't want them to see our mess. Kennett, who was laying down on the bed, asked, 'Want to come lay down?'

'No, I don't fucking want to come lay down. You know why? Because I'm fucking pissed, that's why. Because nobody gives a fuckin' damn about how Adelaide is after the surgery. Just because I'm functioning fine doesn't mean I'm doing great. Just because I'm not committing suicide over my face being scarred, just because I didn't go home to Pittsburgh and give up, just because I still try to get on the bike … Everyone thinks, *Oh Adelaide is strong. This is such small stuff and she needs to just get over it.* And you know what? It isn't bipolar. It isn't always bipolar. I'm allowed to be fucking pissed. Adelaide got fucked over by the court system, Adelaide got fucked over by the insurance companies, and now, Adelaide gets fucked over by the DMV. There are thousands, thousands, of people worldwide who care about what happened to me. They've stepped up to help me however I may need help, but the fucking DMV? No, they're fuckin' robots. And guess what? I'm not. And just because it's been a year doesn't mean I am suddenly all better about this. I'm not a robot about it and I don't have to be. So there. I'm fuckin' pissed and that's my soliloquy.'

I stomped downstairs. Halfway down to the first floor, I started up again, 'Go tell that to my parents … who think I should be all better and don't want to spend time out here. I am fuckin' pissed because I don't want to be crying. You always tell me not to cry and to get mad instead, so now I'm mad. Really mad. And I deserve to be mad. I'm not mad at you, just pissed. And you know what? You can be pissed with me. It isn't just me that's hurt – you got hurt, too. You can be pissed right alongside me, but I am not just going to lay down and cry.'

I didn't cry that night and I didn't get to retake my license photo. When it came in the mail, I just tucked the new ID under my old ID with the nicer photo showing through the clear plastic sleeve of my wallet. Eventually, once my emotions had settled, I just took out my expired license and left the legal one. But that would be half a year later.

The surgery did bring my lip down substantially, and the scar down my face is a little less wide. The skin flaps on my throat from the tracheotomy are non-existent and I often forget I have any scar on my stomach. Yet, once everything had healed up, my life and mood remained the same. I still thought about my scar, my deformed lip, and reckless drivers. Underneath all of it, my PTSD and bipolar remained, both of which were triggered by my appearance in the year that followed this final surgery.

I'm not able to distinguish if the nerve that lifts my lip up into a smile is still severed or if the lack of movement is from the lumpy scar tissue that runs beneath my cheek. I'm disheartened the most by this when I apply lipstick, because it seems futile. Why draw attention to something deformed?

My jagged eye socket doesn't faze me, but if I open my mouth and feel the bones above my left gums with my finger, I get freaked out. Just like my eye, there are several sharp edges and the skin that covers them is thin. It makes me question how in the world the bone hasn't just worn through the gum tissue.

After the crash, I cared for my face with anti-scar gel so it could heal properly and then, over time, I looked in the mirror enough times to adjust to the new reflection. Every face changes with age – mine just underwent an extreme alteration without the help of Botox or time. I've since accepted the image I see in the mirror and won't go through more surgery.

The double takes won't ever go away entirely. One day, years later, when I walked to the library, I noticed a large fire truck parked on the street across from the library. Nobody seemed to be in a panic, so I pondered what the firefighters were doing while I finished my walk. I was hypersensitive when I walked into the library because I was sick with a head cold that left me sniffling at frequent intervals and I didn't want others to notice. Inside, there were three firefighters. One was getting a library card while the other two stood around. I returned a cookbook and then took inventory of the movie carousel to see if there was something good. When I crouched down, I was oddly aware that one of the firefighters was paying attention to me. At first, I thought, *Shit, did I sniffle? Did he hear me?* I didn't see his face; I simply felt his presence and gaze.

I walked out of the library, crossed the street, and passed the coffee shop again. My mind wandered. Firefighters had shown up at the scene of my crash. Early in the year, I'd been contacted over Facebook by an old co-worker who was an EMT when I'd been hit. He reached out because he realized he had been the second ambulance to my scene after I'd been carted off. I prodded him a bit about his memory and he wrote, 'I remember seeing skin and hair around the outside of the window of the car, which was a bit disturbing. Also, the firefighter wasn't sure you would survive because you were presumed to have brain injuries and such.'

A few steps later, I wondered if any of the firefighters at the library had been at my scene. I thought, *No, their fire truck wouldn't have traveled that far. It would have been a fire truck from Lyons or Hygiene, which are both closer towns.* Then it hit me: *The firefighter in the library was curious about my scar! Of course. Even though he wasn't at my scene, firefighters are used to witnessing grim events. He was probably just wondering what caused my scar.*

I have a similar experience when I see an acquaintance for the first time after the crash. I know that they question what happened in my life since they've last seen me. Kids under the age of ten are hilarious because they lack a social filter and they actually do ask for the backstory. Often a parent in the background starts apologizing before I can even tell them what happened.

I am never upset with people for noticing my scar. If I was in their position, I would be similarly intrigued. The best experience I had was when a bold stranger said, 'I like your scar!' a number of years after the crash. It left me beaming for the rest of the day. It may not have been a socially acceptable thing to say, but acknowledging the scar is a way of acknowledging that I went through something traumatic – a reminder that I conquered an extremely tough situation. It took me a long time to accept my scar, and a longer time to finally appreciate it as a badge of honor, not something to try to hide. I may still be upset about the loss of my smile and the jaggedness of the bones on the roof of my mouth and surrounding my eye socket, but I have made peace with the scar itself.

I tell Kennett about encounters in which strangers bring up my scar. I've semi-jokingly floated the idea past him of getting a tattoo next to it. Not to cover it up, but to add to the story. If I did, the tattoo would be a small bike riding up the scar as if the scar was a mountain road.

Appearances have a strong power over us. Appearances are how we make a first impression, how we impress people, and how we show some of our personality. Initially, I felt a sense of self was stripped from me with my injuries. Now that those injuries have had time to heal, I've had time to come to terms with what's left and what I'll have to deal with for the rest of my life. Instead of wishing for my circumstances to change, I'm thankful I still have the opportunity for a long life.

Most people probably don't think they would be capable of living a happy life after losing a limb, being paralyzed, or having serious facial disfigurement. The life changes that one has to confront are enormous following a permanent, traumatic injury, yet the majority of people find a way to move on. Reaching a new normal is possible even under seemingly hopeless situations. I occasionally mourn my old self, even after the long letting-go process that I have been through. Those moments are fleeting.

CHAPTER 18
RACING AGAIN

*'I feel alive and in my body when I put in a hard workout,
hit a new goal, or compete. Who the hell doesn't crave that
feeling of momentarily being on top of the world?'*
A quote from an interview I gave

By New Year's Eve, a little over two months after the crash, I was exhausted. I was past the hardest physical aspects of the recovery, but I was still low on energy as my body continued to heal. Galen and Joslynn were throwing a party downstairs as I sat in our bedroom with the door shut. I had no desire to close out 2015 socializing with acquaintances and strangers.

Propped up by pillows on the mattress, I searched online for a race that I could look forward to and train for. After enough googling, I found myself on the website for Vineman, a full-distance triathlon at the end of July in California. The trauma surgeon had told me I'd be back to 100% by June, so I felt Vineman was a realistic goal.

I clicked through all the links on the page multiple times – course, results, date, gallery, registration price. Then, I considered the added benefit that Vineman was the same day and location as a women's-only triathlon my friend, Krista, would be competing in. It could be exciting to travel with her.

Kennett came to check in on me and he and I discussed the pros and cons of signing up for the race. This wasn't a local 5K, meaning that I would have to be very well trained just to complete it. Vineman was the same distance of triathlon as the one I had been training for on the day of the crash.

'So you're okay if I sign up? The entry fee increases tomorrow, so it makes sense to sign up now.'

'Yeah, do it,' Kennett said.

'I think I can be ready by then, do you? Do you think I could be competitive for the prize purse? It's split between any women who finish under 10:30,' I said.

'Of course. You have plenty of time to get back in shape. I think it's a great idea. You should sign up.'

'Really? Will you help me train?'

I knew the answers to all of the questions I had asked – especially the last one. From the day I met Kennett, he had supported my training and coached me. It was part of our dynamic as a couple.

The race would also be a big financial commitment, as many triathlons are. Not only was the entry fee considerable, but the travel costs associated with getting to and staying in Santa Rosa were large. Kennett didn't hesitate to tell me I should just sign up for it already.

After Kennett left the room, I rang in the New Year, at 10 pm, by purchasing my entry and going to bed. Vineman would become my drive to train again. I treated it as a comeback. If I could complete it, the crash would be conquered once and for all.

As I began training in the spring, Kennett also started throwing swims and short runs into his cycling plan. My crash had prevented him from training properly for the 2015 cycling season. Given that his season was already off to a slow start, he thought he might as well try racing a triathlon. Kennett picked his first race to be Ironman 70.3 St. George, which was in early May and half the distance of Vineman – a perfect race to prep myself for longer-distance racing. We both signed up.

As the North American continental championship, St. George consistently draws a strong field of athletes to Utah, which did not deter Kennett, who spent months leading up to the race focused on what kind of finish time he would need to qualify as a professional. I don't recall having any particular goals for the race since it was my first triathlon back.

When race week arrived, we drove the van out west, which put us in St. George by mid-afternoon on Thursday. Oh my god – was it *hot*. And the bikes took forever to get set up. And I was cranky. I had to figure out how to put a new bottle between my aerobars, which was fine except it required I use a straw. Because my lips were torn up in the crash, straws were hard for me to use; I attempted creating suction but failed to draw up any liquid. The heat, the long day of driving, and my inability to use something as simple as a straw – another reminder that my face had been fucked up six months ago – were all too much to bear. I began sobbing and we hadn't even left the campsite.

We were parked at a campsite near the base of Snow Canyon, a 3.5-mile climb that was supposed to be the toughest part of the course. I would struggle more on the 10-mile downhill section that followed it. Uncomfortable at high speeds because I hadn't been able to stop in time on the downhill when my crash occurred, it made sense that I would be hyper-sensitive in similar situations. To help me overcome this fear, Kennett and I rode to the top of the climb and turned right, exiting the canyon and onto a wide highway road with rumble strips on the shoulder.

The downhill was long, gradual, and led back into town where the run would start. Kennett and I only descended a mile before I had to stop and collect myself. I think I rode that small section multiple times over the next two days before the race in practice, hoping I could overcome my fear. On flatter roads, I practiced sipping water from the straw in my bottle until I had better success.

Race day was 90 degrees, but I managed to stay hydrated as long as I focused on getting suction on the straw. I powered up the Snow Canyon climb, passing a number of competitors in the process. When the gradient reversed and we headed downhill into town, all of them passed me back. It was incredibly frustrating and I couldn't do anything about it. When I got to the final turns into town, I took a deep breath. About 3 miles into the run, I saw Kennett heading the other direction toward the finish line.

He ended up placing first overall amateur and qualified as a professional triathlete, which often takes people years to achieve.

Now, we were a triathlete couple. I had followed Kennett into cycling and fell in love with both him and the sport, but bike racing had also caused tension throughout our entire time together.

When we first started dating, I didn't understand why Kennett needed to leave all day for a training ride. When he signed a contract with the Swedish team in 2015, we fought about him leaving for months on end to race. Most recently, after my crash, I had grown extremely jealous and resentful when he would ride. When Kennett found the initial quick success in his first triathlon, it felt like a clean slate for us. I could finally see that all his hard work was paying off. And, as opposed to the Swedish pro team fiasco, which only caused him and me stress, triathlon would be something we could share together, unhindered by false promises and someone else's unreliable timeline.

We got ahead of ourselves when Kennett became a pro. Given how well he had done at St. George – a competitive race – we figured he would be winning prize money in the pro field for the rest of the 2015 season. Kennett, always one to follow his lofty dreams, helped convince me that he could make a career out of being a professional triathlete. During a June afternoon at work, he and I took a ten-minute break to walk around outside in the sun and talk about the future.

Changes were occurring at the office and we didn't want to be part of the drama. But more than that, we were both unhappy with life. The stress of the crash, the loss of a dream when the Swedish team folded, and the feeling of failure as a bike racer were all causing Kennett to be depressed. I was in a similar state of mind. I wanted time to enjoy life. After a near-death experience, sitting in a cold office building when the sun was shining outside wasn't my idea of living the dream. We decided that day to quit our jobs, and after our walk we marched into our manager's office to give our two weeks' notice.

Less than a week after our last day at work, we began driving to Oregon and California to visit family and race. Kennett would race Vineman 70.3 and two weeks later I would race Vineman full. Maybellene sat on the bed at the back of the van as we drove cross-country with bikes, wetsuits, and four weeks' worth of supplies.

The swim for Vineman took place in the Russian River, so shallow in spots that my hands hit the bottom. The morning fog meant I could only see one buoy ahead of me, which was magical. As the fourth female out of the water and onto the bike, I was off to a good start. The Vineman bike course meanders through Sonoma's wine country, which was supposed to be the main feature of the race, hence the name. Earlier, when I had pre-ridden the course, I kept thinking, *Maybe the real reason everyone likes this course is because they get drunk on wine afterwards and forget the pain before pulling out their credit card for the next year's registration.* I didn't feel good on the bike and I was getting passed left and right for what seemed like endless miles. The road surface was incredibly rough; cracks, potholes, and large bumps dominated the course. One section of the road was so rough that the bridge of my nose ended up getting bruised from the way that my helmet visor banged up and down on it. For something I had looked forward to so much, the experience of racing Vineman wasn't living up to my expectations. I just wasn't in the right mindset either.

I passed through an aid station about halfway through the bike course when a lanky volunteer, perhaps a runner of about forty-five years old, took on a coaching role as he shouted to me, 'Great job, lady. You're still the fifth girl out there.' It might have been the gel that I had just eaten, the encouraging words he said, or simply a section of smooth road, but my mind eased up and I briefly began to enjoy myself again.

Ten miles later, I was hurting again. *Really, Adelaide? This is what you decided to do with your life after nearly losing it? This is hell!* After the race, I rationalized that my negative mindset was caused by getting passed by so many people. I finished as the fourth female and I was twenty-second out of the water overall, meaning that roughly 270 men passed me on the bike. As a steady stream of people overtook me during the five hours it took to complete the bike leg, I lost motivation and grew increasingly frustrated. Our month-long trip in the van prior to the race had meant I trained very little on the bike, and none of the training I did was high-quality riding. Yet it didn't occur to me that a big reason I might not have liked the bike course, and the race in general, was because my body was overly stressed from PTSD.

I raced twice more in 2015, and while the improved results were a sign my fitness was returning, I still couldn't seem to find the power I was accustomed to having on the bike prior to my crash.

Kennett and I got excited with training in the beginning of 2016 when my second surgery and the civil lawsuit were behind us. I assumed I had emotionally moved past the crash as well. Kennett started getting coached and in mid-May I also began training with the same group. I learned to push myself more than ever and enjoyed the training and life routine that Kennett and I fell into. On top of other training that deviated depending on the week, Tuesdays, Thursdays, and Saturdays were always early-morning swims, while the main focus on Wednesday was a hard group run. Training at a more consistent level gave me predictability in my life that continued to benefit my mental health.

One of the biggest hurdles in training was finding the desire to ride. I figured the motivation would come if I just continued to train consistently. Instead, I just grew increasingly more frustrated that I didn't feel as strong on the bike as I had prior to my crash. This was more than a feeling – I trained with a power meter that confirmed that my output was significantly less than it had been back in 2014. Additionally, I didn't feel comfortable on my triathlon bike, so I spent more time on my road bike. In doing so, I was training the wrong muscles because I wasn't spending time in the aero position that triathlon requires.

Bike intervals in particular made me anxious. Before I'd even leave the house, I would become frantic that I wouldn't be able to produce the watts that were outlined in my training plan. This stress was unusual and unproductive. When I started training for bike racing under Kennett's guidance, I was always excited to break new power records. I would ride so hard that a few times I threw up after an all-out climb or an interval. To me, that was a sign of success. I had pushed myself to my max.

Athletes and coaches both understand that some training sessions are harder than others. All athletes have days when they miss their desired splits in the pool, their power numbers on the bike are low, or their prescribed run plan falls to pieces. I should have been comfortable giving a solid effort on the intervals regardless of the outcome. Instead, my anxiety wreaked havoc on my nervous system, making it near impossible to do my bike workouts properly.

I fought myself on the bike. I desperately wanted to have the same desire to push myself to the max as I had early on in cycling. I just didn't know how to regain that excitement and willpower. Meanwhile, I was making significant improvements in swimming and running. Over the course of the season, I decided I wanted to qualify as a professional triathlete. It would put me in a more competitive field and give me some perks in terms of planning races with Kennett, who was already racing in the pro field. In order to qualify, I had to place top three amateur female at a race with a prize purse larger than $20,000 for the pros. Kennett and I traveled to Los Cabos, Mexico, for our last race of the season. I placed fourth – an encouraging result.

At the start of 2017, Kennett and I planned a trip down to Tucson. The first week, we trained with three friends, while during the second week we were joined by several additional teammates and our coach for a more structured training block. One teammate who was joining us for the trip wasn't a Boulder local so I'd never met her. I checked in with the coach.

'This girl coming in from out of town … is she a good rider?'

'Yes, she is a strong rider and I think you'll enjoy going out with her. I've talked with her and she's very nice.'

'I meant is she a *good* rider? Can she handle her bike?' I needed to know that she was a safe rider, knew how to point out potholes and glass to those riding behind her, and could handle her bike in traffic calmly and smoothly.

'I'm sure you guys will be matched in pace. I've never seen her ride but I think she'll be fine.'

I left it at that, but I knew I wasn't going to be comfortable riding with most of the people who were coming to the camp. During the first week, I made sure to stay nearby the guys while riding. I trusted them, especially Kennett. If they did intervals on one stretch of the road, I went there, too. I lightheartedly said I didn't want to be riding next to people I didn't trust as being skilled bike handlers. However, once everyone arrived, I was the low person on the totem pole. I was the only non-pro in the group and had only been allowed to come because I was Kennett's wife, so I tried my best to fit in even if it was at a cost to my perceived safety.

Kennett and I had been to Tucson in 2014 for training and bike racing – trips that I still look back upon with fond memories. This time around, as a triathlete, I was having the same amount of fun. We stayed at an Airbnb close to Saguaro National Park where we could ride quiet, cactus-lined roads. I got two of my highest volume weeks of training during that 2016 camp. After two weeks of riding, I'd drastically increased my average cadence, which made each pedal stroke feel smooth and powerful. As an added bit of confirmation, I hit a personal best effort for a twenty-minute effort on my bike. My first race of the season was going to be Texas 70.3, and as I rode I daydreamt about crushing the bike course and qualifying as a professional.

On the penultimate day in Tucson, our training group set out to Kitt Peak, a 120-mile round-trip ride that included a 10-mile climb at the mid-point. I wasn't nervous for it, but I also wasn't fond of being on other people's schedule for that long of a ride. It was hard for me to wait for others when we took pit stops to pee, take off clothes, or get food. I knew we had many more miles to go before being done and each stop made the day a little longer. At the same time, I was thankful to be riding with a group for the motivation it provided when I got tired. We were traveling on a desolate highway road with little traffic and even fewer buildings. I stayed in the main group of riders while Kennett went ahead with a faster teammate.

On our way back into Tucson, the ride began to crumble apart. One person got dropped and another got a flat but didn't have a repair kit with him. Our group now shrank to five people, including myself. After spending twenty minutes trying to fix the flat tire, we gave up when it became apparent that it was impossible – the short valve on the tubes we had wouldn't work with his deep rim wheels.

Spending all that time off the bike wasn't ideal. I think I ate something but had failed to drink. In the meantime, the person who had been dropped pulled up beside us in the passenger seat of a car, having hitched a ride. She had also flatted and wasn't able to fix it, so she had flagged down a driver.

Now that the riders with the flats would have to hitch rides back into town, our group dwindled to four. It was about a mile later when I reached down to grab my water bottle and hit a tar bump in the road, which sent me flying off the bike. I was the third person in our single-file paceline and my crash caused the person behind me to also hit the pavement. Immediately afterwards, I sat up. I raised my knees toward my chest, twisted my wrists to check for broken bones, and wrapped my arms around my knees to survey the scene. I asked the rider who was behind me if she was okay. She seemed to be uninjured. I was visibly shaken and looked down to see my arms and legs covered in road rash. My bike had some scratches, and I hoped that was all. Just a little road rash, a few paint scratches, and a ripped-up jersey – at first it appeared that I'd escaped without any major damage.

The two other riders with us, who had trained with me for almost a year, looked down at me while I was still sitting on the pavement and compassionately asked how I was doing. It was not an, 'Are you injured?', but a deeper question of how I was handling this crash after my history with getting hit by the car.

'I'm fine. I'm just done. I'm done with this ride. There is nothing else I'm going to get out of riding for two more hours. Give me a minute more on the ground and we can go to the gas station. It's only a mile away. I'll probably just wait and get a ride back from there. There is no training benefit I'm going to get from continuing on so I'm just going to call it.'

I was angry at how the ride had transpired, but I couldn't just sit on the side of the road and run through my list of grievances. We had to get moving. My training partners handed me my sunglasses and the lens that had fallen out. I tucked them into my pocket, noting they might be another casualty of the crash.

The other triathlete who crashed began panicking over her bike. Like mine, her bike had scratches on it, and she was concerned that the carbon frame might have been cracked. Her concern was understandable; as the only person in the training group from abroad, she was out of her element and wouldn't have known where to take the bike to get it fixed if it indeed was cracked. I'm sure she was already stressed from two weeks away from home in England, having to meet new people in a new environment. Plus, unlike mine, her bike was brand new. As I picked myself off the ground, I looked over at her again and saw that she was on the phone with her boyfriend overseas.

I rose and picked up my bike off the ground, then lifted the rear wheel to see if it would spin. I noticed that my right arm couldn't support the bike by itself, so I set the bike down and used my other arm. I'd deal with the injury later and applied the brakes to ensure that the bike was safe to ride the few miles to the gas station – the only sign of civilization around. As far as I could see in every direction, there were only cacti, brush, and distant brown mountains on the horizon.

When we mounted our bikes and began the ride to the gas station, I realized that I couldn't safely ride back to the house even if I'd wanted to; my elbow was in serious pain, forcing me to put all of my weight into my left arm. Quick to assign blame, I began tallying everything that had been poorly planned leading up to and during the ride. I was certain that all of these elements, such as doing our hardest ride after an intense training week when everyone was at their most tired, contributed to my lack of attention when it came to looking out for the tar patches.

My cell phone didn't get service, so once we parked our bikes against the gas station wall, one teammate gave her phone to me so I could call Kennett. Kennett doesn't check his phone very often, and didn't pick up on this occasion, so I also called Chris, whom Kennett had been riding with.

Kennett and Chris were still out riding themselves, so I just left voicemails. Inside the gas station, we all searched for food. The teammate from overseas called her boyfriend back again. I wandered back to the chip aisle by the refrigerated beer section where she was standing. When I motioned for her phone, she handed it to me so I could tell her boyfriend that she was in good hands and that we would take care of her. It didn't immediately dawn on me that *I* needed someone to take care of *me*.

I brought trail mix and soda, and awkwardly carried my stash out to the gas station porch with the others. Two teammates took off to finish the ride while we waited to be picked up. I cracked a few jokes while I cradled my elbow close to my body, though I was becoming exhausted putting on a good face. Sharp pains shot up through my elbow if I didn't hold it dead still. After calling Kennett and Chris again, neither of whom answered since they were still riding, I called the only other person I knew in Tucson, who didn't pick up either.

Finally, I got ahold of Kennett, who drove out to pick us up. I kept up my cheery mood forty-five minutes later when Kennett got out of the car. I didn't want Kennett to associate this second crash with my near-death crash. If I could prove that I was strong, he wouldn't worry too much. He loaded up the car with bikes, dropped the other teammate back at the house, and continued straight on to the hospital ER.

X-rays showed a minor, clean elbow break on my radial head. I called my mom from the hospital room to tell her what had happened and for the first time, seemingly out of nowhere, I began crying. I had held my composure all afternoon but once I heard my mom's concerned voice, my resolve cracked. After hanging up, I calmed down and talked more with Kennett as we waited on the nurse to return, munching on the trail mix I had bought at the gas station hours earlier. By late evening, we walked out of the hospital with a sling, a prescription for medication, and a bag full of bandages for the road rash I had sustained.

Even though the break was minor, bones take six weeks to heal. In the days that followed, I calculated how quickly I could recover, hoping that I could still race Texas 70.3 in early April. I was solely focused on my physical injuries, unaware that PTSD was about to rip apart my life. I thought to myself, *It's just an elbow, right?* I had no clue how wrong I was, or what misery and emotional pain the next few months would hold.

On the drive home to Colorado two days later, Kennett admitted that, before we had left on the trip, he had been concerned that training hard for two weeks in Tucson would cause a bipolar episode. He thought I'd find it difficult staying in a house with other triathletes and that the high-volume training we'd be doing would tire me out to the point of exhaustion. He had braced himself, figuring we might not make the entire two weeks of the trip before having to head home. Contrary to what Kennett assumed, I had a phenomenal time on the trip. Yet I had also been nervous that fifty hours of training in two weeks would exhaust me, causing an episode. Because of this, I monitored my energy levels carefully. If anything, I became hypomanic from the rush of endorphins that back-to-back workouts provided. If I hadn't broken my elbow, it would have been more proof to Kennett that I could self-manage my bipolar and he didn't need to worry about me. Unfortunately, the crash changed the outcome of the trip significantly.

The anger I felt in the first hours after the crash didn't dissipate; it grew until any positive attitude I had left from the training camp became dwarfed by rage. I spent a month and a half after the crash depressed but simultaneously furious. My anger was directed at our coach, who had sent us out on the ride without the car support for later in the day, which we would have benefited from.

Before the crash I had already decided to stop getting coached because we couldn't afford it anymore, but simply not having contact with the group wasn't enough to ease my anger. I held onto it, blaming the coach for the crash even though he had nothing to do with it.

My anger was also directed at the teammates, most of whom didn't reach out to see how I was doing in the days and weeks after the crash. I even directed anger at myself for not possessing the superhuman healing powers needed to recover in time for Texas 70.3, a race that I had spent months visualizing and dreaming about. All this anger was unfounded, but the most unfair part of it was when it got directed at Kennett. I didn't like that he still wanted to be part of the coaching group. Irrationally, I felt it was unsafe for him. What if he was given a training session that led to an injury?

In mid-April, a new psychiatrist was recommended to me. I had stopped seeing my previous psychiatrist the year before because I didn't like that he was heavy on prescribing pills and was not personable with me. At the time, I also didn't think I needed help.

Kennett came with me to the appointment with my new psychiatrist, during which we discussed my anger and extended period of bipolar depression following the crash, as well as how it all impacted Kennett. The psychiatrist adjusted my dose of Lamictal and also encouraged me to see a trauma therapist who specialized in brainspotting. I was still in denial about needing help with PTSD, and also in denial that seeing a psychiatrist or therapist would solve any problems with bipolar.

I left the office with a slip of three local recommended therapists, though I was hesitant to call any of them. I hadn't had good experiences with therapy in the past, but Kennett and my new psychiatrist were adamant that I try again. A week later, I still hadn't called any of the therapists, so Kennett took it upon himself to make an appointment for me. He informed me that he had done so, and, as I looked at her website, I quickly picked apart the therapist he had chosen on my behalf. I just didn't like the look of her. I decided that she wouldn't understand anything about bike racing or triathlon, and, in my jaded view, her website made it appear as though she was into healing with spirituality. *Not my type of person*, I thought. *I get to choose who I see, not Kennett.* In defiance, I picked my own therapist from the two that remained on the psychiatrist's list and made an appointment for later that week. Kennett chalked this up as a success.

I began seeing Faith, a therapist that specializes in treating trauma victims with brainspotting. Brainspotting is similar to another, better-known type of trauma therapy called EMDR. As I sat in Faith's office, I was told to locate a point in my field of vision where I feel an emotion most strongly. Faith used a two-foot-long metal pointer with a small red rubber tip to keep my eyes focused on that one spot for an extended period of time while we talked through the most recent crash, my reaction to aggressive drivers, and my general anger toward people and the world. By keeping the eyes focused on this single point, the mind is better capable of healing itself by bypassing the conscious brain and accessing the subcortical brain.

In addition to brainspotting, Faith taught me how my post-traumatic stress disorder manifests in my day-to-day life. Our natural tendency when experiencing a stressful situation is to resort to fight, flight, or freeze. I went into that first appointment agitated and left calm and relaxed.

In subsequent appointments, Faith explained that my body immediately linked the second crash with my first major crash. While I don't recall any thoughts I had during my first crash, I was still conscious. As a result, my brain realized that I might die, or, more accurately, was in the process of dying. Since then, I'd subconsciously associated being in a bike crash with dying. When I hit the pavement in Tucson, more than two years after being hit by the red Fiat, my subconscious brain immediately thought my life was in danger.

I questioned Faith on this, telling her I had been trying to keep the atmosphere calm after I had broken my elbow. I hadn't even cried until talking to my mom hours later. This wasn't an image of someone who thought they were dying, right? She explained that I had been exhibiting a flight response, which includes dissociating from the event. However, once the immediate danger was taken care of, my reaction was reduced to a fight response. That was apparent during my phase of anger over the month and a half it took for my elbow to heal.

With Faith's help, I was slowly able to reduce the triggers I have resulting from both crashes. She pointed out that I might not even know what was triggering me in certain circumstances. After a few months of therapy, I realized that when I rode with another cyclist I almost always chose to ride on the outside, closer to traffic. As someone who has been in a crash with a car, this seems like an odd choice.

However, being on the outside meant I was further from intersections where a car could pull up from the right-hand side to turn onto the road I was riding. To this day, I am more sensitive to movements on the right side of my body when I ride.

In the process of working with Faith, I felt supported and was able to refocus on training. I missed Texas 70.3 because of my elbow but raced St. George 70.3 again. At the start of the race, an official stood in front of my start wave at the edge of the water and warned us about the wind that was supposed to pick up by the time we were on the final descent of the bike course into town.

The final descent that the official was talking about was the same one I had feared in 2015 – my first race back. This time, it seemed nobody could stop talking about the wind that was supposed to appear mid-morning. They even moved the race start time to get everyone on the course earlier in the day. It was a relief that, once I got on the bike course, I was able to focus on my effort instead of panicking that I might get blown around in the last few miles. I handled the bike a little slower than others, but I ended up being just fine on that windy descent. I finished fifth overall female, still just shy of becoming a professional. This result, along with the fourth overall at Los Cabos, was confirmation that I was on the right track. I wasn't too concerned about missing out on the pro status. This wasn't something that I felt needed to be rushed.

The next race, Raleigh 70.3 in North Carolina, was a month later and I had more training under my belt for it. When Kennett and I began our first pre-race ride from our host's house, I panicked that my brakes weren't working sufficiently. I cried within the first few miles and asked Kennett to stay with me for the entire ride. Faith had taught me that being near Kennett while riding calmed my nervous system and subconscious brain. Sure enough, I relaxed and fell into his draft, allowing him to put in a harder effort while I tagged along behind.

I had traveled to Raleigh feeling nervous about being on the bike, but come race day, my mind settled into the goal of qualifying for my professional license. I felt that the time had come and I was ready to take the next step. I cruised through the 1.2-mile-long warm-water swim without any issues other than losing my cap in the last few hundred meters, making it through transition to my bike in a good position. The 56-mile bike course had lots of rolling hills, but most of the descents had a clear line of vision and weren't long enough for me to hit uncomfortable speeds. I felt more relaxed than I had at St. George. Something about North Carolina, and being back on the East Coast in general, puts me in a good mood. I fell into a rhythm of knocking off one hill after the next, avoiding the large drafting packs that went by from time to time. Two or three other girls were in my vicinity throughout most of the ride, but they began to fade away during the later miles of the course. Because of the congestion on the course – 1,750 people were competing that day – I had to hold back a bit to avoid getting in others' draft zones. No matter, I felt like it was wise to conserve for the run, and when one girl passed me near the end of the bike course, I let her go without chasing.

Coming off the bike, I knew I was near the front of the women's field, but I wasn't sure of my exact place due to the sheer mass of athletes on the bike course. I could have been in second or fifth. Near the first mile of the run, I noticed I was making quick work of the girl who had passed me at the end of the bike course. She was skinny and long-limbed; she looked fast. I wasn't sure if it was wise to pass her this early, but I did so anyways. Two miles later, at the first turn around, I saw that she was already over a minute back, and I continued pulling away throughout the remainder of the race. By this point, the temperature was a sweltering 85 degrees with high humidity, and each aid station was a momentary relief from the heat. While there are no certainties in tackling a half marathon after hours of swimming and riding in the heat, I was confident I would hold her off. The only thing that would stop me was a freak cramp or failure to hydrate.

Four hours and forty-three minutes after the start gun went off, I began sprinting down the finishing shoot. There was one more woman in front of me that I had to catch after all. I made the pass just in time before crossing the line and buckling over from exhaustion. It turned out that that last woman was in the pro field, and it wouldn't have mattered if I hadn't passed her. While Kennett and I weren't completely sure until nearly an hour later when the official results were released, I felt an overwhelming sense of relief realizing that I had come in first female in the amateur division and had qualified for my professional license. Goal completed! Now I could spend the rest of the year adjusting to racing in the pro field, without putting any pressure on myself, and refocusing my attention on therapy.

The sessions with Faith over the next few months didn't go as well as I had hoped, and I became disheartened about the effectiveness of therapy. We talked about how the goal in brainspotting was to reduce my triggers and keep me from feeling like I was in a constant state of being threatened. However, some threats are real. She said brainspotting could help me feel safe on a quiet road without cars because there was no rational reason I should feel threatened. However, a busy road with drivers zooming past, heads down, looking at their phones? That is a real threat, and brainspotting couldn't totally rid me of the fear I experienced in those situations.

Faith questioned me about whether I wanted to continue as a professional triathlete, during which I would continue to put myself on the road – an inherently dangerous thing to do. Faith recommended that I might want to ride inside on the trainer, at least while I was going through the emotional sessions of brainspotting.

I took her advice and chose to ride indoors when I wasn't feeling motivated to be outside. Some days, especially around the most emotional therapy sessions, I would ride inside with music or a movie on for entertainment. Each time I got on the trainer, I was excited to not have to ride outside, but five minutes into the workout I would become bored and regret not choosing to go outdoors.

Riding outside had mixed results. Sometimes, I made it through a workout feeling calm and proud of myself for riding. Other times, I would have unexplainable panic attacks. I still did my intervals near where Kennett was riding, so he could stop and calm me down if my panic got too intense.

None of this was conducive to racing well. My first professional race was Ironman Coeur d'Alene 70.3 on June 25th, 2017 in Idaho.

I hated the bike course, even though the hills would have suited me well in the past. I felt weak and out of shape. It seemed like I never wanted to train hard on the bike anymore and it showed in a poor bike split that day. As hard as the bike course was, I had my best run ever and, like Vineman, I have very fond memories of the race.

The question I got from other people continued to be, 'Is it worth it?' There are plenty of other sports to compete in and outdoor activities to do in Boulder. I hated these conversations and having to debate whether it was worth riding when it obviously caused me stress.

I took each of these discussions as a personal affront because I was being asked to give up something I still loved. Internally, the debate wasn't if I should keep riding. It was, *How do I get my sheer love for cycling to return to the point where I can train at the level I want to?* Even riding inside meant giving up quality time outdoors, and therefore wasn't a long-term solution. Why did I have to give up something else? I was the victim in the whole situation and I didn't *want* anything else taken away from me.

The assumption that I would feel better not riding was flawed. I liked that I'd be able to compete as a professional in triathlon. It was a long-term dream that I had never acted on because, with untreated bipolar, I wasn't able to stick to a training schedule. While I still struggled with bipolar, it was no longer the cause of my holdup. I felt that I had conquered it, to an extent, and that it wasn't fair that I had another emotional disorder – PTSD – keeping me from pursuing my dreams and my life.

Boulder is a cycling mecca. I knew if I gave up cycling, I would feel jealous of every rider I saw – never mind the envy and sense of loss I would feel not being able to leave the house with Kennett when he went out on his daily rides.

I stopped therapy with Faith in the fall of 2017 and, while I think the trauma therapy helped me, I haven't fully overcome these issues – partially because, as Faith told me, many of the fears that I have while riding are real. The threat of being run over by a distracted, drunk, or aggressive driver is not imagined.

In 2018, I went for a Sunday ride – one that I was excited for. The roads are quiet on Sundays, so I felt at ease, especially as I took the sweeping turns on the descent down Sunshine Canyon. At the base of the descent, a yellow Jeep swung left, abruptly crossing in front of me as I was going around 30 mph. When I saw the windows and the tires only a few feet in front of me, I wondered which I'd crash into. I braked and swerved and the driver did the same. Quick actions meant we avoided a crash, but I stopped to yell at the driver as he pulled into the dirt parking lot for his hike. He was a younger kid, maybe still in college, and he was so incredibly sweet as I told him he could have killed me. I lost my composure and started bawling.

At this point, the driver got out of the car and told me I should set my bike down against the wooden rail. He asked if I needed a hug and I said yes. I got a hug from this complete stranger and after he said he was sorry multiple times, I reached for my bike. My leg shook uncontrollably when I tried to clip into the pedals to ride home. When I got in the house, I took a small dose of the pain medication that has been sitting in my closet since the first weeks after my crash. I just wanted to calm myself down and dull the memory, because these negative experiences aren't the ones I want to focus on.

The majority of memories I have on the bike now are those that I never want to dull. As I write this, I can think back to earlier today when I rode up Lefthand Canyon just north of Boulder. The temperature was in the nineties and the sun beat down intensely, but as I climbed further up the canyon the breeze cooled me off. When I passed another cyclist headed the other direction, I nodded and did a mini wave with my fingers, which I kept rested on the aero bars. I looked down and saw my hands covered with sweat. When I glanced down later, my hands had dried off from the air flowing past as I pedaled. Most of the cars gave me plenty of space as they passed, and I also nodded at the drivers as an acknowledgement that I appreciated their patience.

I was supposed to climb at a moderate pace for forty minutes, but I felt so good that I treated it as a mini interval, pushing the pace as I went. I feel an internal drive, the one I had been desperately missing after my crash, more often now. I've started riding with new people recently, learning to put my trust in them and not just in

Kennett. I ask friends if they want to go 'play bikes', because that is how I like to treat it.

If I can go out and enjoy someone else's company while riding, that can be a fantastic day. Reaching a new level of fitness means I have a huge smile across my face when I tell Kennett about my training day. (He will forever be my coach, so I always give him updates.) Joking with Kennett as we take the bike path to the gym makes me feel lighthearted.

I'm not trying to prove anything as a professional athlete except that I can push my own limits, physically. I may have made a 'comeback' by returning to triathlon and competing at a high level, but that didn't signify true recovery. I still struggled with PTSD the day after winning Raleigh, and I still deal with it today. The healing process is agonizingly slow and there is no finite end point to it; each day that is just a little better than the last is a victory when it comes to managing PTSD and regaining my love of riding.

CHAPTER 19
THE FIGHT

'You people down in Boulder need to keep your bikes down there IN Boulder ... We don't like you comin' up here ... on our roads and riding them races ... It's the silliest thing I ever heard of ... so ... just STAY down there ... in BOULDER and do your races ... down there IN Boulder. Okay?'

A voicemail left on my phone when I promoted the Gebhardt Automotive Cycling Classic in 2014 before my crash

I saw Faith consistently throughout the spring and summer of 2017 to manage my PTSD. Trauma therapy was frustrating because it brought all of my emotions front and center, which was the point, yet dealing with those emotions and trying to ride daily didn't always work. Faith explained it best: 'I wouldn't be able to treat a victim of domestic violence if she was still living with her abuser. It just wouldn't work because she'd still be exposed to the person or trigger that caused the trauma in the first place. To fully treat your PTSD, it would mean that you could never ride in traffic again. A quiet bike path not exposed to any cars would be fine, but commuting to the grocery store or riding up a mountain pass would not.'

I'll never be cured of PTSD because, as Faith explained, I'm constantly exposed to the thing that nearly took my life: cars. Trauma therapy did help to minimize my PTSD to a degree. Kennett began seeing Faith shortly after I did in the spring of 2017 for his own PTSD and anger toward drivers. However, after a handful of office visits with Faith, he decided to redirect his therapy sessions to managing his anxiety caused by my bipolar. For years, he had felt anxiety when leaving for a long ride while I was at home suffering from bipolar depression, and things had reached their worst point ever during that spring when I broke my elbow. By focusing on this separate but, to him, important issue, he never fully addressed the PTSD that was caused to him by my crash in 2014. It would finally catch up to him right before his first attempt at an Ironman, though not in a way that most would expect.

By the summer of 2018, almost four years had passed since the crash and Kennett and I were still trying to forget about it, which was hard because we were both out riding on a regular basis. I had a three-hour ride to Carter Lake on this particular day and Kennett was tapering (resting) for Ironman Whistler that weekend, a race that we were leaving for the very next day. He decided to keep me company for an hour, then turn around for home.

We headed out on US 36 since it's the main road out of town, ducked off it at the first intersection, and turned east on Neva Road. The quieter country roads that we took north and east allowed us to ride side by side and hold a conversation. Nearing an hour into the ride, we continued along a false flat uphill, riding two abreast – which is, of course, legal in Colorado and every other state.

The two-lane road we were on had minimal traffic and was populated with a few older farmhouses tucked away back into the hills. We were about to leave Boulder County, and it is well understood in the cycling community that we are less welcome in Larimer County, which borders us to the north.

Before my crash, in the fall of 2013, we had a serious road rage incident in Larimer County. A car laid on the horn the entire way around our group of four cyclists. The driver had an entire lane to pass us, but instead he chose to intimidate us. Next, he immediately veered in front of us and slammed on his brakes, attempting to cause us to run into the back of his car. One of our friends, Steven, had to brake so hard to avoid going through the rear window that he burned off the tread on his tire, creating a flat spot.

The car came to a stop and Kennett pulled up to the driver's open window and began screaming at him. The driver, who was in his sixties, got out of his car, yelling about how we were hogging the road and that we had no right to be riding out there. After a few minutes of this back-and-forth yelling, I had to make sure Kennett and the other two guys I was riding with stayed back instead of continuing to engage in a verbal fight with the man; after all, we had called the police by then and just needed to wait for them to arrive to issue a citation. Kennett, in particular, had a difficult time calming down and each time the driver got in Kennett's face, just inches away, I worried that the two would start throwing punches.

When the cops finally arrived over an hour later, we found out that the driver had been traveling from church to his next destination – working with therapy horses. It was hard to believe that someone could hold so much hatred in their heart between trips from church and a volunteering position. I believe the driver was eventually cited for careless driving.

Most avid cyclists have had many encounters such as the one described above, and this wasn't the first or last incident that Kennett and I have had either. In 2013, the driver was behind the wheel of a sedan. On our Tuesday ride in 2018, just before Ironman Canada, the vehicle in question happened to be a white truck. Just about anyone who rides in Boulder knows that pickup-truck drivers in Larimer County often end up being particularly aggressive to cyclists.

When the white pickup came alongside Kennett and me, he laid on the horn for three full seconds. After he came around us, Kennett flipped him off, and then the driver pulled over onto a gravel patch that was on the right-hand side of the road in front of a house.

I had been riding on the outside, nearest to the cars, which left Kennett closest to the pulled-over truck when we came up to it. The driver had opened the door and already stepped out part way into the road. I sensed Kennett was going to attack the driver and my split-second thought was, *That guy could be carrying a gun. Please don't be dumb, Kennett.* Even before Kennett had come to a stop, I was screaming at him, 'Kennett, don't! Kennett, stop!'

Kennett skidded his bike to a stop and unclipped his cleats so he could have both feet on the ground. I can't say exactly what happened from there because it all went by so quickly. Kennett yelled, the driver yelled, and then they were grabbing at each other. The driver was shorter than Kennett, maybe in his forties with long, grayish-black hair. Kennett had the guy by his hair and I could see that he had even pulled some of it from the guy's scalp. As a female with long hair, I know how much it hurts to have hair pulled out and I knew, even if they stopped at that very moment, that Kennett had already caused harm. I think the guy had Kennett by the shoulder of his jersey. A switch in Kennett's brain had flipped and he wasn't concerned about the consequences.

'STOP! KENNETT! STOP IT! KENNETT, STOP IT!'
I screamed at him.

Suddenly realizing that this was a bad idea, particularly the day before traveling to a race, Kennett told the driver he was going to let him go, and did. They backed away but continued to argue and threaten each other with a further fight. I tried desperately to diffuse the situation.

'Sir, you came around us very aggressively. Listen, he was just trying to protect me. I almost died on the side of the road after being hit by a car.' I pointed to my scar. I pointed in the direction of Hygiene Road. He shouted over me.

'You shouldn't fucking be on the road! This is my fucking house. You came at me [referring to Kennett]. I live here and you cyclists are always taking up the fucking road. If you're so scared of cars, then get off the road. You shouldn't be allowed on it, anyway. You're fucking stupid to be riding on a road with cars.'

Ohhh, he wasn't just pulling over to start a fight or yell at us. He was home. Geez – Kennett really didn't need to attack him, I thought to myself.

'Sir ...' I tried to interject, but he continued yelling over me, and Kennett continued yelling over him. He and Kennett were inches apart at one point, screaming in each other's faces, and I was worried that Kennett would attack him.

The driver said he was going to call the cops and took pictures of us. I told him we would gladly stay until the police came and we backed away as he continued to provide the police with his information. We stood 50 feet from the driver and Kennett decided to also call the police on my phone. Then, each party waited. The driver got back in his pickup and pulled it into his driveway. Apparently, he *had* been trying to intimidate us or start a fight by pulling over halfway into the street and stepping out at us. He then came in our direction but said calmly that he was just going to check on the mail. As he opened the mailbox, he muttered about how maybe the police didn't need to come after all. It would be another twenty or thirty minutes before they came, and by then he was doing yard work as we waited on the side of the road in the sun.

Two police officers arrived and we were asked to fill out witness sheets. I thought to myself, *This is what it's like to fill out a witness statement. This is difficult; even though it just happened, I can't give exact details. It all happened so quickly.* A third officer came up in another patrol car. For several minutes, they rotated talking to us and talking to the driver. It was obvious that those first two officers understood what it was like to be a cyclist and the harassment we deal with on a daily basis. One of the officers, who told us that his girlfriend rides centuries and gran fondos, later explained to the driver the rights that cyclists have, including the right to be on the road as well as the right to ride two abreast when it doesn't hold up traffic.

The third cop that showed up seemed to scowl at Kennett and me. The questions he asked were more accusatory. 'You could have just kept riding. Why didn't you?' Kennett explained that by continuing on, it would give the driver an opportunity to get back in his truck and run us over. 'Well, why were you riding side-by-side? When you ride two abreast, you end up being in the middle of the road.' Kennett and I showed him, by placing our bikes on the road, just how little room we took up riding side by side, and that we hadn't been anywhere close to the yellow centerline of the road, or even in the middle of our lane of traffic. However, the officer didn't seem to understand that riding two abreast was even legal.

When we explained that Kennett gets protective of me, the officer asked, 'If you were trying to protect her, then why would you let her ride on the outside, closer to traffic?'

I stepped in for that question and explained, 'Officer, when I was in a crash four years ago,' pointing to my scar, 'the car came up from my right-hand side. Ever since then, I am particularly sensitive to movements on the right when I ride. While it may not be the safer position, it feels safer to me given my history.'

During this mini interrogation, we were forced to defend ourselves for doing something completely legal, without causing harm to anyone, to someone who didn't fully understand the law.

Finally, we got to the most important question. What did we want the outcome of the incident to be if we had a choice? The officer who asked directed the question at Kennett, but I kept trying to insert myself, like a smart kid raising their hand wildly in a science class. I didn't trust Kennett to make a good decision because he had just started a nasty skirmish.

'Sir, I would like us to be able to talk with the driver. I don't think we need to press charges, but I'd like this to end on a civil note.'

'I think that is a good idea. He needs to be okay with that, too. We'll go talk to him. You wait here.'

When the officer came back, he told us that the driver was willing to talk to us. Then, he got more stern and told us not to be defensive and escalate anything. Our cleats clicked against the gravel as we left our bikes and walked over toward the house.

Given how hot the day was, the entire group of us – Kennett, me, the driver, and the police officers – all stepped into a shady spot beneath one of the trees.

'Sir, my name is Adelaide. I'm sorry with how this turned out.'

'Hi, my name is Robert.'

'We didn't realize you lived here. After honking your horn and pulling over so abruptly, we assumed it was an aggressive move. We probably overreacted because I was nearly killed by a car, like I mentioned earlier. Kennett was just trying to be protective of me, and it got so out of hand. I just want you to realize we weren't trying to annoy you. Riding side-by-side may seem like we are ignoring you, but when we can do it, depending on the road visibility, it actually saves you time because you only have to pull over into the other lane to pass one person instead of staying out further into the road passing one person and then another on top of that.'

The police officers had been quiet, but then the one who had asked the tougher questions tilted his head a small degree and said, 'Huh, I never realized that.' I thought, *Wow – if nothing else, there was a small breakthrough in understanding between all of us.*

Kennett said, 'Yeah, if there is a pack of several riders, it helps a driver to only have to pass six bike-lengths of cyclists riding two abreast instead of needing to go around twelve bike-lengths of cyclists riding single file.'

He turned to the driver. 'My name is Kennett. I'm sorry, I've had so many bad incidents with aggressive drivers that I'm sure they influenced how I reacted.'

I told the driver that my wish was that he be patient with other cyclists, especially females on the road. Honking a horn next to a cyclist can be startling and it is terrifying to have a huge truck next to a cyclist when they think the driver is aggressive. Kennett acknowledged that the driver is probably slowed down every day because his home is on a route trafficked heavily by cyclists, which must get frustrating.

Everyone agreed that this was the best outcome that could have happened as a result of the fight. It actually made me wish for a bigger assembly of cyclists, drivers, police officers, and maybe even lawyers. I bet, given the animosity between these groups, clashes would break out in such an environment, too. But how else do you bring humanity and empathy to the issue of sharing the road and acknowledging human lives? I have spent five years considering this dilemma.

After Kennett, Robert (the driver), and I each said our piece, we dispersed. Kennett and I went to collect our bikes as the police officers walked the same direction to their squad cars.

I turned and asked, 'Would you mind telling Officer Fisher I said hello and that I'm doing well? He'll know my name. He was the first responder to my scene and, along with a select few people, he helped save my life.'

The officer told me to hold on and grabbed his phone. 'You can tell him yourself.'

So, I briefly got on the phone to say thank you to Bill Fisher. Earlier in the year we had been emailing about meeting for a coffee, but it had yet to happen. In one email, he told me that talking to other officers about my crash was therapeutic for him. It was important to me that he eventually see my face intact, which would hopefully dull the memory he has of me ripped open from glass, slumped against the wheel well of the Fiat.

In the weeks after my crash back, I always understood that I was not the only person who was hurt when I went through the driver's-side window of that red Fiat. I got so much support through the healing process, yet others were left alone with their thoughts and horrific memories. I've always wanted to make sure I reciprocate in the little ways I can. When I got to thank Officer Fisher over the phone, we recommitted to meeting for coffee later that summer, during which he finally got to see me healthy and fully alive.

After the call with Officer Fisher, Kennett and I rode off. I needed to start my first forty-minute effort. Kennett was supposed to turn around to ride home but he offered to continue riding with me. He felt bad that I might give up on my intervals and that he had subsequently wrecked my ride. While I wanted the company, it was 90-some degrees outside. I knew the extra time outdoors would just drain him and it was only days away from him racing the longest distance he had ever done before. We split up and I rode my intervals as planned, but with a little less energy behind each pedal stroke. I didn't give up on my ride or turn around with Kennett because I wasn't experiencing the same PTSD I used to live with.

During the remainder of that ride, what I *was* trying to wrap my head around was what Kennett had just done. I wasn't sure who laid hands on who first, but ultimately I knew Kennett had started that fight, discounting the driver's initial aggression while in his vehicle. I recalled my co-worker Tim, who pulled me aside in the office after my crash and said to me, 'I'm worried about Kennett. Even before you'd been hit, he would come back to the office after lunch rides and he would be extremely angry with drivers. You need to make sure he gets therapy. Otherwise, there is going to be one day when a driver does something to him and he is going to hurt them. He won't even realize what is going on because he'll lose control.'

I'd *tried* to get Kennett to get outside support. We had each gone to a therapist who specializes in a trauma therapy called EMDR shortly after the crash, but neither of us connected with her. When we had gone together to see a sports psychologist, I took over almost every session with tears and complaints about how unfair the legal system was. When I saw Faith after I broke my elbow in 2017, I convinced Kennett to see her for a few sessions, but it apparently wasn't close to enough. As I continued through my three-hour ride, I tried to remember exactly why Kennett had gone to see Faith. Was it specifically around PTSD from the crash? Or was it therapy for how to manage living with me given my bipolar and *my* PTSD? I thought it was the latter, but honestly it didn't influence the decision that I came to by the end of that ride: Kennett needed to go back to therapy.

The next day, we flew to Seattle and drove north to Whistler, Canada. We lugged two bikes, two bags, and two carry-ons across the bus to the airport, across the airport to the check-in, and from Seattle's baggage claim to the car rental. Nothing had wheels on the bottom so we carried all of it. It bugged my shoulder a bit, but Kennett's chest started to bother him.

By the next morning, his chest hurt a lot, so we paid for him to see a doctor in Whistler Village, who told him he had torn his intercostal and that it would probably take ten days to heal. Then, we spent money on an anti-inflammatory cream. Kennett told me there was a 2% chance he'd be able to race given the injury since he wasn't able to swim. Over the weekend, I got frustrated. We'd spent money to travel to the race with the assumption that Kennett would make it back with race earnings. Instead, we were spending even more money to get him medical care.

We talked about what might have caused his injury. He had done a short swim after returning from that Tuesday ride and that was the first time he'd noticed it hurt. After some discussion, we figured he'd got hurt when he was yanking the driver over in the brief fight they'd had.

Even though I was annoyed, I reminded myself that this was Kennett's PTSD. He had supported me through every single time I had had PTSD. Kennett rode with me the first time I went outside and the first time I went past the crash site. There were outbursts at home, many tears shed over how unjust the legal system was, and temper tantrums in mediation when I wasn't acknowledged as a victim. I needed to understand that Kennett got in the fight because he was still affected by my crash and hadn't focused on his own recovery.

I tried to be extra peppy and supportive, since he was hurting both physically and mentally. While he started the race, he couldn't finish the swim. Over the next week, I found myself in multiple conversations trying to answer the question about how Kennett tore his intercostal.

I told Lydia about the altercation during our ride after it happened, but kept my mouth shut around other friends. Krista, who had moved out of town, came back into Boulder for a visit the week after Whistler. As with many things we have shared with each other, I told her all of the details over a run. I knew she and Lydia could see the compassionate side of Kennett and that they'd understand what fueled his fight. Both Lydia and Krista have a version of the second-hand trauma Kennett struggles with. Slowly, I shared it with other friends who had known us since 2014.

I didn't want people we train and socialize with to criticize Kennett for getting in a fight with a driver, because I didn't think they could understand the root of the problem. I knew if the crash had happened to someone else, I would have struggled to comprehend the impact it would have, not just on the injured person, but on their community.

I've chosen to see the fight in a positive light. For a brief moment under the trees, there was empathy between cyclists, a driver, and the police. I don't have the answers to improve relations between cyclists and drivers, nor do I have the solution to keep cyclists safe.

I'm grateful that I still have the ability to ride. As Faith mentioned, I don't think it is possible for me to continue riding and not have triggered responses to aggressive or careless drivers on the road. For that matter, I am pretty sure I have more intense reactions when I am in a car as well. For as difficult as it is, I don't think giving up riding entirely is a solution for me. There was enough taken away from me on the day of the crash – my smile, my confidence, parts of my relationship with Kennett – and I do not want to feel any more loss from the crash. Instead, I have chosen to do what is in my power to make cycling safer, including leading by example to encourage others to ride, and advocating for cycling safety within my community.

EPILOGUE

*'One day, careless driving causing serious bodily injury will
cause someone to lose their license.'*
Brad Tucker, 2018

In March 2019, Bicycle Colorado – a bike advocacy group for
which Brad, my lawyer, is the president – asked me to speak at the
Colorado State Capitol in Denver to testify on behalf of a proposed
Vulnerable Road Users Bill. After years of struggling against a
broken system, I now had the opportunity to help fix it. This is what
I said:

> *'My name is Adelaide Perr. I'm a vulnerable road user and I'm here
> asking you to vote yes on HB-175. Today is day one for a young woman
> in North Boulder who was riding to work when an impatient driver pulled
> in front of her. I got home from a run this morning and saw my husband
> a few hundred feet away, standing by the street as she was loaded into an
> ambulance. When he walked over to me, I hugged him. As he cried, he said
> the woman looked like me. Her eyes were rolling back in her head and she
> was trying to move her arm. She was bleeding heavily from her face. I'm
> here because this bill is important, and I'm worried about my husband who
> is at home suffering from PTSD today. In 2014, I was the one on a bike
> ride, when a driver ran a stop sign and pulled abruptly into my lane of
> traffic ... I'm not just asking for your support on HB-175 to keep me safe.
> Every day that my husband leaves for a bike ride, I make sure to give him a
> kiss because I worry he is going to be killed. Please help keep unsafe drivers
> off the roads and make the consequences for injuring someone severe.'*

On May 29th, Governor Polis signed the Vulnerable Road Users Bill into law. With this law, a driver who is found at fault for causing serious bodily injury to a vulnerable road user – including pedestrians, people in wheelchairs, and cyclists – will receive a Class 1 Traffic misdemeanor and twelve points on their license, allowing courts to suspend their driver's license. We have allowed careless driving to become an accepted, and even expected, part of our culture. Thousands of lives are lost every year because of it, while hundreds of thousands more – vulnerable road users and car occupants alike – are left with permanent, disabling injuries. Protections for road users cannot come too soon. The bill was signed into law in the morning, and by that afternoon a cyclist in Denver had already been run down by a careless driver.

***

After the fight in the summer of 2018, Kennett began seeing Faith for PTSD therapy again, this time focusing solely on reducing his reactivity when getting buzzed or honked at. In 2019, he went on to place second at Boulder Ironman and third at Boulder Ironman 70.3. He still enjoys riding, though never to the same degree he did before my crash. Despite trauma therapy, he still has anger toward aggressive drivers, and from time to time our mutual anxiety comes out when he leaves for training rides.

With school shootings and now coronavirus, I think I am especially sensitive to other people's trauma. My own near-death experience has made me more empathetic to what others are going through. Additionally, PTSD surfaces in strange ways – ever since the Covid-19 pandemic, I've had trouble getting out the door on rides again. I know that the only reason I survived in 2014 was because of how quickly I received help. With the fear of Covid-19 and people wearing masks, would somebody jump in to save me if I was hit again and left to die on the side of the road? The night on the ventilator was the worst night of my life – and that was with Kennett by my side. I cannot imagine what it is like for those who are isolated because of the virus. The anxiety is there just under the surface, and it has made riding extremely difficult to enjoy again.

While Kennett continues to train as a professional triathlete, I've started from scratch too many times now. Being a full-time athlete was both mentally unsatisfying and emotionally draining. You put all of your energy into your physical abilities, and when you get injured or have a bad race performance, your world comes crashing down. I'm glad I pursued my athletic dreams and reached a level I always believed was possible, but now I'm ready to move on.

I'm working toward returning to my education background as a teacher or counselor so that I can pass on the tools and lessons I've picked up over the past five years to the next generation. I will always have a passion for hard exercise (and competition to a degree) and I'm staying physically strong enough to do what my friend Emily refers to as 'stupid adventures' – big runs, rides, or other outdoor sports that are planned last-minute – without waking up injured the next day.

***

Writing this book was not, as many people suggested, a therapeutic endeavor for me. I gave up on it over a dozen times, abandoning my manuscript for up to half a year before finding the emotional energy and motivation to give it another shot and complete a third or fourth round of edits. The first part of the book, where I was in a sedated coma, was the easiest section for me to write because it involved interviewing and writing about others. It turns out it is extremely difficult to work through one's own experiences and emotions to weave a cohesive story. To accurately tell the story, I also had to share a lot of my flaws and memories I'd prefer to forget. On top of all that, I often worried about whether my writing was strong enough to convey what I wanted, because since the beginning my goal was to help others through this book. If you read this book and took away just one thing from it to help yourself or the community you embrace, then I'd say it was worth it.

ACKNOWLEDGEMENTS

There are two types of acknowledgements:

There are those people who have helped with the book. They include my writing coach, Doug, who made this a much more cohesive book; several people who willingly met me for coffee so that I could interview them; and friends who agreed to read sections of the book and provide feedback or encouragement to continue. Of course, Kennett dealt with it day in, day out. I gave up on this book more times than I can count and he hasn't left me yet.

Then, there are those people who saved my life and who supported me in the aftermath of the crash. Many are not mentioned in this book, but please know that if you reached out afterwards, you helped me see the good in humanity and I am very grateful. So many people wrote messages online to Kennett and me. I've read each note multiple times. The EMTs, surgeons, and nursing staff are my heroes. I cried off and on for days when I learned my oral surgeon had died of cancer at a young age – cancer that I believe he knew about when he treated me. Even though he was struggling with his own mortality, he helped me regain my life.

Connect with the author:
website: www.adelaideperr.com
Instagram @Adelaide_Kennett